Structural Adjustment and Intersectoral Shifts in Tanzania

A Computable General Equilibrium Analysis

Peter Wobst

Research Report 117
International Food Policy Research Institute
Washington, D.C.

Dissertation, University of Hohenheim (D100).

Library of Congress Cataloging-in-Publication Data

Wobst, Peter.
Structural adjustment and intersectoral shifts in Tanzania: a computable general equilibrium analysis / Peter Wobst.
    p. cm.
  Includes bibliographical references.
  ISBN 0-89629-120-0 (paper)
  1. Tanzania—Economic conditions—1964- 2. Tanzania—Economic policy. 3. Equilibrium (Economics)—Mathematical models. 4. Tanzania—Politics and government—1964- I. International Food Policy Research Institute.

HC885 .W63 2001
330.9678—dc21   2001016691

In memory of my dear brother Joachim

Contents

Tables

Figures

Acronyms and Abbreviations

Ag	Agriculture
BOT	Bank of Tanzania
CCM	*Chama cha mapinduzi*
CES	Constant elasticity of substitution
CET	Constant elasticity of transformation
CFNPP	Cornell Food and Nutrition Policy Program
CGE	Computable general equilibrium
C.I.F.	Cost, insurance, freight
CTRAD	Retail and wholesale trade
ERP	Economic Recovery Program
ESAF	Enhanced Structural Adjustment Facility
ESAP	Economic and Social Action Program
FAO/WFP	Food and Agriculture Organization of the United Nations/ World Food Programme
f.c.	factor costs
F.O.B.	Free on board
FY	Fiscal year
GAMS	General Algebraic Modeling System
GDP	Gross domestic product
GDP at f.c.	Gross domestic product at factor costs
GFCF	Gross fixed capital formation
GNP	Gross national product
GNP at f.c.	Gross national product at factor costs
HIPC	Heavily Indebted Poor Countries
IDA	International Development Association
IMF	International Monetary Fund
ISI	Import substituting industrialization
LES	Linear expenditure systems
LFS	Labor Force Survey
LOP	Law of One Price
Macrosam	Macroeconomic social accounting matrix

Microsam	Microeconomic social accounting matrix
MM	Marketing margins
NESP	National Economic Survival Program
NLP	National Land Policy
OGL	Open general licenses
OHC	Own-household consumption
PPA	Participatory Poverty Assessment
PRGF	Poverty Reduction and Growth Facility
Protosam	Raw (unbalanced) microeconomic social accounting matrix
ROW	Rest of the world
SAF	Structural Adjustment Facility
SAM	Social accounting matrix
SAP	Structural adjustment program
SDR	Special Drawing Rights
SSA	Sub-Saharan Africa
TOT	Terms of trade
TSh	Tanzanian shillings
URT	United Republic of Tanzania
US$	U.S. dollar
VAT	Value-added tax
WFP	World Food Programme

Foreword

Like many socialist countries, Tanzania shifted from a centrally planned economy to a market-oriented economy in the late 1980s and early 1990s. Reforms, which proceeded in fits and starts, included devaluation of the currency, reduction of tariffs, changes in the domestic tax system, and increased investment in infrastructure. In this research report, Peter Wobst attempts to determine how this structural adjustment affected agriculture in Tanzania, as well as growth, equity, and poverty alleviation—in other words, the economic well-being of the people in this extremely poor country.

Many developing countries have had tax and subsidy systems that handicap farmers and push down agricultural production. Although not their major focus, structural adjustment programs have often included policy changes that tend to correct such biases. Wobst finds that by 1992 reforms had largely eliminated the bias against agriculture in Tanzania and even in some cases protected that sector. His analysis also reveals that currency devaluation has stimulated total agricultural production in Tanzania but harms farmers who do not produce goods for export. Policymakers could help this group of farmers, however, by improving transportation, communication, and marketing infrastructure so that they can market their goods more effectively domestically.

In addition to policy consequences, this report presents methodological advances that should be of great value for policy analysis in Tanzania. Wobst constructs a computable general equilibrium model of the Tanzanian economy, as well as an updated social accounting matrix, which provides a detailed picture of the socioeconomic structure of Tanzania.

This report is part of a larger IFPRI study of macroeconomic reforms and regional integration in Sub-Saharan Africa that seeks to help policymakers understand the effects of reforms on agricultural performance, natural resource use, poverty, and income growth. It should be of interest not only to those concerned with recent economic developments in Tanzania, but also to those concerned with the broader issue of macroeconomic reforms and their ultimate effects.

Per Pinstrup-Andersen
Director General

Acknowledgments

I am indebted to Professor Franz Heidhues for accepting my thesis at his institute and his kind support throughout the period of its completion. I am also indebted to Professor Sherman Robinson, who observed my endeavors on a day-to-day basis and encouraged the continuous progress of my thesis through his discussions, suggestions, and advice.

I am deeply grateful to all my colleagues in the Trade and Macroeconomics Division of the International Food Policy Research Institute for their encouragement and the friendly working environment they provided, as well as their constructive discussions and intellectual stimulation. I particularly wish to thank Dr. Andrea Cattaneo, who may have lost confidence, but never hope or temper, in guiding me.

I would like to thank the German Agency for Technical Cooperation (GTZ) for its financial support of my data collection in Tanzania, and Professor L. A. Msambichaka who served as my local supervisor during this time. Special gratitude goes to Mr. John Komba, former head of the National Accounts Section at the Bureau of Statistics. He represents the many people I had the opportunity to meet and whose expertise I profited from while working in Dar es Salaam. I also thank Nicholas Minot of IFPRI, Channing Arndt, and an anonymous external reviewer for their comments on this report. Last but not least, special thanks go to Oskar.

The author alone accepts all responsibility for the ideas expressed in this work and for any errors or omissions.

Summary

In 1986 the United Republic of Tanzania began a remarkable transition from a planned economy with a single-party political system to a free market economy with a multiparty democracy. This political and economic transition started with Tanzania's first structural adjustment program after the failure of the Ujamaa experiment under President Julius K. Nyerere. After 15 years of continuing reforms, the economy is now widely liberalized and shows substantial development in sectoral and overall economic performance. However, little is known about the interrelationships among macroeconomic reform policies and intersectoral behavior and the related linkages with the economy at the microeconomic household level.

This study analyzes the effect of stabilization and structural adjustment policies on overall economic growth, sectoral performance, welfare, and income distribution in Tanzania. It was conducted for a multicountry project entitled Macroeconomic Reforms and Regional Integration in Southern Africa that covers six countries in the region. After a brief discussion of Tanzania's political and economic developments since independence in 1961, the study reviews policy programs implemented and economic performance achieved since the beginning of the reforms, highlighting economic fluctuations under changing political conditions. The report reviews the computable general equilibrium (CGE) methodology, which has been widely used and continually advanced for development analysis throughout the last two decades. The general CGE approach and the underlying database 1992 social accounting matrix constructed under the same project are described along with the country-specific features of the Tanzanian CGE model.

The report comprises three parts that address (1) trade liberalization, industrial protection, and the bias against agriculture; (2) exchange rate devaluation in an import-dependent economy; and (3) devaluation under decreasing marketing margins. The part on agricultural bias examines the traditional analytical issues of agricultural versus nonagricultural economic growth and the problem of adverse agricultural terms of trade due to a biased domestic policy regime and external economic conditions. The part on exchange rate devaluation is motivated by Tanzania's history of substantial currency adjustments under structural adjustment programs, the importance of the exchange rate issue for export-oriented economic growth in Tanzania, and, consequently, the continuous challenge of the external stability of the Tanzanian shilling (TSh). The third part focuses on macroeconomic policies, such as devaluation of the real exchange rate, in conjunction with complementary policy measures, like the improvement of the transportation and communication infrastructure.

The analysis of the policy bias against agriculture, or "urban bias" as coined by Lipton (1977), advances the traditional partial equilibrium work in this field led by researchers at the International Food Policy Research Institute and the World Bank at the end of the 1980s and early 1990s. This study offers three major improvements. First, the applied CGE model is an economywide, multimarket approach that captures all sectoral and intersectoral price linkages simultaneously rather than analyzing each commodity market separately. Second, the modeling approach used permits different degrees of tradability through imperfect substitution between domestic and foreign goods, the so-called Armington assumption (Armington 1969). Partial equilibrium analysis, in contrast, distinguishes tradables and nontradables, with tradables defined as perfect substitutes in all markets. The Law of One Price applies to these commodities, meaning that world market prices directly determine domestic market prices. Third, the CGE framework determines changes in the exchange rate endogenously rather than estimating these changes from a separate model. The results of the analysis show that although the removal of the distorting trade taxes has a positive effect on the agricultural terms of trade, the removal of other commodity taxes—mainly levied on nonagricultural commodities—is unfavorable for agriculture. The existing tax scheme is generally mildly biased toward rather than against agriculture. The analysis also shows that production effects are generally dampened through intersectoral repercussions in the general equilibrium framework when compared with partial equilibrium results. Overall, the results suggest that the exchange rate—which significantly affects the agricultural terms of trade and was heavily devalued early in the liberalization process—as well as foreign trade taxes, which are low following economic liberalization, essentially eliminated the policy bias against agriculture in Tanzania.

The second part of the analysis evaluates the gradual elimination of the existing foreign trade deficit through real exchange rate devaluation, a crucial part of any World Bank/International Monetary Fund structural adjustment program. The results highlight two particular aspects: (1) the relative effect of devaluation on agricultural versus nonagricultural production, and (2) the relevance of the economy's degree of import dependency. The degree of import dependency depends not only on the share of imports within a certain commodity market, but also on the degree of substitutability of foreign and domestic commodities. Furthermore, the import content of production plays a crucial role, as does the composition of total imports, that is, the shares of intermediate goods, luxury goods, and other types of imported goods. Tanzania relies heavily on imports that cannot be substituted by domestic production. Therefore, the main contribution to closing the external trade deficit through devaluation has to come from the export side, requiring exports to more than double. Thus, under structural adjustment total absorption in the economy falls for three reasons: decreasing imports, decreasing production through a fall in imported intermediate inputs, and increasing exports. As a result, overall economic welfare decreases along with decreasing absorption. However, the relative burden on different household groups depends on their income sources, especially for wages, salaries, and capital income from agriculture versus nonagriculture and export versus nonexport sectors. A devaluation is likely to boost agriculture rather than industrial sectors because of the important role of export agriculture. The gap widens between export and nonexport agriculture, with devaluation favoring, in relative terms, export-oriented producers over nonexport-oriented producers. In absolute terms, devaluation leaves nonexport-oriented producers worse off than they were before adjustment because of worsening production opportunities. In general, devaluation of the real exchange rate causes substantial structural changes, with both winners and losers.

The third part of the analysis addresses the design of macroeconomic policies that aim at structural adjustment in conjunction with complementary policies that ease the negative distributional effects of policies associated with structural adjustment. In the context of devaluation, this report looks at the supplementary impact of the improvement of the transportation and communication infrastructure, which is particularly important because Tanzania is a large country with long transport routes and poor physical infrastructure, leading to high marketing costs. The analysis compares a devaluation that reduces the existing trade deficit by 50 percent under the initial marketing costs with four subsequent scenarios with gradually reduced marketing costs, which finally reach half of their initial level. The results reveal that more efficient trade and transportation services substantially reduce the per unit cost of marketing by reducing demand for and prices of marketing services. More efficient services also release productive resources to more cost-effective sectors of the economy with additional factor resources available, resulting in an increase of the overall level of economic activity. Better marketing infrastructure also produces more cost-effective international trade, thereby requiring a much lower depreciation to achieve the same reduction in the trade balance. Improved infrastructure particularly favors agriculture compared with nonagriculture and nontraded rather than traded agriculture. Consequently, the poorest households, which are engaged in small-scale farming of nontraded food crops, gain the most from an improved infrastructure environment because they obtain more effective market access and participation. The analysis shows that complementary policy measures, such as an infrastructure investment program aimed at improving marketing services, have a substantial effect on the structural and sectoral performance of the entire economy and, therefore, on the impact of other macroeconomic policies such as a devaluation. Complementary policies make structural adjustment easier, more efficient, and, above all, more equal in terms of income generation and distribution, which particularly favors the rural poor. In other words, appropriately designed structural adjustment can benefit agriculture and the poor through lower adjustment costs and fewer negative welfare effects.

The findings of this analysis have some important policy implications and lead to suggestions for further economic policy research in Tanzania. Major structural changes in Tanzania's economy took place during the political and economic transition, and these changes require further study by the research community and policymakers. The extensively liberalized economy remains extremely vulnerable to internal and external shocks and changes in its underlying macroeconomic policy environment. Furthermore, the effects of macroeconomic policies cannot be analyzed in isolation, but must be viewed in their overall economic context, including complementary policy measures that can help to enhance their effectiveness and ameliorate the costs of adjustment, especially for the poor.

CHAPTER 1

Introduction

This study analyzes the effect of stabilization and structural adjustment policies on overall economic growth, sectoral performance, welfare, and income distribution in Tanzania. To address the analytical interests of the study, a computable general equilibrium (CGE) model was formulated that incorporates country-specific features designed to capture special economic conditions and institutional characteristics of the Tanzanian economy. As the initial data set for the CGE policy analysis and for the calibration of the model, a social accounting matrix (SAM) was constructed based on 1992 national accounts data. The study focuses on the impact of internal and external macroeconomic shocks and policies on the economy, especially the agricultural sector and rural households. Policy changes and macroeconomic shocks considered in the study include changes in the domestic tax structure, devaluation of the Tanzanian shilling, reduction of tariff barriers, and decreasing marketing costs through increased investment in infrastructure.

Motivation

In the late 1980s and 1990s, Tanzania experienced a remarkable political and economic transition from a socialist country with a centrally planned economy to a multiparty democracy with a liberalized free market economy. With the Arusha Declaration in 1967, the government had inaugurated an era of economic socialism based on self-reliance, including Tanzania's Ujamaa policy and villagization program.[1] Internal and external economic shocks throughout the 1970s led the country into economic crisis in the early 1980s. The authorities initially reacted to the economic breakdown with self-guided adjustment efforts, but in 1986 they finally agreed to the first stabilization and structural adjustment program (SAP), which was guided by the World Bank and International Monetary Fund (IMF).

Under Ali Hassan Mwinyi, the second president, who in 1985 succeeded Julius K. Nyerere, president for 24 years, economic reform started with the 1986–89 Economic

---

[1] Ujamaa is the Kiswahili word for familyhood and relationship and became a synonym for Tanzania's socioeconomic system after 1967.

1

Recovery Program (ERP) and was accompanied by political changes in the late 1980s and early 1990s. During his second term of office, however, President Mwinyi's government demonstrated a much lower commitment to economic reform. As a result overall macroeconomic performance deteriorated and jeopardized the ERP's achievements of the late 1980s and early 1990s.

In 1995 Benjamin Mkapa, the third president, was elected in Tanzania's first free and democratic presidential elections. Mkapa restored the international donor community's confidence in Tanzania's commitment to economic reform when he approached the IMF for assistance in launching the 1996/97–1998/99 ERP under the Enhanced Structural Adjustment Facility, now called the Poverty Reduction and Growth Facility. In April 2000 the International Development Association (IDA) and the IMF "agreed to support a comprehensive debt reduction package for Tanzania under the enhanced Heavily Indebted Poor Countries (HIPC) Initiative." Assistance will depend on several conditions, however, "including the adoption and implementation of a participatory poverty reduction strategy paper" (World Bank 2000a).

This brief overview of the economic and political milestones since independence in 1961 illustrates the tumultuous developments Tanzania has faced during the past four decades. Economic performance under the SAP has improved substantially in many respects, but recent occurrences, such as the 1996/97 drought and the 1997/98 El Niño floods, reveal the economy's continuing vulnerability and the need for sound macroeconomic policy measures and supporting economic analysis.

Despite macroeconomic reforms and market liberalization, many countries of Sub-Saharan Africa (SSA), of which Tanzania is one of the poorest, have experienced only moderate improvement in their general social and economic conditions. Even economies with growth rates above the international average continue to fall behind in absolute income gap measures because they start from extremely low levels of production and income per capita.[2] As Heidhues (1998, p.175) states, "If liberalization and globalization lead to a widening of income gaps between countries and within countries, we are moving away from the central objectives of development policies." Although increasing evidence suggests that the policy elements of the so-called Washington Consensus—macroeconomic stability and outward-oriented trade and market policies—are conducive to economic growth in these economies, one has to carefully address Heidhues's concerns.

This study is motivated by these considerations and aims to develop an analytical framework that incorporates the political, institutional, and infrastructural deficiencies typical of Tanzania's economy. To complement the strategy and policy measures of the Washington Consensus, understanding the particular behavior of Tanzania's economy and its response to policy measures is necessary.

---

[2] All 49 SSA countries combined, excluding South Africa, represent less than 1 percent of international trade. Their total 1997 gross domestic product (GDP) at factor costs (US$169.1 billion) was barely more than South Africa's (US$124.5 billion) in 1995 constant U.S. dollars (World Bank 1999b).

Objectives

An analysis of macroeconomic stabilization and structural adjustment policies attempts to quantify their main economic effects by emphasizing growth, equity, and poverty alleviation. The main analytical focus is on trade liberalization measures, such as devaluation of the exchange rate and reduction of tariff barriers; the economy's responsiveness to these measures; and Tanzania's potential for enhanced foreign trade. The economy's responsiveness to changes in the domestic tax system and increased investment in infrastructure is also emphasized.

One of the study's principal objectives is to analyze macroeconomic and aid policies to determine their effect on overall economic growth and sectoral performance as well as welfare and income distribution among different socioeconomic household groups. From a technical perspective, the study seeks to construct an individualized CGE model that reflects particular country-specific features of the Tanzanian economy in addition to a Tanzanian SAM that constitutes the calibration point for the CGE model and provides the underlying database required for any empirical analysis of the links between macroeconomic policy and economic performance. Together, the CGE and SAM provide a comprehensive tool for quantitative, multisectoral policy analysis that could be applied by Tanzanian researchers.

Methodology

The objective of stabilization measures is to achieve macroeconomic stability with respect to the government budget, the balance of payments, foreign trade, and monetary issues, while structural adjustment measures seek to achieve shifts of resources among sectors in order to adapt the structure of the economy to changes in national and international economic environments. CGE models capture both stabilization and structural adjustment features. On the one hand, CGE models incorporate the macroeconomics of the national economy, specifying key determinants as endogenous variables, and on the other hand, they allow any degree of sectoral disaggregation that is suitable for the analysis of intersectoral shifts.

The core features of CGE models guarantee the integration of macro, market, and micro levels into the modeling procedure. Through a functional specification that assumes product differentiation, CGE models capture a variety of sector and market linkages within the economy and linkages with the rest of the world. In this study the CGE approach reflects Chenery's (1975) view of "neoclassical structuralism." The model incorporates both a neoclassical foundation and some structural rigidities. The major rigidities of the Tanzania CGE model applied in this study are (1) foreign trade restrictions following the Armington assumption, where imports and exports are imperfect substitutes for domestic produce; (2) high import dependency due to fixed relative input-output ratios, that is, intermediates cannot be substituted by labor or capital, and imported intermediates can only be substituted by domestic goods according to their relative substitutability; (3) segmented factor markets, which restrict migration between agricultural and nonagricultural sectors;

3

(4) fixed sectoral capital, which captures the rigid investment structure of the economy; and (5) minimum quantities of marketed and nonmarketed household demand in order to guarantee minimum levels of food consumption. Furthermore, one single good in the model appears in a variety of states, namely, as domestic produce, export, domestic supply, import, composite aggregate, and final consumption good. In accordance with the wide product differentiation, the model features the same variety of endogenous prices that are associated with their respective good.

Considering the completeness of the functional specification of CGE models, including the wide variety of endogenous variables, CGE models are the most appropriate tool to analyze the effect of macroeconomic policies on markets and sectoral adjustment processes as well as their impact on individual household welfare. The microeconomic foundation of the CGE specification guarantees the simultaneous interaction among the microeconomic, market, and macroeconomic levels of the economy that capture all horizontal and vertical linkages among sectors, factors, households, and other agents of the economy. Although the CGE approach has a neoclassical structure and solves for relative prices under market-clearing conditions, it allows the specification of additional market constraints in order to capture the broad variety of market imperfections, rigidities, and inefficiencies typical of developing economies.

Researchers have applied SAM-based CGE models to a broad variety of developing economies for many different analytical purposes. The applications to Tanzania comprise a series of models developed at the Research Department of the Norwegian Statistics Office to analyze land degradation effects,[3] along with a model by Sarris (1994b; 1996) developed as a part of the Food and Nutrition Policy Program at Cornell University.[4] These earlier applications are advanced to meet the analytical objectives of this study. First, both approaches are based on a SAM for 1976 tax year data, the latest year for which an input-output table for Tanzania is available, while this study applies a newly constructed 1992 SAM. Furthermore, both approaches show a limited sector disaggregation and only a limited focus on agriculture and its subsectors. The model applied in this study features a more disaggregated labor market and household specification than the land degradation models. In addition, the land degradation models are "closed" regarding their foreign trade and balance of payments specification, which makes them less suitable for the analysis of trade liberalization policies. Sarris's model incorporates the specification of enterprise investment behavior at a highly sophisticated level, the functionality of the commercial banking sector, and the role of the central bank. On the one hand, the statistical data available in Tanzania barely meet the requirements of Sarris's model specification and, on the other hand, his specification of the intertemporal investment process, which drives the dynamics of the model, is too narrowly focused for considering the distributional issues addressed in this study.

---

[3] See Balsvik and Brendemoen (1994); Aune et al. (1997); and Grepperud, Wiig, and Aune (1999) and refer to the discussion of these approaches in the section on existing CGE model applications to Tanzania in Chapter 3.

[4] For a discussion of this approach, see the section in Chapter 3 on existing CGE model applications to Tanzania.

4

As with all CGE models, the model applied in this study is neoclassical in structure and follows the approach in Dervis, de Melo, and Robinson (1982). In addition, it incorporates various country-specific features in order to capture Tanzania's particular regional and national economic conditions. The model incorporates own-household consumption, which considers the production of nonmarketed food crops and their contribution to total household consumption and nutrition.[5] In an economy in which 85 percent of the population lives in rural areas and mainly engages in food cropping, the appropriate specification of own-household consumption behavior is essential for household-specific welfare analysis. The model also contains explicit marketing margins for domestic supply, export, and import commodities in order to capture the extreme differences between producer and consumer prices due to high transportation and other marketing costs in an economy with poor infrastructure and long transit distances. Moreover, the model specifies a commodity-specific food aid variable to simulate food aid injections in circumstances of production failures caused by a drought or other events that decrease agricultural productivity. Taking such productivity decreases into consideration becomes important in the context of Tanzania's agriculturally dominated economy, which remains vulnerable to internal and external shocks. Finally, the model incorporates a European-style value-added tax (VAT) with a rebate mechanism to capture Tanzania's introduction of a VAT tax in 1998 and to analyze alternative domestic tax scheme scenarios.

Hypotheses

From the mid-1980s Tanzania experienced an almost complete economic transition from a centrally planned economy to a free market economy. At the same time, Tanzania experienced a variety of internal and external economic shocks that reverberated throughout the entire economy. Major quantitative changes in key variables of the Tanzanian economy in the 1990s include (1) changes in the domestic tax system, (2) infrastructure investment, and (3) devaluation of the exchange rate. The analysis of this study starts from two main hypotheses, namely:
  • Although macroeconomic stabilization and structural adjustment measures do not always address agriculture directly, they have a substantial impact on economic performance and income distribution within agriculture.
  • Indirect linkages among sectors and market segments are important and, consequently, a general equilibrium approach to analysis is much more suitable than a partial equilibrium approach.[6]

---

[5] This is sometimes termed "autoconsumption" and represents the share of total production that is not marketed but is consumed by the producing household itself. This substantial part of national production used to be neglected in the national accounts statistics and has only recently been added to the official national accounts data as nonmonetary GDP, accounting for more than one-third of the monetary GDP for 1987–96 (see URT 1997, Tables 1 and 2).

[6] Examples of such links include food crops versus cash crops, agriculture versus nonagriculture, traded versus nontraded, and monetary versus nonmonetary.

The analysis will address these two hypotheses as they relate to policy issues in the context of Tanzania's economic transition. Such issues include tax reform, infrastructure development, factor productivity, and the foreign exchange market. These policies affect the entire economy and can be best captured in the applied CGE framework. Indirect linkages and an endogenous exchange rate included in a CGE model are especially important when measuring the policy bias against agriculture. Partial equilibrium approaches in the Krueger, Schiff, and Valdes (1988) tradition tend to overstate the bias against agriculture (Bautista et al. 1999). Moreover, absolute and relative effects of macroeconomic structural adjustment policies on farmers compared with nonfarmers and food crop versus cash crop activities can be captured using the CGE mode. These impacts are diverse among the different groups and sectors, and the CGE approach indicates the economic source of the major effects.

Organization of the Study

Chapter 2 presents an overview of Tanzania's historical transition from a centrally planned economy to a free market economy since independence in 1961. It focuses on failures in the immediate postindependence period, the economic breakdown, and the subsequent structural adjustment efforts. It also points out recent economic developments, the current state of the economy, and policy measures applied since implementation of the first World Bank/IMF-guided SAP in 1986. Chapter 3 presents a methodological overview of SAMs and CGE models and provides a literature survey on CGE applications in the context of research on African development issues. Chapter 4 documents the construction of the 1992 SAM for Tanzania, emphasizing the SAM balancing procedure using a new cross-entropy estimation approach. Chapter 4 also presents the general CGE specification with emphasis on the country-specific elements that the model incorporates to capture the particular behavior of the Tanzanian economy. Chapter 5 contains the analyses conducted. It presents motivation, experiment design, results, and conclusions for each policy under consideration. Chapter 6 concludes by reviewing conclusions that can be deduced from the analysis.

CHAPTER 2

From African Socialism to a Free Market Economy

Tanzania has experienced a transition from a one-party, socialist system with a centralized economy to a multiparty democracy with a free market economy. This chapter describes the political and economic developments since independence in 1961 and the role of IMF/World Bank-guided SAPs. It highlights Tanzania's current economic performance and presents prevailing policies directed at further liberalization, economic growth, and poverty alleviation.

President Julius K. Nyerere's 24-year socialist leadership from 1961 to 1985 bestowed a peaceful socioeconomic environment, despite great ethnic diversity and economic deficiencies that have typically led to political instability in many African countries. After independence, however, the promotion of economic development failed, making Tanzania one of the six poorest countries in the world for the last two decades. At varying levels of intensity, Tanzania has received a great deal of attention from the international donor community over the last three decades. However, the international business community has not sufficiently noticed or promoted Tanzania's economic potential.[7]

Many recent political and economic developments in Tanzania bode a prosperous future, at least in the medium term. Abundant natural resources, a peaceful socioeconomic environment, and successful steps toward liberalization and modernization of the economy augur the success of future development. Despite poor past economic performance, Tanzania need not be just another case of a planned economy that failed in its macroeconomic transition toward an open market economy.

---

[7] The Scandinavian countries were especially supportive of the African socialism experiment, as was, for example, the former German Democratic Republic until the Federal Republic of Germany started paying more attention to Tanzania. Private companies, by contrast, have been rather reluctant to invest in the country, and foreign direct investment played only a minor role in Tanzania's economic development throughout the 1970s and 1980s. Only recently, in conjunction with the ongoing privatization and liberalization process, have foreign companies reconsidered their financial engagement in Tanzania. This is especially true for South African investors since the end of apartheid and the improvement of South Africa's political and economic relationship with most countries in southern Africa.

The disappointing efforts of one decade of structural adjustment do not indicate irrevocable failure of beginning the process of convergence with other more developed economies. To achieve a substantial economic boom, however, Tanzania must overcome the negative economic consequences of earlier experiments in socialist planning and distinguish between the positive and negative elements of that legacy.

Economic Development before Structural Adjustment

This section reviews economic and political developments in Tanzania between independence in 1961 and 1985, when political reorientation led to the first IMF/ World Bank-guided SAP in 1986. The section highlights the different states of the economy (1) immediately after independence, (2) under the socialist regime established by the Arusha Declaration in 1967, and (3) under the self-guided adjustment efforts of the early 1980s.

Independence, 1961

Eager for the political change that led to freedom and independence in 1961,[8] the new government was overextended and unprepared to guide and control the national economy. Consequently, the new leaders adopted the existing colonial-style economic structure. Although Tanzania was a British protectorate rather than a colony, and not as important to the United Kingdom as neighboring Kenya, agricultural production was clearly oriented toward Europe's demand for raw materials and basic products such as sisal, cotton, coffee, and tea. Between 1960 and 1962, agriculture contributed more than 50 percent to gross national product (GNP), and sisal, coffee, and cotton contributed about 60 percent to total foreign exchange earnings (Taube 1992). Tanzania neglected not only to satisfy its own national food requirements, but also to diversify its export products and promote light manufacturing for potential gains through import substitution before and shortly after independence.

Politicians were soon overtaken by the reality of severe deficiencies in the supply of food products, energy, housing, manufactured goods, and health and educational services, as well as intermediate inputs and implements for the agricultural sector. Between 1961 and 1966 Tanzania's economy operated primarily under free market conditions, and the government adopted the World Bank's "transformation approach" to agricultural development as a component of its first five-year plan (Wenzel and Wiedemann 1989).[9] However, between 1962 and 1963 Tanzania implemented the Agriculture Products Board Act, which reintroduced

---

[8] On December 9, 1961, and December 10, 1963, Tanganyika and Zanzibar, respectively, became independent. On April 26, 1964, Tanganyika and Zanzibar formed a confederation to become the United Republic of Tanzania (URT) and join the British Commonwealth of Nations.

[9] The transformation approach promoted modern, large-scale cash crop farms under the supervision of foreign agricultural experts, but it lacked the necessary financial support because of the sudden withdrawal of foreign aid by the former German Democratic Republic and the United Kingdom.

government marketing boards for "scheduled" crops. The National Agricultural Products Boards managed maize, wheat, rice, cashews, and oil seeds through market purchase; price regulation; and regulation of storage, transport, and processing (see Bryceson 1993).

Arusha Declaration, 1967

In 1967 the ruling government party, Chama cha Mapinduzi (CCM), passed the first national economic declaration establishing Tanzania's era of economic socialism.[10] The Arusha Declaration, named for the location of the conference, clearly meant to address the deficiencies in Tanzania's economic development, but it explicitly endorsed socialism and a planned economy, which the country's new leaders thought appropriate at the time. With the best of intentions, a particular African style of socialism was formulated, embedded in traditions found in Tanzania's family, village, and societal structures. Ujamaa, a Kiswahili word meaning familyhood and relationships, became the expression for Tanzania's socioeconomic system and a synonym for Tanzanian socialism.[11]

Within the Ujamaa policy, the Ujamaa village was believed to be the most productive and efficient unit for fulfilling the requirements of a population scattered across a huge and widely inaccessible country. Even today, 85 percent of Tanzania's population lives in rural areas and is mainly engaged in agricultural activities, generating about 50 percent of gross domestic product (GDP). Some households rely mostly on subsistence production because they are too isolated for extensive economic transactions. The Ujamaa policy incorporated Tanzania's villagization program, which resettled almost 7 million people within one decade.[12] Villagers from remote areas were concentrated in large Ujamaa villages created in locations with greater accessibility to input and output markets. Improved economic infrastructure—such as transport systems, water and energy supply, and health and education facilities—was meant to increase the availability of productive inputs, the capacity of human capital, and the sales prospects for agricultural production. Accordingly, overall national productivity and efficiency in agricultural production would theoretically increase, leading to a rise in per capita income, improved equity of national income distribution, and increased economic welfare.

---

[10] In 1967 the Tanzanian government consisted of the Tanganyika African National Union representing Tanganyika and the Afro Shiraze Party representing Zanzibar, which were separate parties until their unification in 1977. In January 1977 the CCM—the Revolutionary Party—was founded and became the Socialist Unit Party of Tanzania.

[11] The Arusha Declaration formulates the following economic principles: (1) public ownership of the major means of production, (2) preferences for cooperative ownership, (3) a "leadership code" to prevent officials from participating in private economic activities, (4) a policy of self-reliance with diminishing dependency on foreign capital, (5) the establishment of Ujamaa villages, (6) emphasis on food crop agriculture and rural development, and (7) public provision of health care and education (Wenzel and Wiedemann 1989).

[12] In 1973 the Tanganyika African National Union Biennial Conference passed the villagization campaign, which decreed that the entire rural population had to live in permanent villages by 1976.

9

The Ujamaa policy was motivated by the strong desire for self-reliance, based on the assumption that agriculture was the main impetus for overall economic development. Unfortunately, the authorities not only aimed to satisfy national food requirements through self-sufficiency, but also to fulfill all other domestic demand through domestic production. Consequently, through this self-reliant approach Tanzania forced its own withdrawal from international markets.

From 1969 to 1980, the economy operated under the second and third five-year plans following the economic development policy as codified in the Arusha Declaration. Ndulu (1994) characterizes 1961–80 as the first periodic thrust in economic development policy after independence that emphasized state-controlled modernization and structural transformation to reduce reliance on the external economy. Although Tanzania experienced reasonable macroeconomic performance until the mid-1970s,[13] unfavorable external conditions wiped out the previous economic achievements and led to the crisis period of 1980–85 (Ndulu 1994). Even the coffee boom Tanzania experienced between 1975 and 1977, when coffee prices tripled because of frost in Brazil, could not compensate for the negative consequences of the two oil price shocks in 1973/74 and 1979, the breakup of the East African Community in 1977, and the war with Uganda that began in October 1978 (Wenzel and Wiedemann 1989).[14]

Economic Breakdown and Self-Guided Adjustment Efforts

During the early 1980s, Tanzania's economic performance deteriorated continuously, and political leaders had to devise alternatives to socialist failures and a worsening world market situation. Despite all efforts under the Ujamaa policy, Tanzania's economy remained highly inefficient, resulting in low product quality by international standards. Moreover, the extremely overvalued exchange rate decreased the country's competitiveness in traditional agricultural export commodities, thereby diminishing export earnings.[15] In addition, Tanzania's terms of trade deteriorated severely during the early 1980s because of collapsing world market prices.[16] Consequently, the trade deficit increased, foreign capital inflows decreased, and overall indebtedness exceeded critical levels.

---

[13] Annual average growth in real GDP was 3.9 percent during 1966–75, to which growth rates in sectoral value-added contributed as follows: agriculture 2.3 percent, economic services 4.8 percent, manufacturing 6.5 percent, and public services 9.5 percent. Inflation averaged 7.5 percent annually, and the external current account deficit averaged 4.5 percent during the same period.

[14] Along with the unfavorable external conditions Tanzania faced during the 1970s, the economy experienced its worst balance of payments crisis during 1978–80 because of both exogenous and endogenous factors (see Pfeiffer 1989 for an analysis of the balance of payments crisis and its underlying endogenous factors).

[15] The high rate of overvaluation resulted from a controlled and, therefore, quasi-fixed nominal exchange rate and several successive years of inflation.

[16] In 1980 the terms of trade had deteriorated by 11 percent compared with their 1973 level and by 21 percent compared with their 1966 level (Taube 1992), although coffee, for example, experienced another price boom in 1986 that caused temporarily favorable terms of trade.

After negotiations with the IMF on a standby arrangement loan failed in 1979, Tanzania launched its first self-guided National Economic Survival Program (NESP) in 1981. The objective of this program was the conditional liberalization of the economy, and it superseded the fourth five-year plan; however, the NESP basically retained the existing economic regime. In 1982 the government adopted a three-year SAP, prepared with the cooperation of the World Bank and based on the advice of the Tanzanian Advisory Group. This SAP was an exclusively national effort, that is, a homegrown SAP, without any World Bank or IMF financial support. At first, the SAP did not result in any significant changes in Tanzania's economic performance because the government was reluctant to implement the policy measures. It was not until fiscal year (FY) 1984/85 that Tanzania launched its first significant reform aimed at liberalizing the economy. The reform package contained the following main policy measures (Taube 1992; Wenzel and Wiedemann 1989):

- Agricultural producer prices were raised by 46–55 percent.
- Cooperation unions for crop marketing were reintroduced.
- The Tanzanian shilling was depreciated by 40 percent.
- The nominal government budget deficit was frozen at the prior year's amount.
- Government wages were raised by an average of 30 percent.
- Domestic trade of food products was liberalized.
- Consumer price subsidies for maize were eliminated.
- The Own-Fund Import Scheme, which allowed imports purchased with foreign currency deposited abroad, was initiated.

Although the international donor community welcomed these measures as a first step in the right direction, they only marginally affected overall economic performance. Consequently, the international organizations increased their pressure on the Tanzanian government to take further action and pursue a stricter coordination of its economic policies.

Structural Adjustment, Political Liberalization, and Economic Performance after 1986

This section first highlights the evolution of Tanzania's SAPs from 1986 until the present and then describes economic performance and the sectoral policies applied under structural adjustment. In addition, Appendix Table A.1 presents selected country data that provide a number of economic and social indicators relevant to this section.

Evolution of Structural Adjustment Programs from 1986

In the wake of political changes in 1985, when Ali Hassan Mwinyi became president after the 24-year rule of Mwalimu Julius K. Nyerere,[17] the new government

---

[17] Mwalimu is the Kiswahili word for teacher, which was President Nyerere's original occupation but became a respectful form of address for him.

11

adopted a three-year ERP (1987/88–1989/90) as announced in the 1986/87 budget.[18] The ERP's medium-term objectives were a positive growth rate in per capita income, a GDP target growth rate of 4.5 percent, an inflation rate below 10 percent in 1989/90, a fiscal government deficit below 13 percent of GDP, an adjustment of the exchange rate toward an "equilibrium" exchange rate in mid-1988, positive real interest rates by mid-1988, an increase of between 30 and 80 percent in nominal producer prices for cash crops, and decontrol of domestic prices over a period of three years. During the course of the ERP, Tanzania obtained an 18-month standby arrangement with the IMF in August 1986 and a Multisector Rehabilitation Credit from the IDA and donor governments in November 1986.[19] Furthermore, Tanzania became eligible for the rescheduling of loans in the so-called Paris Club, including the postponement and cancellation of existing principal and interest in October 1986. Finally, in July 1987, under the Structural Adjustment Facility, the IMF approved a 67.9 million Special Drawing Rights (SDR) loan in support of the ERP.[20]

As discussed by Taube (1992), the Tanzanian ERP of 1986/87–1989/90 reflects the theoretical debate on macroeconomic stabilization and structural adjustment in the 1980s. It had a medium-term horizon, and it aimed not only at outward orientation and monetary stability, but also at economic growth issues. The program tried to avoid excessive stabilization and aimed instead at expansionary stabilization and adjustment for growth.

The objectives of the ERP were incorporated in the 1988/89–1992/93 five-year development plan and were reinforced by the Economic and Social Action Program (ESAP) in 1989. Within the scope of the two programs, the government strove for a general reduction of state controls and the promotion of private sector activities. In this context, it declared the rehabilitation of key infrastructure components a priority to support future economic development, especially transportation facilities like roads, railways, and ports. The economy initially responded positively with an average annual GDP growth rate of around 4 percent during 1986–94. However, during its second term (1990–95), the Mwinyi administration showed a much lower commitment to reforms, which led to deteriorating macroeconomic management, worsening macroeconomic performance, and instability.[21] In reaction, the IMF, World Bank, and most bilateral donors sharply reduced their support, suspended payments for development projects

---

[18] The ERP documentation specifies four general objectives: (1) increase the output of food and export crops by providing appropriate incentives for production, improving market structures, and increasing the resources available to agriculture; (2) rehabilitate the physical infrastructure in support of directly productive activities; (3) increase capacity utilization in industry by allocating scarce foreign exchange to priority sectors and firms; and (4) restore internal and external balances by pursuing prudent fiscal, monetary, and trade policies (URT 1986).

[19] In particular, 64.2 million Special Drawing Rights (SDR) through the IMF; US$100 million through IDA; and US$50 million provided by the Federal Republic of Germany, the Netherlands, Switzerland, and the United Kingdom.

[20] The section mainly draws on Appendix 1 in Wenzel and Wiedemann 1989.

[21] Annual inflation, measured as a GDP deflator, increased from 21.8 to 25.3 to 40.6 percent during 1990–92; exports of goods and services at constant 1995 U.S. dollars declined from US$643.1 million in 1989 to US$592.4 million in 1990, US$385.4 million in 1991, and US$353.4 million in 1992; imports increased by 3 percent annually during the same period; and GDP at factor costs experienced an 8.4 percent decrease from 1991 to 1992.

and balance of payments assistance, and refused any further financial assistance (World Bank 1999a).

The first presidential and parliamentary multiparty elections in November 1995 confirmed the majority of the ruling CCM and elected President Benjamin Mkapa.[22] The Mkapa government immediately approached the IMF to revive Tanzania's economic reform efforts of the late 1980s, which first resulted in Tanzania's acceptance of the obligations of Article VIII, Sections 2, 3, and 4 of the IMF Articles of Agreement, effective from July 15, 1996.[23] By signing Article VIII, Tanzania regained the confidence of the international donor community in its serious commitment to pursue sound economic policies. In November 1996 the IMF approved a three-year credit under the Enhanced Structural Adjustment Facility (ESAF)[24] to support Tanzania's new ERP for 1996/97–1998/99.[25] The new ERP emphasized fiscal performance and structural reforms, namely:

- building administrative capacity for improving development management;
- maintaining a stable fiscal stance and using public resources more efficiently;
- promoting the private sector by deregulating investment and divesting parastatals;
- providing greater support for primary education and basic health care;
- supporting the development of basic infrastructure, especially to give impetus to rural agricultural development;
- restructuring the financial sector to respond to the needs of the private sector (World Bank 1999a).

The ongoing ERP is well under way, and the third and last tranche of the ESAF credit was disbursed in February 1999. The IMF and other donors have expressed their satisfaction with recent economic developments in Tanzania, especially considering the negative effects of the 1996/97 drought and the 1997/98 El Niño floods. During their Article IV consultations with Tanzania in February 1999,[26] IMF executive directors "commended the Tanzanian authorities for their steadfast implementation of prudent macroeconomic policies and progress in structural reforms during the past three years,

---

[22] The first local multiparty elections had already been held in late 1994.

[23] "IMF members accepting the obligations of Article VIII undertake to refrain from imposing restrictions on the making of payments and transfers for current international transactions or from engaging in discriminatory currency arrangements or multiple currency practices without IMF approval" (see IMF Press Release Number 96/42, July 25, 1996, at http://www.imf.org).

[24] "ESAF is a concessional IMF facility for assisting eligible members that are undertaking economic reform programs to strengthen their balance of payments and to improve their growth prospects. ESAF loans carry an interest rate of 0.5 percent per annum, and are repayable over 10 years, with a 5-1/2-year grace period" (see IMF Press Release Number 96/55, November 25, 1996, at http://www.imf.org).

[25] The total three-year credit had an original equivalent of SDR 161.6 million and was approved in three annual loans of SDR 51.4 million in November 1996, SDR 71.4 million in December 1997 (including an SDR 20 million increase to deal with the effects of the 1996/97 drought), and SDR 58.8 million in February 1999 (augmented by SDR 20 million to deal with the effects of the 1997/98 El Niño floods). Tanzania joined the IMF in 1962. Its current quota is SDR 146.9 million (see IMF Press Releases Numbers 96/55, 97/54, and 99/6 at http://www.imf.org).

[26] "Under Article IV of the IMF's Articles of Agreement, the IMF holds bilateral discussions with members, usually every year" (see IMF Public Information Notice 99/28 from March 31, 1999, at http://www.imf.org).

despite the severe economic disruptions caused by adverse weather conditions" (IMF 1999). In particular, the executive directors welcomed the continuous overall growth, increasing gross reserves, strong fiscal stance, tight monetary policies, and recent structural reforms, namely, introduction of the VAT on July 1, 1998; the effectiveness of the government's cash management system; and the progressing privatization of parastatal entities. However, the positive indications of an ongoing economic transition process and the first signs of improved macroeconomic stability should not detract from the indisputable necessity of further joint efforts between Tanzanian authorities, international financial institutions, and bilateral donors to promote further reform. A first promising sign of continual joint endeavor is the IMF's consideration of Tanzania's eligibility under the HIPC Initiative (IMF 1999).[27] Whatever the next multilateral loan is called and under which facility it might be scheduled, in the short and medium term Tanzania will depend heavily on another phase of international financial, as well as technical, assistance until its administrative capacity and economic structure allow for a more self-reliant and sustainable development path.

Economic Performance and Policies Applied under Structural Adjustment

This section provides an overview of Tanzania's economic performance under structural adjustment, focusing on recent developments, followed by a detailed description of sectoral, structural, and macroeconomic policies implemented during this period.[28]

General Economic Performance. According to the *Policy Framework Paper for 1998/ 99–2000/01*, published in January 1999, the general performance of the Tanzanian economy under the ERP 1996/97–1998/99 was satisfactory (IMF 1999; URT, IMF, and World Bank 1999; World Bank 1999b).[29] Since the mid-1990s, the Tanzanian government has pursued substantial structural policy reforms to achieve further trade liberalization, enhanced fiscal consolidation, streamlining of the civil service sector, privatization of parastatals, tight monetary growth, better delivery of social services, and poverty alleviation. Even though the 1996/97 drought and the 1997/98 El Niño floods had a negative effect on economic performance, real per capita income improved between 1995 and 1998, while inflation declined and the external position continued to strengthen.[30] Government savings were about 1 percent of GDP for both

---

[27] Tanzania's eligibility under the HIPC Initiative may be decided at the upcoming midterm review of the current ESAF arrangement.

[28] Tanzania's serious commitment to the transition process and the actions that have been taken to implement the economic reforms are summarized in Appendix Table A.2.

[29] The description of the current economic performance of the Tanzanian economy in this section draws heavily on the *Policy Framework Paper 1989/99–2000/01,* Public Information Notice Number 99/28 of the IMF, and Press Release Number 99/6 of the IMF, the most recent official documents available.

[30] According to the most recent available data in *World Development Indicators 2000,* GDP per capita, measured at purchasing power parity in current international dollars, increased from 461 to 472 to 473 to 480 for the years 1995–98; annual inflation with respect to consumer prices decreased from 28.4 to 21.0 to 16.1 to 12.8 percent during the same period; and the trade deficit in constant 1995 U.S. dollar decreased from US$984 million to US$800 million to US$589 million to US$417 million during 1995–98 (World Bank 2000b).

fiscal years; inflation was at an annual rate of 12 percent by the end of June 1998 and 7 percent by the end of December 1999, the lowest rate in 20 years; international gross reserves increased by more than 10 percent and outperformed the target of an equivalent of three months of imports of goods and nonfactor services (4.1 months by the end of December 1999); and the Tanzanian shilling nominally depreciated by only 7 percent against the U.S. dollar during 1997/98, which translates into a real appreciation given the inflation rate of 12 percent during this period. However, agricultural growth was far below target, mainly because of climate-related factors, and total GDP growth of 3.4 percent in 1997/98 could only be achieved through much higher growth in some nonagricultural sectors;[31] exports declined by 19 percent in 1997/98; the current account deficit, excluding official transfers, increased to 14.2 percent of GDP; and government revenue fell by 1.2 percentage points to 12.3 percent of GDP (IDA/IMF 2000).

GDP Development. The growth of GDP at factor costs during the prestructural adjustment period was characterized by high volatility. After moderate GDP growth from independence in 1961 until 1976, the average annual growth rate sank to 1 percent in 1977 and 1978, then recovered to previous levels in 1979 and 1980, and finally became negative in 1981 (–0.5 percent) and 1983 (–2.4 percent). However, in 1984 and 1985, the two last years before the implementation of the ERP, GDP growth was 3.4 and 4.6 percent, respectively, which amounts to an increase of 5.8 percentage points from 1983 to 1984.

GDP increased substantially after implementation of the 1986 ERP, but collapsed during the early 1990s, the second term of the Mwinyi government (Figure 2.1). Following implementation of the 1996 ERP, GDP growth regained levels that translate into positive per capita growth, but remained below targets, mainly because of adverse weather conditions during FY 1996/97 and 1997/98. In FY 1998/99, GDP continued to grow at the previous year's level, and for the two following fiscal years it was projected to grow between 5.2 and 5.9 percent per year.

Although these growth rates look promising at first sight, Tanzania's population continues to grow at high annual rates.[32] Furthermore, with a real GDP per capita of current US$129.50 in 1995, which translates into a US$461 purchasing power parity, Tanzania has one of the lowest per capita GDP levels in the world. It requires substantial and continuous growth over a medium-term horizon even to reach the still poor SSA average of about US$500 in real GDP per capita (UNDP 1996; URT 1995c; URT 1996b; World Bank 1996b).

---

[31] Agricultural GDP growth slowed from 4.8 to 3.2 to 2.2 percent between 1996 and 1998, but still contributed between 46 and 48 percent to total value-added during this period (World Bank 2000b).

[32] Even though the population growth rate decreased by 0.1 percentage points annually during 1994 to 1998 from 3.0 to 2.6 percent, it still shows extremely high levels that constitute the gap between the real GDP growth rate and the per capita growth rate. If the annual real GDP growth rate falls below 2.6 percent, the per capita growth rate will be negative. However, this is not a well-substantiated figure, because the last census was in the mid-1980s.

Figure 2.1—Annual growth rate of GDP at factor costs, 1989–99

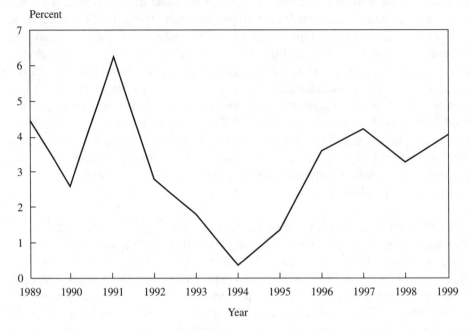

Source: BOT (1991): *Economic Bulletin*, vol. 29, no.3, Table 1.9.
Note: Figures are for total GDP at constant 1992 prices for the Tanzanian mainland, including an approximately 27 percent share of nonmonetary GDP for the relevant period. In consideration of an annual population growth rate of 2.8 to 3.0 percent, all total GDP growth rates lower than 2.8 to 3.0 percent translate to negative per capita GDP growth rates.

As mentioned in the *UNDP Development Co-operation 1995 Report*, agriculture remains the most important source of economic growth, but some nonagricultural activities show promising growth rates as well, especially the mining and tourism sectors:

> The positive growth performance in the economy was due mainly to strong growth in the agricultural sector, which comprised 55.2 percent of GDP and which experienced real growth of 7 percent during the year, but was shared by almost all sectors except public administration, construction and manufacturing. The economy's positive performance can be seen in the following sectors: Mining and Quarrying (5.9 percent); Electricity and Water (4.4 percent); Wholesale/Retail Trade, Hotels and Restaurants (5.7 percent); Transport and Communications (9.3 percent); and Finance, Insurance, Real Estate and Business Services (8 percent) (UNDP 1996, pp. 20–21).

Because of unfavorable weather conditions during the 1996/97 and 1997/98 cropping seasons and other potential setbacks in agricultural production for external or internal reasons, the shift from dominating growth in agriculture to dominating growth in nonagriculture continued in 1996–98.

Price and Market Reforms. In the context of the 1986 ERP, an additional Agricultural Adjustment Program was formulated to complement the macroeconomic adjustment process and generate a sufficient supply response. The main objectives of the program were to (1) liberalize the marketing and pricing of food grains, (2) initiate the liberalization of the major export crop markets, (3) remove the monopoly export power of the crop marketing boards, (4) restructure parastatals in agriculture, and (5) improve the efficiency of export crop tenders and auctions and crop processing industries (World Bank 1994a). Most domestic market controls on food crops were abolished in 1989, including the restrictions on the marketing and transportation of food grains. Producer prices for the main agricultural products were liberalized between FY 1991/92 and FY 1993/94. The marketing of nontraditional export crops was also liberalized in the late 1980s. In 1990 this liberalization was extended to traditional export crops such as coffee, tobacco, cashews, and cotton. During the 1991/92 marketing season, private traders were allowed to buy cashew nuts, and in 1993 private marketing of all major traditional export crops was permitted. The list of items subject to price controls was reduced from 400 to 2—petroleum products and electricity—throughout the liberalization process. In addition to price and market liberalization of agricultural commodities, subsidies for agricultural inputs such as fertilizer were phased out (World Bank 1996b).

Import Rationing. Permission to import from own funds—foreign currency deposited abroad—was given in 1984 and accounts for one-third of total imports today. In the context of the 1986 ERP, quantitative import restrictions were replaced with a system of open general licenses (OGLs). The negative list for imports under the OGLs was substantially reduced in 1992, and the share of nonoil imports subject to licensing under the OGLs was only 20 percent of total nonoil imports. In July 1993 the OGL negative list was further reduced and included goods for health or security reasons or because they were considered luxury goods. In February 1994 the negative list was further shortened and restricted to health- and security-related goods; crude petroleum and luxury goods no longer require import licenses (World Bank 1996b).

Tariff Rates. Before June 1988 the tariff system contained 20 different rates with a maximum tariff of 200 percent. The system was reduced to four nonzero tariff rates by 1990, and the maximum tariff rate was steadily reduced to 50 percent in July 1994 and to 30 percent in June 1997.[33] Despite the rate reductions, the share of collected import duties in total tax revenue increased from an

---

[33] The effective tariff schedule as of July 1996 is ad valorem for most items with four bands at 5, 10, 20, and 30 percent. Capital goods are taxed at 5–10 percent, and intermediate and consumer goods are taxed at 10–30 percent (IMF 1998).

average of 14.1 percent during the prereform period 1981/82–1985/86 to 26.3 percent during the reform years of 1986/87–1995/96 (URT, IMF, and World Bank 1999; World Bank 1996b). This substantial increase primarily reflects increased import volumes, but may also reflect more efficient tax collection following the tariff rate harmonization.

Export Taxes. Export taxation was suspended in 1982 and reintroduced with the 1996/97 budget for traditional goods (cotton, coffee, tobacco, tea, sisal, cashew nuts, and minerals) at a rate of 2 percent of their export value. Its expected contribution to total revenue collection was estimated at TSh 1,800 million or 0.3 percent.[34]

The reintroduction of an export tax on traditional export agriculture increased the degree of taxation of agriculture yet again, compounding other financial burdens placed on agricultural producers, such as the increase in the minimum wage,[35] increased duties on imported assembled vehicles, stamp duty (1 percent), and contributions to crop marketing authorities. Consequently, many producers are concerned about how agricultural products will sustain increased competitiveness in international markets (see Tanzanian government 1996/97 budget summary in Coopers and Lybrand 1996).

Input Subsidies. Fertilizer prices were highly subsidized during the preadjustment period. Because of subsidization, farmgate prices fell by around 50 percent between 1976 and 1984. Although explicit subsidies were abolished in 1984, "repeated currency devaluation overtook the increases in the fertilizer selling price permitted to the Tanzania Fertilizer Corporation so that by 1988/89 there was an implicit subsidy of up to 80 percent" (World Bank 1994b, p. 78). From 1990/91 onward the subsidy was phased out with 70, 55, 40, and 25 percent for the respective fiscal years and with zero subsidy since 1994/95. The elimination of fertilizer subsidies in combination with continued inflation and subsequent currency devaluation caused rapid increases in local input prices for the different varieties of fertilizer. In 1991/92, for example, the domestic market prices for fertilizer (in nominal terms) rose an average of 85 percent and from 32 to 91 percent in 1992/93.[36] However, despite these sharp price increases, the supply of fertilizer in the mid-1990s still did not meet demand, mainly as a result of extremely poor supply channels (World Bank 1994b).

Exchange Rate Policy and Foreign Exchange. The exchange rate was effectively unified in August 1993 when the official rate was set on the basis of rates prevailing in the foreign exchange auction introduced in July 1993. The foreign exchange

---

[34] Taken from a speech on FY 1996/97 by the minister for finance (see URT 1996b).

[35] The official monthly minimum wage increased from TSh 17,500 to TSh 30,000 in July 1996.

[36] The GDP deflator for this period ranges around 30 percent inflation annually.

market was further liberalized when the auction was replaced by an interbank market for foreign exchange in June 1994.

Furthermore, the surrender requirement on proceeds from nontraditional exports was abolished in July 1993 and for traditional exports (except coffee) in June 1994. The exchange system for payments and transfers for current international transactions has been completely liberalized, and no limits are imposed on current payments and transfers.[37] Administrative controls on imports have been removed, and trade restrictions on foreign exchange remain only for petroleum products and a few goods restricted for health and security reasons (URT, IMF, and World Bank 1999; URT, IMF, and World Bank 1996).

Table 2.1 presents the exchange rate development of the Tanzanian shilling since 1985 when the first ERP was implemented. The shilling experienced rapid devaluation between 1985 and 1989, followed by two years of mild depreciation and two years of moderate depreciation before the exchange rate market was fully liberalized in 1993/94. Since that time depreciation of the exchange rate shows a stable path at low levels. The liberalization of the foreign exchange market not only contributed to this stability, but improved political circumstances as well. The influence of the 1995 national elections on monthly exchange rate figures for 1995 and 1996 is shown in Table 2.2.

The first free and democratic elections in Tanzania under a multiparty system were held in October 1995. From a stable position during the first four months of 1995, the exchange rate depreciated during the pre-election period and then reappreciated after the elections, which restored the former united CCM party and elected Benjamin Mkapa as the new president.[38]

Domestic Tax Policies.[39] Total tax revenue declined substantially from prereform years until the first half of the 1990s. Tax revenues as a share of GDP declined during 1982–86 (16.5 percent), 1987–92 (14.2 percent), and 1993–96 (13.1 percent). Weaknesses in tax administration and the proliferation of exemptions caused the worst performance in FY 1992/93, with a revenue-GDP ratio of only 11.4 percent. The decline in performance was also caused by structural changes in the economy, as the composition of output shifted toward sectors that were more difficult to tax. For example, the GDP share of manufacturing and mining declined throughout the 1980s, while the GDP share of agriculture and the nonmonetary informal sector both increased.

---

[37] A measure that is in accordance with the obligations of Article VIII, Sections 2, 3, and 4, of the IMF Articles of Agreement, accepted by Tanzania in July 1996.

[38] This information is based on BOT 1998, *Economic Bulletin* for the quarter ended September 30, 1998, vol. 28, no. 3, Table 4.3; OANDA (1999), Classic 164 Currency Converter, available at http://www.oanda.com, accessed May 30, 1999; and the author's calculations.

[39] Data on domestic tax policies are based on IMF (1996b); Coopers and Lybrand (1994, 1995); Tanzanian government budget summary 1994/95, 1995/96; and World Bank (1996b).

Table 2.1—Annual exchange rates, 1985–98

Year	1985	1986	1987	1988	1989	1990	1991	1992	1993	1994	1995	1996	1997	1998
Rate	16	52	84	125	192	197	234	335	480	523	558	596	625	681
Percentage change	—	225	62	49	54	3	19	43	43	9	7	7	5	9

Source: BOT, several quarterly *Economic Bulletins*; author's calculations.
Note: Exchange rates are official mean selling rates for U.S. dollars in Tanzanian shillings for the end of each period. Data are rounded to the closest integer.
— Not available.

20

Table 2.2—Monthly exchange rates, 1995–96

Year	Jan.	Feb.	Mar.	Apr.	May	Jun.	Jul.	Aug.	Sep.	Oct.	Nov.	Dec.
1995	538	545	545	551	581	603	601	616	614	610	586	558
1996	542	542	542	550	606	620	596	591	590	597	594	596

Source: BOT 1997, *Economic Bulletin* for the quarter ended December 31, 1996.
Note: Exchange rates are official mean selling rates for U.S. dollars in Tanzanian shillings for the end of each period. Data are rounded to the closest integer.

Domestic sales tax revenues declined from 8.2 percent of GDP during the prereform period to 3.6 percent of GDP during the reform period, while income tax revenues declined from 5.1 to 3.6 percent for the same periods. Although trade tax collection improved from 2.3 percent to 3.6 percent of GDP for these periods, the rise could not compensate for the losses in income and consumption taxes, which constitute more than 60 percent of total tax revenue for the periods under consideration.

Before the reform period, the sales tax schedule contained more than 26 rates with a maximum rate of 300 percent. Until 1995, the number of sales tax rates was gradually reduced first to seven and then only two ad valorem rates for imported and domestic goods (25 and 30 percent) and three rates for services (5, 10, and 15 percent).[40] Excise duty, generally 30 percent, is levied on petroleum products, alcoholic beverages, cigarettes, cosmetics and perfumes, and soft drinks. Since 1992/93 several measures have been applied to simplify the confusing tax structure, and tax rates have been substantially reduced. The list shown in Appendix Table A.4 summarizes the major steps of tax reforms in the 1990s.

Agricultural Stocking Behavior. The national Strategic Grain Reserve holds a total stock of 150,000 tons of staple food crops for emergency situations. Because Tanzania generally has a positive overall food balance, the annual emergency grain procurement targets can usually be fulfilled by domestic production. Tanzania does not rely on regular annual shipments of food aid. However, the adverse weather conditions of two recent cropping seasons (the 1996/97 drought and the 1997/98 El Niño floods) forced the government to request international assistance under the Food and Agriculture Organization of the United Nations/World Food Programme (FAO/WFP). Since early 1998, three FAO/WFP crop and food supply assessment missions have taken place to monitor the situation and implement assistance measures.[41]

Foreign Aid and Private Capital Flows. Throughout the first 10 years of structural adjustment between 1986 and the end of 1995, Tanzania accumulated a total medium- and long-term external debt of US$6.3 billion. About 50 percent of this debt was owed to bilateral official creditors, 40 percent to multilateral creditors, 3 percent to the IMF, and the remaining 7 percent to private financial institutions and suppliers. The major multilateral creditor was IDA, to whom Tanzania owed US$2.2 billion, 35 percent of its total debt, or 75 percent of its total multilateral debt.[42] During 1991–95, Tanzania borrowed on extremely concessional terms with an average commitment structure as follows: interest rate of 1.3 percent per year, repayment period of 36 years, grace period of 9 years, and a grant element of about 70 percent (IMF 1996a).

---

[40] Some goods bear specific rates, however.

[41] For detailed information, refer to the three special reports on the *FAO/WFP Crop and Food Supply Assessment Mission to Tanzania,* February 19, 1998; August 3, 1998; and February 15, 1999 available at http://www.fao.org.

[42] Detailed information on the composition of the external debt can be found in World Bank 1996b, pp. 26–32.

Throughout the 1996 ERP period, Tanzania received substantial foreign assistance, and its debt position continued to worsen. The total debt stock reached nearly US$8 billion in 1996/97, or some 110 percent of GDP. Public debt service of US$316.3 million in 1996/97 was equivalent to 25.2 percent of export earnings. The IMF estimates total debt in 1998/99 at a similar absolute level as in 1996/97, even after the debt relief that followed recent IMF negotiations and the rescheduling of flows in accordance with the Naples terms of the Paris Club agreement. Assuming strong GDP growth, total debt will fall below 100 percent of GDP, and total public debt services will amount to 21.6 percent of export earnings instead of 29.1 percent without debt relief.[43]

The comparison of Tanzania's debt situation before and after the 1996 ERP reveals that the overall debt situation hardly improved through the SAPs. As soon as Tanzania regained the attention of the international donor community through its good governance and the application of reform policies, its balance of trade position deteriorated because of a new foreign capital influx. Tanzania has to be extremely careful in deciding where to invest this additional capital. A substantial share of this capital should be invested in sectors that will yield significant profits. In the long term, this should result in a reduction in the country's overall national indebtedness.

Land Policies (IMF1996b; URT 1995b; World Bank 1996b). The land surface of mainland Tanzania is approximately 881,300 square kilometers, while the islands of Zanzibar and Pemba make up an additional 2,000 square kilometers. Inland lakes comprise another 61,500 square kilometers. With the exception of a few mountains, most of the country forms a plateau at 1,020 to 1,650 meters above sea level. Forty-six percent of the total land area is forests and woodlands, while 40 percent is permanent pasture.[44]

Although Tanzania has about 487,100 square kilometers of potentially arable land, 1992 Ministry of Agriculture statistics show that only 10.1 percent of this area is under cultivation. Of this area, nearly 93.4 percent (46,000 square kilometers) is used for small-scale farming by landholders who cultivate the land mainly under customary tenure. The remaining 6.6 percent is used for large-scale farming under granted rights of occupancy.

Figure 2.2 shows the actual land use of the total mainland Tanzania area, including water areas, accounting for 942,800 square kilometers. Only 3 percent of the total mainland Tanzania area is cropped, although an additional 6 percent is considered suitable for arable farming.

---

[43] For the most recent figures on Tanzania's debt situation and for a 15-year projection, see URT, IMF, and World Bank 1999. Because neither GDP nor foreign trade development can be projected reliably and because it is equally difficult to assume the volumes of loans throughout this period, these projections are somewhat arbitrary; however, a total debt stock representing only 52.4 percent of 2015/16 GDP while paying just 7.7 percent of export earnings in public debt service tempts one to hope.

[44] For a detailed description of the nine different physiographic regions and the seven different agroecological zones in Tanzania, refer to Appendix Table A.3.

Figure 2.2—Land use in mainland Tanzania

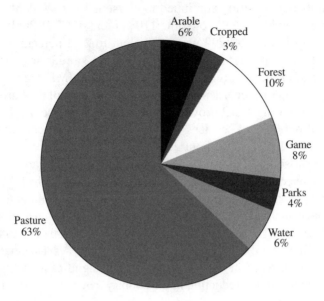

Source: World Bank (1994b).

Although land in Tanzania is not scarce, within the arable and cultivated areas the country faces increasing problems, such as soil fertility losses, soil erosion, deforestation, water pollution, and the development of industry and mining. The increasing pressure led to the adoption of a sustainable National Land Policy (NLP), which the cabinet approved in March 1995. The NLP declares that "all land in Tanzania is public land vested in the President as trustee on behalf of all citizens." The policy allows the individualization of village land, stating that "individuals should be allowed to obtain individual titles within areas not designated for" other uses (URT 1995b, p. 7). The NLP is viewed as an instrument of compromise to help heal the myriad grievances that have come to characterize land policy in Tanzania. Its success in making land tenure more secure will depend on how it is implemented. The most serious challenge to the NLP's implementation is the lack of administrative capacity and information, including insufficient land survey data.

However, compared with many other developing economies dominated by agriculture, Tanzania has a relative abundance of land and has some unexploited potential for future land use. Environmentally friendly and economically sustainable land use is all the more important as land ownership is the single most important safety net in Tanzania: 98 percent of all rural households own some land—5.18 acres on average according to the 1995 rural Participatory Poverty Assessment (PPA) survey.

Credit Policy—Rural Credit. Eighty-nine percent of the villages surveyed in the 1995 rural PPA survey mentioned lack of credit as a constraint to agricultural production. A total of 58.7 percent of households in the lowest expenditure quintile and 39.1 percent in the highest quintile reported that credit was not available during the 1993/94 season. The main sources of credit for those who did borrow were family, friends, traders, trade stores, private moneylenders, or cooperatives. Farmers in the lowest quintile borrowed to buy seasonal inputs (fertilizer, agro-chemicals, and seeds). Farmers in the highest quintile borrowed primarily to hire labor to work on their land. Commercial credits in rural areas are relatively rare. In the PPA survey, 57 of 77 village focus groups that participated had no knowledge of the Cooperative and Rural Development Bank or the National Bank of Commerce, and 65 groups did not know about the postal bank (World Bank 1994b).

Private Banks. Even though the Financial and Banking Institution Act was approved in 1991, the first two private banks in Tanzania began operating only in late 1993. Their operations concentrated on trade financing and mobilizing foreign exchange deposits, mostly in the Dar es Salaam area. Five new private banks and several other private financial institutions have entered the market since mid-1995 and expanded private banking operations. The market share of private banks in domestic credit increased from about 3 percent in June 1994 to almost 30 percent in August 1996. The share of private banks in deposit mobilization rose from about 12 to 23 percent during the same period.

Interest Rate Structure. Both deposit and lending rates were deregulated in 1994. As a result, lending rates at first rose, but then fell below their pre-1994 levels. Unlike the lending rates, deposit rates edged down in 1995 because of predictions of a lower inflation rate. They have continued to fall steadily since deregulation, and their 1997 and 1998 levels did not even compensate for inflation. Comparing actual saving and lending rates reveals that while saving is hardly worthwhile, borrowing for investment purposes is fairly expensive and can be profitable only when marginal returns to investment exceed international levels. Table 2.3 details the development of the interest rate structure between 1992 and 1998.

General Domestic Credit Performance. During the last five years, the restructuring of parastatal enterprises has had a significant influence on credit performance. The importance of parastatal restructuring to the health of Tanzania's financial system is evident in that until 1990, about 80 percent of the loan portfolio of the National Bank of Commerce consisted of loans to only 20 borrowers, of which 19 were parastatal enterprises.

Table 2.3—Deposit and lending rates, 1992–98

Interest rate structure	1992	1993	1994	1995	1996	1997	1998[a]
Deposit rates							
Savings	26	24	24–26	15–27	11–22	7–13	2–12
Short term							
(1–3 months)	16	16–18	16–19	13–33	2–33	4–14	4–14
Fixed (3–6 months)	17–30	22–25	17–31	15–35	8–34	3–29	4–13
Lending rates							
Short term	18–31	22–31	28–39	28–45	28–46	21–28	15–28
Medium and							
long term	29–31	21–39	24–39	31–40	29–38	21–32	20–32
Housing mortgages	9–29	9–29	29–33	29–33	0[b]	0[b]	0[b]

Source: BOT (1998), *Economic Bulletin*, for the quarter ended March 31.
[a] End of September 1998.
[b] No mortgage rates after the collapse of Tanzanian Housing Bank.

CHAPTER 3

The General Equilibrium Approach

The first sections of this chapter describe the general equilibrium approach to modeling. First, in general terms, it explains the choice of methodology used in this study. Second, it looks at the historical development and current state of CGE modeling, including

- review of the development of empirical economic modeling to identify the different strands and stages of CGE modeling, such as
  — theoretical developments,
  — nature of CGEs,
  — different types and broad range of applications;
- discussion of existing CGE applications to Tanzania;
- placement of the specific approach chosen here within the broad field of CGE applications;
- discussion of the potential for future methodological development.

Motivation for the Choice of Methodology

CGE modeling, a powerful methodological tool for policy analysis, is widely used in various fields of economic research, including development economics focusing on agriculture. A CGE model is an appropriate instrument to analyze external shocks and domestic policies in which multisectoral linkages are important. Country-specific applications of empirical models serve as a laboratory for a wide range of policy simulations for analyzing the effects of various policies on the domestic economy. A detailed institutional specification and a country-specific set of variables and parameters adequately characterize the economy under consideration. Such an applied CGE model supports quantitative analysis of changes in economic core variables due to sector-specific and macroeconomic policy measures, as opposed to only determining the direction of change or simply conducting qualitative analysis.

Development and Current Stage of CGE Modeling

Forty years after Johansen (1960) formulated the first CGE model applications of the CGE approach are numerous. Applications cover a variety of (1) countries and regions; (2) model features concerning factor markets, macroeconomic variables, specification of agents, and sector disaggregation; and (3) policies under consideration, such as those regarding domestic taxes, foreign trade, labor markets, production technologies, and the natural environment. Furthermore, a variety of enhanced modeling approaches emerged during the 1990s. Some approaches have incorporated money, assets, and financial markets to connect the microeconomically focused Walrasian CGE model to Keynesian macroeconomic models that focus on stock equilibriums. Other approaches taken during the 1990s moved from single-period models appropriate for comparative-static analysis to multiperiod dynamic models.

In examining the CGE-related literature of the past 40 years, one observes different stages of development of the underlying theoretical models; existence proofs; and computational, algorithmic, and programming issues. To capture important aspects of this literature, the following sections emphasize theoretical developments, present the various applications, focus on the development of agricultural CGE models, and discuss the reconciliation between macroeconomic models and the microeconomically based CGE approach.

Theoretical Developments

The relevant theoretical development for the CGE literature began in the late 1930s and consists of both pure theoretical work on general equilibrium issues as well as empirical work on different model specifications and solution techniques. In 1941 Leontief developed the first empirical model of a national economy. His work, *The Structure of the American Economy 1919–29,* represents the classic input-output study (Leontief 1941). It was influenced by the recession of the 1930s and was applied to policy simulations during World War II. Stimulated by Hicks's publication of *Value and Capital* in 1939 (Hicks 1939), Samuelson, Arrow, Debreu, Hahn, McKenzie, and Negishi pushed forward the development of general equilibrium theory. Little work had been done prior to Wald's (1936) proof of the existence of a static market equilibrium under perfect competition, but in the 1940s and 1950s mathematicians and economists competed to develop the proofs of existence, uniqueness, optimality, and stability of equilibriums under general equilibrium conditions (Felderer and Homburg 1984; Weintraub 1983).[45] Negishi's (1960) theorem established "the equivalence between the Arrow-Debreu equilibrium problem and a specific mathematical programming problem" and represented "the theoretical foundation for the use of mathematical programming models in general equilibrium"

---

[45] Hicks' contribution is considered the culmination of classical general equilibrium theory initiated by Walras (1874) and Pareto (1909). In the 1940s the application of differential calculus as the standard analytical technique in economics was widely replaced by convexity theory and topology. Arrow (1952) and Debreu (1951) formulated the two fundamental theorems of welfare economics that established the Arrow-Debreu (and Hahn) general equilibrium approach and led to Debreu's fundamental *Theory of Value* (1959). Arrow and Hahn (1971) summarize this modern tradition of general equilibrium theory. Excellent recent surveys are Weintraub (1983, 1985) and Mas-Colell (1985).

(Ginsburgh and Van der Heyden 1985). Prior to Negishi, linear programming approaches maximized utility subject to the production possibility frontier plus additional market constraints that picked up shadow prices (Lagrange multipliers). Within this programming model environment, without multiple consumers and no endogenously specified prices, it could be proved that shadow prices equal market prices if the model did not contain any price wedges. In 1958 a study by Dorfman, Samuelson, and Solow (1958) thoroughly treated this early stage of a definite, defined, multisectoral market equilibrium. In the wake of the Negishi theorem, other theorists developed more advanced multisectoral linear programming models (for detailed surveys, see Ginsburgh and Waelbroeck 1981; Taylor 1975).

At the same time as economywide programming models were being developed, Johansen explicitly formulated the first CGE model in 1960, solving for equilibrium prices directly, without reference to shadow prices in a programming model. Dixon et al. (1992) pointed out that Johansen's 20-sector model (1) was general in terms of specifying cost-minimizing industries and utility-maximizing households, (2) "employed market equilibrium assumptions in the determination of prices," and (3) was computable in that it generated a multisectoral numerical description of the Norwegian economy. The Johansen approach took the logarithmic derivatives of a nonlinear general equilibrium specification and derived a linear approximation of the nonlinear model that could be solved by simple matrix inversion (Johansen method). Dixon et al. (1982) further developed the Johansen approach in their multisectoral ORANI model for the Australian economy.[46] Moreover, Hertel and his colleagues at Purdue University use an ORANI-inspired approach in multicountry models for a wide range of applications (for a survey, see Hertel 1997a).

After Johansen's linear approximation in 1960, more than a decade passed without significant adaptation of his approach or further development in empirical CGE modeling. Instead, the 1960s brought development of theoretical proofs concerning general equilibrium models. Empirical applications mostly used linear programming and input-output methods. Scarf (1967a, 1967b, 1973) initiated a second approach in solving general equilibrium models by developing a fixed-point algorithm capable of solving a nonlinear CGE equation system directly, without a prior linear approximation. The Scarf algorithm was based on specifying an excess demand system characterized by non-negative solution prices, consistent with Arrow-Debreu theory. With its finite convergence properties, the algorithm guaranteed a solution for a wide variety of CGE models in a finite number of steps. Shoven and Whalley (1972, 1973, 1974), students of Scarf at Yale, adopted the algorithm, and through their contributions further expanded the CGE application in North America (Dixon et al. 1992). However, the Scarf algorithm does not typically converge quickly and turns out to be computationally inefficient for all but extremely small models.

---

[46] See Taylor and Black (1974), Taylor (1975), and Keller (1980) for their public finance analysis. Succeeding the ORANI model, Adams et al. (1994) developed the more dynamic model, MONASH, that forecast the development of the Australian economy up to 1996–97.

In addition to the Scarf algorithm, two other direct approaches were used in the 1970s to solve nonlinear, empirical, general equilibrium models. The first approach is a Walrasian tâtonnement process in which sectoral prices change iteratively as a function of sectoral excess demand. Numerous applications show that the tâtonnement process provides solutions for general equilibrium problems, but becomes difficult when there are large cross-derivatives in the excess-demand equations, such as when cross-price demand or supply elasticities are significant. The second approach also treats the general equilibrium problem as a system of algebraic constraints, but uses the matrix of the first partial derivatives, the Jacobian matrix. The particular algorithm most widely used was the Powell algorithm.[47]

Ginsburgh and Waelbroeck (1981) developed another approach toward a solution that adopts the Negishi theorem. Their approach specifies the CGE model as a nonlinear programming problem, but it also (1) incorporates endogenous prices, (2) includes multiple consumers, and (3) allows for price wedges. Robinson (1989, p. 888) describes this type of CGE model as one that "sought to simulate the workings of a market economy, solving for both market prices and quantities simultaneously. These computable general equilibrium (CGE) models can be seen as a natural outgrowth of input-output and LP models, adding neoclassical substitutability in production and demand, as well as an explicit system of market prices and a complete specification of the income flows in the economy."

Devarajan et al. (1997) present a simple nonlinear programming model that represents their basic, fully specified, open-economy trade model in the tradition of Ginsburgh and Waelbroeck.[48] The 1-2-3 model developed by Devarajan et al. includes one country, two production sectors, and three goods, of which E is exclusively produced for exports, D is exclusively produced for the domestic market, and M is imported and not produced domestically. The model is a generalization of the Salter-Swan model that strictly distinguishes between tradables and nontradables (see Salter 1959; Swan 1960). However, as in common partial equilibrium approaches, the Salter-Swan model does not incorporate different degrees of tradability. As soon as a good is tradable, the law of one price holds and world market prices fully determine domestic prices, whereas for nontradables world prices do not matter at all. In addition, the strict Salter-Swan model holds little relevance for empirical work because the GDP share of goods that are not traded at all is typically low. The dichotomous classification of goods as either completely tradable or not tradable at all is too extreme. The 1-2-3 model overcomes this shortcoming of the Salter-Swan approach by incorporating a constant elasticity of transformation technology for the production decision between E and D, and a constant elasticity of substitution aggregation function that defines the composite consumer good Q as a combination of D and M. With

---

[47] Adelman and Robinson (1978) and Dervis, de Melo, and Robinson (1982) present the first applications of the Powell algorithm in a mix with tâtonnement.

[48] This model is the basic 1-2-3 model developed by Devarajan, Lewis, and Robinson (1990) and supplemented by Go and Sinko (1993). It draws heavily on the influential contribution to computable general equilibrium modeling in development economics by Dervis, de Melo, and Robinson (1982).

this functional specification, both trade shares and elasticities of substitution (transformation) determine to what extent world market prices influence domestic market prices—goods vary in their degree of tradability.[49]

Devarajan et al. (1997) show how to solve the 1-2-3 model analytically and numerically.[50] The numerical solution is derived by implementing the model in a common Windows-based spreadsheet program (Microsoft Excel) using a standard personal computer. They thereby demonstrate the relative simplicity and convenience of their spreadsheet approach, which can be copied by any modeler without further knowledge of complicated programming languages. However, larger CGE models are commonly programmed and solved in a variety of user-friendly software packages explicitly designed for CGE problems.[51] The programming language applied in this study is the General Algebraic Modeling System (GAMS), a software package originally developed at the World Bank "to make the construction and solution of large and complex mathematical programming models more straightforward for programmers and more comprehensible to users of models from other disciplines, e.g., economists" (Brooke, Kendrick, and Meeraus 1988, p. xiiv). The GAMS programming code for the Tanzania CGE model applied in this study is available from the author upon request.

Nature, Types, and Applications of CGE Models

This section describes the nature of CGE models and categorizes the large variety that has emerged during the last three decades as a result of advancements in the underlying general equilibrium theory, changes in the analytical focus of policy analysis, and rapid development in computer capacity.

The Nature of CGE Models. The previous section described the mathematical structure of CGE models as a system of nonlinear algebraic equations that can also be

---

[49] For further analysis of the properties of the basic 1-2-3 model, refer to de Melo and Robinson (1985, 1989); de Melo and Tarr (1992); and Devarajan, Lewis, and Robinson (1990, 1991, 1993).

[50] They present an excellent graphical solution including two simulations on (1) an increase in foreign capital inflow, and (2) an increase in the world price of the imported good. Furthermore, they solve the model algebraically before proceeding to the numerical implementation of the model (see also de Melo and Robinson (1985, 1989).

[51] Besides the General Algebraic Modeling System (GAMS) software, which is applied and described in this study, two CGE modeling packages, the General Algebraic Modeling Package (GEMPACK) and the Mathematical Programming System for General Equilibrium Analysis, are readily available. GEMPACK is mainly applied by the Australian ORANI modelers as well as the Global Trade Analysis Project researchers at Purdue University (see Global Trade Analysis Project homepage at http://www.agecon.purdue.edu/gtap). The GEMPACK software is especially suitable for "linearizers" in the tradition of Johansen and is described in detail in Harrison and Pearson (1994), whereas GAMS and GAMS-based software packages—like Rutherford's (1987) Mathematical Programming System for General Equilibrium Analysis, which combines an efficient solution algorithm with an interactive user-interface—are most suitable for "levels modelers" of the Devarajan et al. (1997) and Dervis, de Melo, and Robinson (1982) type. Beyond these standard software packages for CGE modeling, some examples can be found that are implemented in mathematical software like GAUSS and MATLAB or in econometric regression packages that include nonlinear solvers.

specified as a multisectoral nonlinear programming model. In addition to their mathematical nature, however, CGE models have additional characterizations. Robinson (1989) lists three types of CGE models.

The first type of CGE model can be placed in the spectrum of models ranging from analytical to stylized to applied (Devarajan et al. 1994). Analytical models are extremely simple and much abstracted from empirical realism in order to derive analytical propositions about their properties. Analytical models surrender empirical relevance to achieve analytical tractability. Typically, analytical models tend to focus on partial rather than general equilibrium issues. Because of their high degree of simplification, they can rarely be tested empirically.

Moving along the spectrum, the next group of models is stylized numerical models. These models are empirical applications of analytical models used to explore the magnitude of the effects of particular causal mechanisms. Although typically larger and more detailed than analytical models, stylized numerical models stay close to their underlying analytical model structure. The art of using stylized models involves incorporating representative economic features that reflect the situation of a class of countries. However, analytical and stylized numerical models usually do not provide sufficient detail to analyze and support specific policy recommendations.

In contrast to stylized numerical models, applied models are much less stylized and are designed to allow for a country-specific analytical focus. They distinguish themselves from stylized models in that they consist of a more detailed specification of the institutional side of the economy under study, which limits their general applicability. Although applied models allow for detailed and country-specific analysis, there is a danger of concealing the basic causal mechanisms of the model without enhancing its empirical significance, something that should be considered while choosing more detailed features for an applied model specification (Devarajan et al. 1994).

A second way to classify CGE models concerns the policy issues that the models analyze.[52] Input-output analysis focuses on real sectoral allocation issues. CGE modeling concerns itself more with distributional issues, with explicit specification of prices and factor incomes.[53] In the late 1970s and the 1980s, policymakers became much more concerned about external macroeconomic shocks and structural adjustment. The two oil crises in the 1970s, the decline in primary commodity prices in the mid-1980s (declining terms of trade), and the financial crisis in many developing countries,[54] which led to severe cutbacks in foreign capital inflows, forced policymakers to deal with structural adjustment issues. Economic advisors and politicians of the affected countries had to restructure production and trade to cope with price shocks and the lower levels of foreign resources that resulted from

---

[52] The entire range of CGE models addressing different analytical issues includes the following models: (1) trade policy, (2) structural adjustment, (3) public finance, (4) environmental, and (5) income distribution.

[53] Early CGE models of developing countries focused on issues of income distribution (see Adelman and Robinson 1978; Taylor and Lysy (1979).

[54] Starting with Turkey in the late 1970s and Mexico in 1982.

changes in the world economic environment. The prevailing task of reform became designing a macroeconomic policy intervention package that would support the necessary structural changes while still supporting favorable medium- to long-term growth prospects. According to Robinson (1989, p. 891), policymakers had to aim at "structural adjustment ... to some shock that requires not only compositional changes in production, resource allocation, demand, and relative prices, but also changes in macroeconomic aggregates such as income, investment, absorption, consumption, and government expenditure." CGE models proved a powerful tool to fulfill these multiple requirements and support macroeconomic policy design.

A third way to classify CGE models involves their underlying theoretical paradigm.[55] The core of CGE models is the multisectoral intermediate input links they adapted from input-output models. In addition, they incorporate nonlinear equations that describe agents' economic behavior (for instance, their substitution possibilities) and endogenous prices. Thus CGE models are structural and have an essential microeconomic spirit. As Dervis, de Melo, and Robinson (1982, p. 6) express this basic theoretical underpinning of multisectoral models: "Walras rather than Keynes is the patron saint of multisector analysis."

Although multisectoral CGE models are based on microeconomic, neoclassical theory, modelers had to abandon some of the strict neoclassical assumptions to meet the imperfections of the actual economies under observation. Instead of perfect competition with perfectly flexible prices and free product and factor mobility, applied CGE models often incorporate structural rigidities that seek to capture non-neoclassical behavior, macroeconomic imbalances, and institutional rigidities typical of developing economies.[56] The relevant theoretical features that describe macroeconomic adjustment, political economy, uncertainty, incomplete markets, and temporary equilibrium are not directly incorporated into the models: they are imposed through ad hoc constraints not directly related to the agents' endogenous rational behavior. The theoretical shortcomings and technical compromises reflect the current inadequate state of the underlying theory (Taylor 1990; Robinson 1989, 1991).

Different Types and Applications of CGE Models. The numerous applications of CGE models that have emerged during the past three decades can be categorized with respect to their scope and issues of interest. Within the African context, the vast variety of applications can be classified into the following most common scopes:[57]

- single versus multicountry (regional) CGE models;
- single-period versus dynamic CGE models;
- nonfinancial (real economy) versus financial CGE models;
- national versus village CGE models.

---

[55] Here the scope of the CGE model ranges from (1) Walrasian/neoclassical models (Yale school), (2) neoclassical structuralist models (Chenery), and (3) macroeconomic structuralist models (Taylor).

[56] These deviations from the Walrasian paradigm and their corresponding methodological problems are criticized in Srinivasan (1982), Bell and Srinivasan (1984), and Shoven and Whalley (1984).

[57] Each application usually represents a couple of the listed categories; for example, an agriculturally focused, nonfinancial, single-country, trade model.

The most common issues of interest in the African context are the following:
- macroeconomic (structural) adjustment issues;
- external shock, foreign aid, and capital inflow issues;
- agricultural development and industrialization issues;
- trade liberalization and spatial trade issues;
- rural-urban migration and urbanization issues;
- welfare analysis and income distribution issues;
- environmental issues.

Other meaningful characteristics could certainly be added to this list, but this survey deals mainly with CGE applications that focus on the analysis of macroeconomic policies for agricultural growth and income distribution in developing countries.[58]

Multicountry CGE Models.[59] CGE models can be divided into single-country and multicountry models. Both types are open-economy models and incorporate the rest of the world as an integral component that guarantees the consideration of all worldwide capital and commodity flows and, consequently, their influence on the economy under observation. Therefore, even a single-country model can be deemed to be a world model, a term referring to a model that incorporates different regions into one model, thereby covering the major actors of the world economy (Deardorff and Stern 1990; Shoven and Whalley 1992; Lewis, Robinson, and Wang 1995; Brown et al. 1996). The analytical focus of the study to be carried out determines whether a single or multicountry model should be applied. Single-country models analyze a single, national focus, while multicountry models address questions such as global trade liberalization, regional trade agreements, interregional migration, and the worldwide sustainable exploitation of natural resources.[60] A combination of single-country and

---

[58] For a general survey on CGE models and their theoretical background, see Robinson (1989). Devarajan, Lewis, and Robinson (1986) include models that are country-focused and exclude models that are issue- or theory-focused, even if applied to a specific country. Decaluwe and Martens (1988) provide empirical surveys, and Bandara (1991) presents the evolution of CGE modeling through more than 60 CGE applications related to different policy issues in LDCs and discusses the appropriateness of using CGE models for policy analysis. De Melo (1988) surveys CGE models with a particular trade focus, Gunning and Keyser (1993) and Ginsburgh and Van der Heyden (1985) concentrate on recent developments in CGE modeling, and Hertel (1997a) presents an excellent survey on CGE models focusing on agricultural policies. Additionally, in 1988 a special issue of the *Journal of Policy Modeling*, vol. 10, no. 3 (continued in no. 4), entitled *SAM-Based Models,* included a variety of contributions on different CGE modeling issues.

[59] In the context of CGE modeling, the terms multicountry and regional are often used as synonyms. However, multicountry is a superordinate concept, because a regional model always deals with more than one country and is thus a multicountry model, whereas some multicountry models deal with multiple countries that are not in the same region, for example, a regional model to analyze the effects of the Asian crisis on Southeast Asian regional trade versus a multicountry model to analyze the effects of the European Union's agricultural policies on Mexico's export performance. However, the basic technical modeling concept for all these CGE models is the same, this chapter uses both terms depending on the context.

[60] For example, Lewis, Robinson, and Wang (1995) analyze the impact of an Asia Pacific Economic Cooperation free trade area on Pacific Rim economies and conclude that the Asia Pacific Economic Cooperation's developing countries would not only gain most from increased regional trade, but that the benefits would be larger the broader the membership of the free trade area. Hinojosa and Robinson (1992) analyze the effects of the formation of the North American Free Trade Agreement on the employment and wage structure in the participating countries. They found that, contrary to common trade theory predictions, wages did not converge in their CGE scenarios but rose significantly in Mexico and the United States. For surveys on this subject see Shoven and Whalley (1992); Brown (1992); Goldin, Knudsen, and van der Mensbrugghe (1993); OECD (1990); and U.S. International Trade Commission (1998).

multicountry models is possible, separating a national economy into several economically distinguishable regions by, for example, different agroeconomic zones, to assess the diverse effects of national policy measures on these different regions.[61] Furthermore, the spectrum of CGE models can be expanded on either side in relation to their regional focus. On the one hand, a new and promising literature on village CGE models has emerged in recent years,[62] but, on the other hand, global CGE models have been constructed that go beyond the common application of multicountry and regional CGE models.[63]

Dynamic CGE Models. The second major characteristic of CGE models is whether they are single-period models for comparative-static analysis or dynamic models for multiperiod forecasting. Single-period models are appropriate when the analytical focus is on reaction to a onetime shock or event, such as an external shock from a change in the trade balance that affects a country's economic performance.[64] This situation requires the implementation of adequate policy measures to adjust to the exogenous event. Such a scenario can appropriately be analyzed in a comparative-static framework in which dynamic macroeconomic issues like inflation and changing investment patterns have only secondary interest. The situation requires analysis of how to change the structure of production, trade, and demand within the same economic environment, rather than an analysis of economic growth under continuing changes in macroeconomic variables.[65]

Some dynamic CGE applications lack a comprehensible justification of why they are designed as dynamic instead of single-period models because they do not show an explicit interest in intertemporal aspects—neither in their analytical focus

---

[61] Isard (1960), who developed the method for the basic multiregion, input-output model, and his coauthors present a detailed overview of applied general interregional equilibrium approaches (Isard et al. 1998). Löfgren and Robinson (1999) present a spatially disaggregated national CGE model that incorporates interregional and nation-region feedbacks to analyze the spatial effects of economic policies.

[62] Taylor and Adelman (1996) make a major contribution to village CGE models and discuss different approaches to constructing village SAMs, the numerical basis of village CGE models.

[63] The World Model by Lewis, Robinson, and Wang (1995) is one of the well-known examples. The most current literature evolves from the Global Trade Analysis Project (GTAP) at Purdue University. GTAP provides "data, models, and software for multiregion, applied general equilibrium analysis of global economic issues" (see, for instance, Anderson et al. 1997 and Huff 1995 for recent applications and refer to the GTAP homepage at http://www.agecon.purdue.edu/gtap/ where the *GTAP Technical Paper Series* can be found). For a survey on GTAP applications, see Hertel (1997b).

[64] A "surprise" in the rational expectation literature.

[65] In this vein, in a single-period CGE framework, each solution, which is reached after an external shock, or the implementation of a domestic policy measure, or both, represents a new equilibrium. However, a CGE model is not associated with a specific time period to reach the new equilibrium, and its time horizon is only vaguely specified (short term, medium term, long term) by the choice of macroeconomic closures, especially the mobility of factor markets. In this sense, a single-period model is "dynamic" enough to serve the analytical purpose addressed here and to answer the question of how to get from one economic situation to another under the same basic economic conditions without considering the time horizon explicitly. Under these circumstances, a dynamic model would add unnecessary additional features that would add little to the issue under study.

nor in their specific model design. The literature also contains multiple examples of reasonable dynamic CGE applications.[66]

Azis (1997) uses a static and a dynamic framework, thereby focusing on both the economic objectives of the study as well as the differences of its results in relation to the different methodological approaches. Likewise, Abbink, Braber, and Cohen (1995) demonstrate under which assumptions a simple static CGE model can be elaborated to a dynamic CGE specification and compare the two versions. Few applications show explicit interest in, and specification of, intertemporal aspects of the development process as, for example, the multisectoral CGE with overlapping generations and intertemporal optimization presented by Keuschnigg and Kohler (1995).[67] Go (1994) offers another example by highlighting the intertemporal trade-offs of tariff reforms when examining the sensitivity of investment and growth to external shocks and adjustment policy. Dynamic CGE models are extremely useful for simulating the overall economic development path of an economy or an entire region as, for instance, demonstrated by Adams and Park (1995). Their CGE approach to modeling development paths provides a dynamic, sequenced, CGE model that emphasizes the implications of Vernon's product cycle for modeling trade and economic development in East and Southeast Asia. Other growth-oriented models focus more on trade and assess, for example, the appropriateness of an export-oriented growth strategy with respect to the volume and structure of foreign trade and its influence on macroeconomic variables like growth in GDP, inflation, interest rates, and the distribution of income (Gibson and van Seventer 1996). Diao, Yeldan, and Roe (1998) construct a dynamic applied general equilibrium model of a small, open economy to investigate the transition path and convergence speed of out-of-steady state growth paths in response to trade policy shocks. Finally, common single-period models are extended to dynamic versions such as the ORANI-Intertemporal, an intertemporal CGE model of Australia that represents an advancement over the ORANI model (Malakellis 1993).

Financial CGE Models. The third type of classification for CGE models distinguishes between financial CGE models with integrated real and financial sectors and real-economy-side CGE models without explicit specification of financial variables. There is an ongoing controversy among CGE modelers about the necessity of "monetizing" models through the incorporation of money, capital, and asset markets to simulate the financial intermediation process.[68] The major aspects of

---

[66] For an early survey on dynamic CGE models (concentrating on tax policy evaluation), see Pereira and Shoven (1988), who review nondynamic CGE models, raise modeling issues regarding the dynamic behavior of agents and markets, discuss implementation and policy issues, and assess the strengths and weaknesses of dynamic modeling. In the final part of a recent book edited by Mercenier and Srinivasan (1994), four authors deal with modeling intertemporal trade-offs. The book is also a comprehensive collection of recent works on applied general equilibrium applications in the context of economic development, comprising four parts, namely (1) Modeling Agriculture Policy Issues, (2) Analysis of Stabilization Programs, (3) Modeling Imperfect Competition, and (4) Modeling Intertemporal Trade-offs.

[67] Keuschnigg and Kohler analyze the dynamic effects of trade liberalization in Austria.

[68] For a review of this synthesis between micro- and macroeconomics, see Robinson (1991, p. 1522), who points out the underlying theoretical tension and concludes that: "We are still far from a theoretical reconciliation between Walras and Keynes and empirical models cannot help but reflect the theoretical gap."

this debate are how to model the linkages between the real and financial side of an economy in a CGE framework and to what extent the integration of financial variables affects the real-economy-side variables of the model. Weighing the advantages of incorporated financial intermediation against the disadvantages of the more complex model structure is crucial. Two interesting attempts to incorporate financial markets into CGE models have been made since the mid-1980s (see Mercenier and Srinivasan 1994). First, Lewis's CGE model of Turkey, which separates the real and the financial sectors (Lewis 1994),[69] includes asset markets, firms that demand funds capable of being loaned, households with transaction demand and liquidity preference, a central bank, and a banking sector. In addition, Lewis's model specifies asset market equilibrium and the linkage between individual prices and the exchange rate in which the latter is determined through demand and supply on the domestic currency market.[70] Second, Fargeix and Sadoulet (1994) present a fully specified financial CGE model of Ecuador to analyze the impact of inflation on capital flight and productive investment and the trade-off between lower inflation and higher interest rates induced by a restrictive monetary policy. Their model incorporates a mechanism of partial adjustment to address the linkages between the level of inflation and the amount of real wages. The Fargeix-Sadoulet model analyzes economic growth and development related to external macroeconomic shocks as well as different mixes of exchange rate, fiscal, and monetary policies.[71]

Agriculturally Focused Trade Models for Structural Adjustment Analysis. This section introduces the extensive group of agricultural and trade-focused CGE models with explicit substitutability incorporated into their trade specification. These models are particularly suitable for analyzing trade liberalization and other structural adjustment policies that are implemented to counteract external economic shocks and aim at improving sectoral performance in agriculture.[72] Robinson (1990) surveys single-country, agriculture-focused CGE models and introduces the theoretical underpinnings of analyzing agricultural trade liberalization with single-country CGE models, developing a model based on the Salter-Swan Australian trade model. The Department of Agricultural and Resource

---

[69] Another more recent CGE model incorporating Turkey's financial markets is presented by Yeldan (1997), who conducts counterfactual and comparative static simulations to analyze (1) the financing of the fiscal government deficit through debt instruments or monetization, (2) the effect of public debt instruments on the financial markets, and (3) the implications of external debt servicing and exchange rate devaluation.

[70] Following the chapter by Lewis in Mercenier and Srinivasan (1994), Lora comments in detail on the advantages and disadvantages of this approach (Lora 1994, p. 137). In a general statement, Lora points out that: "Compared to their real counterparts, financial submodels are still in a very experimental state, bearing little resemblance to the structure and behavior of the actual financial sectors of the economies under scrutiny."

[71] The chapter by Fargeix and Sadoulet in Mercenier and Srinivasan (1994) is followed by valuable comments by Taylor and Bourguignon who both emphasize the crucial importance of the choice of macroeconomic closures and the subsequent effects on the simulation results (Taylor 1994; Bourguignon 1994).

[72] The literature in this survey is oriented to the particular interests of the current analysis, concentrates on developing economies, and emphasizes the southeast African context in which the Tanzania study is embedded. For a more extensive survey refer to Hertel (1997a), which focuses on industrial economies.

Economics at the University of California at Berkeley has accumulated an extensive literature on trade-focused CGE analysis of income distribution and welfare effects resulting from external shocks. Adelman, Bournieux, and Waelbroeck (1986) promote an industrialization strategy led by agricultural development. In the presence of a low-growth world economic environment, they find that this strategy yields higher growth rates, better income distribution, and more rapid industrialization and, consequently, a stronger balance of payments than a purely export-oriented industrialization. Adelman and Robinson (1987) assess macroeconomic adjustment and income distribution under alternative macroeconomic closures for the saving-investment balance and the balance of trade. They show that the choice of closure significantly influences the functional distribution of income, whereas size effects of income distribution are largely insensitive to the closure settings. In addition to pure income distribution effects, Adelman and Berck (1988) analyze different food security policies in a CGE framework and find that poverty-reducing development strategies are superior to price variance-reducing strategies or food aid. In the tradition of Adelman and her coauthors, other Berkeley researchers continue to analyze the income distribution and welfare effects of stabilization policies and structural adjustment programs within CGE frameworks (de Janvry, Fargeix, and Sadoulet 1988). More recent works, such as the study of climatic change by Winters et al. (1998), integrate current aspects of interest but still focus on income distribution and welfare effects.

In the context of Sub-Saharan Africa, Benjamin (1996) conducts a CGE analysis on the links between adjustment and income distribution in the agricultural economy of Cameroon.[73] The work on Cameroon CGE models goes back to the first application by Condon, Dahl, and Devarajan (1987) as an example of the implementation of a CGE model in GAMS.

CGE models have been applied only sparsely to southern Africa, and there is hardly any officially published work on Angola, Burundi, Lesotho, Malawi, Mozambique, Namibia, Swaziland, Uganda, or Zambia, although some of these economies appear in cross-country studies or can be found in so-called gray literature publications. Beginning in the mid-1990s, a few CGE articles have analyzed Botswana, Kenya, Rwanda, South Africa, Tanzania, and Zimbabwe. Some work on Kenya deals with energy taxation and technical change related to an oil import-dependent economy.[74] In post-Apartheid South Africa, researchers have recently

---

[73] Some recent country-specific CGE applications that analyze the effects of alternative trade regimes on income distribution and equity are presented in Wang and Zhai (1998) for China and in Bautista and Robinson (1997) for the Philippines. There are also numerous applications in the context of Southeast Asia, especially to India, the Democratic People's Republic of Korea (North Korea), and Indonesia. This literature is extensive and growing.

[74] On this issue, see Mitra (1994) and Semboja (1994). For an analysis of technical efficiency change in Kenyan agriculture and its influence on the poorer segments of the population, refer to Akinboade (1994). For a classical example of temporary windfall gains during the Kenyan coffee boom in the late 1970s see Bevan, Collier, and Gunning 1986.

shown concern about economic restructuring, new outward-oriented trade strategies, and openness toward world markets.[75] In Zimbabwe researchers have concentrated not only on the common restructuring of the economy based on macroeconomic policy, but also on the conditions for land reform intended to achieve distributional and environmental improvements.[76]

In this sparse literature of CGE applications in central and southern Africa, the fully specified financial CGE of Rwanda by Decaluwe and Nsengiyumva (1994) stands out. They analyze a financially repressed economy that sets interest rates administratively and controls the volume and distribution of bank credits, as applied in Rwanda until 1987. This analysis emphasizes the resulting excess demand for credit by firms and the effects on selected sectoral productivity. Finally, Unemo (1995) studies the environmental impact of government policies and external shocks in Botswana, which represents the first environmentally focused CGE analysis of macroeconomic policies in southern Africa.

Existing CGE Model Applications to Tanzania. This section describes the literature on CGE model applications to Tanzania. First, the Research Department of Statistics in Norway is analyzing structural adjustment policies, particularly their effect on natural resources and soil degradation (Balsvik and Brendemoen 1994; Oygard 1995; Aune et al. 1997; Grepperud, Wiig, and Aune 1999). Second, Sarris (1994b, 1996) analyzed macroeconomic policy reforms, especially their influence on rural informal credit markets and household welfare, applying a dynamic and financial CGE model.[77] Each of these studies is described below.

The first CGE model of Tanzania accounts for the effects of land degradation and follows the basic approach developed by Dervis, de Melo, and Robinson in 1982 (Balsvik and Brendemoen 1994). This dynamic model does not incorporate a submodel for simulating the soil degradation process, but rather treats soil degradation as an exogenous variable in the agricultural production function. Because of the focus on soil degradation and its influence on overall economic performance, this model neglects some CGE features relevant to structural changes of the economy and related

[75] Naude and Brixen (1993) provide a traditional CGE analysis on economic restructuring and income redistribution and highlight the importance of a flexible exchange rate regime on South Africa's mining sector. Coetzee et al. (1997) also point out the crucial effects of South Africa's exchange rate policy on the sustainability of trade liberalization, while Gibson and van Seventer (1996) provide five-year projections for a growing mining sector and an exchange rate devaluation. An article by Coetzee, Swanepoel, and Naude (1997) expresses the interest in and popularity of CGE models in this regard. They build a minimalist CGE model for analyzing trade liberalization in South Africa. This model is a suitable pedagogical tool meant to encourage other researchers in this emerging field.

[76] See Davies, Rattso, and Torvik (1994) for a five-sector CGE model of Zimbabwe with endogenous import rationing; Davies and Rattso (1996) analyze the impacts of land reform on income growth, poverty reduction, and land degradation; and Rattso and Torvik (1998) disentangle market liberalization effects from coinciding drought effects in 1992 and 1995.

[77] Sarris's study of Tanzania is part of a major research program under the Cornell Food and Nutrition Policy Program on the effect of SAPs on the poor in Africa (see http://www.nutrition.cornell.edu/cfnpp.html).

welfare analysis. On the production side, labor markets are not differentiated and the nominal wage is set exogenously, which translates into a distorted labor market not necessarily in equilibrium. On the consumption side, the model specifies only one representative household, making it unsuitable for determining how macroeconomic policies affect different socioeconomic groups. Furthermore, the model is very closed compared with many CGE models that focus on trade: (1) the model determines world import prices and world export prices exogenously,[78] and (2) it also determines the exchange rate and foreign savings exogenously.[79]

An advanced version of this model incorporates a separate soil model that specifies a tropical soil productivity calculator to establish a two-way link between the economy and the environment (Aune and Lal 1995). In this version soil degradation is no longer determined exogenously but endogenously through a natural soil productivity variable. The underlying nitrogen cycle determines soil productivity because nitrogen limits plant growth and is the most important reason for the decrease in agricultural productivity. In this framework, Aune et al. (1997) analyze the interdependence of soil productivity and economic growth under structural adjustment conditions. In particular, they analyze the removal of subsidies on agrochemicals, a depreciation of the exchange rate, a reduction in government spending, and fiscal policy reforms. They then compare their results with those generated by a conventional CGE model with constant soil productivity. For a 10-year simulation, the study applies an endogenous soil degradation variable and finds that GDP levels are substantially lower, proving the importance of soil productivity for economic growth in Tanzania (Aune et al. 1997).

A recent paper based on the same type of model analyzes maize trade liberalization and fertilizer subsidies in Tanzania, which are two alternative policy reforms with the objective of stimulating agricultural production (Grepperud, Wiig, and Aune 1999). The study finds that sustainable agricultural growth in Tanzania can be achieved only through greater application of fertilizer, expansion of the land area under cultivation, and technological change in production. The results indicate that fertilizer subsidies are preferable to trade liberalization, because fertilizer subsidies improve agricultural growth

---

[78] This is unlike many trade-focused CGE models that define a downward sloping world demand curve for export goods, thereby allowing for a limited effect of the country's export supply on world market prices. However, the model applied in this study, although allowing for a downward sloping demand curve, does not employ this feature and works with fixed world prices for imports and exports as well.

[79] Fixing the nominal exchange rate and foreign capital inflow restricts the model's trade responsiveness to macroeconomic policies because it quasi fixes the trade balance at its initial nominal value in domestic currency. A fixed nominal exchange rate and fixed trade balance violate the pure Dervis-de Melo-Robinson specification of a CGE model—the model is not homogeneous anymore. Because the model has no other numeraire (fixed domestic price index) except for the fixed nominal exchange rate, the real exchange rate is endogenous and has to adjust in order to clear the trade balance condition. Furthermore, the model has fixed nominal wages, which translates into exogenously determined employment. Fixed nominal wages and a fixed nominal exchange rate, in turn, translate into a real wage in foreign currency, although the wage is a mix of foreign and domestic commodity prices. This is a model closure applied by Rattso (see, for instance, Davies, Rattso, and Torvik 1998) in the tradition of Taylor (1990, 1991). Taylor's models are, however, investment driven rather than savings driven, and he keeps careful track of the implicit linkages between exchange rate, trade, and wages. It is an extremely "structuralist" model type, which Balsvik and Brendemoen do not point out explicitly, although their results and conclusions might be driven and misled by this closure specification.

more and enhance intensive agricultural production. However, fertilizer subsidies favor traditional export agriculture rather than food cropping, while trade liberalization favors the latter. This integrated modeling approach reveals the importance of variables other than economic ones for macroeconomic and sectoral policy analysis and exposes the deficiencies of pure economic model specifications.

Sarris's work on CGE applications to Tanzania analyzes the effect of macroeconomic policies on household welfare in a dynamic framework with explicit financial markets. This CGE analysis is based on a 15-sector SAM for Tanzania for 1976 with 5 agricultural sectors, 6 labor categories, 3 capital categories, and 6 households (Sarris 1994a). Sarris (1994b) describes in detail the applied model and its calibration with respect to the underlying SAM. The analysis focuses on the depreciation of the exchange rate, changes in public spending, financial sector reforms, and external shocks for the five-year period 1977–81. The results indicate that the effects of individual policy measures often partly offset each other and that the net effect of a combination of policies depends on their relative emphasis. The study supports the view that "recent positive post-1986 developments are certainly related to adjustment policies, especially the devaluation of the official exchange rate; and in fact they could have been even better, had it not been for the adverse external developments" (Sarris 1996).

The study has two conceptual shortcomings. He mentions that Tanzania experienced its worst economic crisis from 1978 to 1984, and that the government has implemented stabilization and structural adjustment measures since the early 1980s. The first shortcoming is that the base year of the underlying SAM is 1976. Because the analysis considers the subsequent five years, it must be interpreted in light of the question: What if Tanzania had adopted the policy measures in 1977? The analysis should not be interpreted by questioning the degree of effectiveness of policy measures in counteracting the negative effects of the economic crisis. The second shortcoming concerns the dynamic dimension of the model. A CGE model is usually not interpreted to provide a solution for a particular period of time like a fiscal or calendar year. The CGE model should provide a new equilibrium in the wake of an external or internal policy shock. It is difficult to explicitly specify the convergence period needed to obtain a new equilibrium; however, the general short-, medium-, or long-term characteristic of any model is determined by its factor market specifications and macroeconomic closure rules. In Sarris's model, the investment structure, which does not show typical short-term rigidity, is specified to allow for significant changes in total investment and its sectoral distribution. This specification is hard to justify as reflecting a one-year adjustment rather than a medium-term adjustment. The five successive runs of the dynamic model can only be interpreted as a five-year period if the underlying model structure represents an annual model that adjusts within one year toward a new equilibrium. Sarris states that his model specification satisfies the requirements for an annual equilibrium, a goal that, without extensive econometrics, proves extremely difficult to achieve.[80]

---

[80] The CGE-based country studies of the Cornell Food and Nutrition Policy Project, which are summarized in Sahn, Dorosh, and Younger (1996), and CGE modeling of structural adjustment policies in general are criticized by de Maio, Stewart, and van der Hoeven (1999) because of the assumptions made about parameters, relationships, and macroeconomic closures in the models. For a reply to the comments of de Maio, Stewart, and van der Hoeven, refer to Sahn, Dorosh, and Younger (1999).

The Current Study within the Existing Literature

This study's approach to CGE modeling follows the Dervis, de Melo, and Robinson (1982) type, which was developed principally at the World Bank in the early 1980s for purposes of structural adjustment analysis. It is an open-economy, single-country model that treats the rest of the world, excluding Tanzania, as one region. The model allows for two-way trade (cross-hauling), assuming that imports and domestic demand as well as exports and domestic supply are imperfect substitutes, respectively (Armington assumption). Producers maximize profits subject to their nested CES production functions, and households maximize utility with respect to interlinked linear expenditure systems (LES) for final and own-household consumption.

The model is nonfinancial because it does not explicitly define money and asset markets, and is thus a real-economy-side model rather than a monetized version. One reason for this choice is that the analysis of structural adjustment policies focuses on real economy effects such as amounts of goods produced and consumer welfare in terms of commodities consumed rather than monetary effects, inflation, and interest rates. The second reason for not choosing a financial CGE approach is the lack of sufficient data on the relevant financial markets. Assessing the financial side of the economy is not only a matter of integrating variables for money supply and demand and other assets. Specifying how the accumulation of savings works in an economy, how the financial intermediary process converts the savings into effective investment, and how the sector-specific returns to investment are rechanneled through the banking system to the initial source of capital would also be necessary. The functional specification of this process requires a comprehensive understanding of the financial markets and their agents, a consistent database of the relevant asset market transactions, and econometric estimations of parameters.[81]

The model is nondynamic and solves for a new equilibrium within a single period given a specified external shock, internal shock, or policy change. The previous section on dynamic CGE models provides some insight into the advantages and disadvantages of making CGE models dynamic for different analytical purposes. Considering structural adjustment analysis, nondynamic modeling is, in general, a reasonable and appropriate approach. Structural adjustment and stabilization programs are usually designed to react to a particular shock the economy experienced and policy measures designed to countervail the negative effects of this single-occurrence shock. The applied policy package is meant to adjust the structure of the economy, under existing macroeconomic conditions, to cope with the particular external or internal event that shocked the economy. In terms of expectation models, the shock is a surprise requiring adjustment to reestablish the economy's macroeconomic balance. Analyzing such policies does not require equilibrium dynamics. Instead, it requires analysis of how the economy will adjust and the nature of the new equilibrium of the

---

[81] See Bourguignon, Branson, and de Melo (1992) for an example of the integration of asset portfolio behavior of macroeconomic models in Tobin's tradition into a CGE model.

economy under certain sectoral and macroeconomic constraints and assumptions. The macroeconomic closure rules of the model and the specification of its factor markets are crucial to describe this convergence process properly and to determine the short-, medium-, or long-term character of the model. Thus, within a certain period, under some given conditions and some applied policies, the shocked economy adjusts to achieve a new state of stability (equilibrium).[82]

To make the model more realistic, the approach used in this study incorporates a number of features to capture economic conditions typical of a developing economy like Tanzania. First, the model explicitly distinguishes between private final demand and own-household consumption. In an agriculturally dominated economy in which 85 percent of the population lives in rural areas and engages mainly in food cropping, home consumption constitutes a significant share of daily food requirements. Consequently, it is useful to include the magnitudes and mechanics of formal and informal production as well as formal and informal consumption to simulate agricultural market behavior appropriately. Even though own-household consumption is not marketed, it is part of the model's real demand side, and therefore influences formal food market behavior. Marketed and nonmarketed consumer goods are of the same origin as production, but are valued at different stages of the marketing chain: nonmarket goods at farmgate prices and marketed goods at consumer prices, including all transport and marketing costs.[83] Second, high transport and marketing costs constitute another important characteristic of the marketing process in developing countries with insufficient infrastructure in transport and communication services. The present approach takes this particular characteristic of the economy into account by incorporating specific marketing margins that are associated with imports, exports, or domestic produce. This specification permits detailed analysis of the economywide effects of investment to improve infrastructure, a key element for achieving sustainable development. Third, the model incorporates a food aid variable, taking into consideration Tanzania's vulnerability to bad weather conditions.[84] This feature of the model permits analysis of an injection of food aid into the market system if domestic food production collapses, and it simultaneously incorporates the related monetary flows. Because food aid can have ambiguous effects on prices, domestic production, and final consumption, an appropriate specification permits the model to realistically simulate the economy. Fourth, the current model specifies a European-style VAT with a rebate mechanism that Tanzania, like many

---

[82] Unlike nondynamic CGE models, dynamic CGE models change some of the underlying economic conditions for each consecutive period to simulate the dynamics of these conditions, such as investment behavior. Such a specification emphasizes a particular interest, a sufficient understanding, and some concrete expectations regarding the development of this economic behavior that is outside the scope of structural adjustment analysis.

[83] The model captures the distinction between marketed and nonmarketed consumption with two interlinked LES demand functions that are based on different prices and show different minimum consumption coefficients that cause different price elasticities for marketed and nonmarketed goods.

[84] Such as the severe droughts in 1996/97 and the El Niño floods in 1997/98.

other countries in Sub-Saharan Africa, recently introduced. This feature allows for tax policy experiments in order to analyze substitution opportunities between the existing domestic tax structure and alternative approaches.

These additional model features seek to Africanize the applied Tanzanian CGE by considering particular economic characteristics typical of the region in general and Tanzania in particular. Such an extended and individualized model serves as a realistic simulation laboratory for analyzing the effect of internal and external economic shocks on Sub-Saharan African economies.

CHAPTER 4

A Social Accounting Matrix and General Equilibrium Model for Tanzania

This chapter describes the Tanzanian SAM and the CGE model developed for this study. The first section introduces the SAM concept and describes the different stages of the construction process for the Tanzania SAM. The second section provides the equations and explains the general functionality of the basic CGE model applied in this study. To capture the particular economic country characteristics, this section also highlights the country-specific features incorporated into the model.

A 1992 Social Accounting Matrix for Tanzania

A SAM is a square matrix consisting of row and column accounts that represent the different sectors, agents, and institutions of an economy at the desired level of disaggregation. It follows the principle of double-entry bookkeeping, reflecting expenditures in the column and receipts in the row accounts, that is, each entry represents a monetary flow from a column to a row. The SAM is a useful framework for preparing consistent, multisectoral, economic data (representing the expenditure-receipt flows among all actors and sectors of the entire economy) that captures both input-output and national income and product data. Once the country data for one particular year is organized in the SAM framework, it provides a static image, a snapshot, of the country's economic structure. The SAM data framework, for its part, provides the statistical basis for the creation of a plausible economic model to analyze policy interventions and external shocks in an economy (King 1985).[85]

On the basis of recently generated national accounts data, a 56-sector SAM is built focusing on the disaggregation of agriculture. First, a highly aggregated macroeconomic social accounting matrix (macrosam) is designed

---

[85] For extended descriptions of the SAM concept see Pyatt and Round (1985) and Reinert and Roland-Holst (1997).

to set the macroeconomic framework that provides the control totals for the disaggregation procedure. Then the sector disaggregation of the microeconomic social accounting matrix (microsam) is presented, and the data sources and the data adjustments made are explained. In summary, the microsam differentiates four household types and five labor categories. Special features of the microsam include nonmonetary, own-household consumption and separate marketing margins on domestic produce, exports, and imports, which play a crucial role in the production and marketing process of African countries facing severe infrastructure deficiencies. As the database is to be used for economic policy modeling, consideration of these features will have a significant influence on the results of the analysis. Because of data insufficiencies, the first microsam obtained from adjusted raw data (protosam) is highly unbalanced. A cross-entropy estimation method is applied to balance the protosam and generate the final estimated 1992 microsam for Tanzania that uses all available information in a consistent framework.

Introduction and Summary

A SAM was constructed for the base year 1992 to provide the starting point for calibration of the Tanzanian CGE model and to provide the initial data set for the CGE policy analysis. Because this study focuses on agriculture, accounting for about one-half of GDP in Tanzania, the disaggregated SAM contains 21 agricultural sectors out of 56 economic sectors. The Tanzanian SAM consists of 56 activity accounts capturing the flows belonging to the domestic production process and 55 commodity accounts capturing the flows belonging to the marketing process of nationally and internationally produced goods.[86] The disaggregation of productive factors is capital, land, and five labor categories, and households are divided into rural farmers, rural nonfarmers, urban farmers, and urban nonfarmers.

The construction of a SAM under poor data conditions is not only an exercise in putting together a complete data set, but also an estimation process on the basis of limited, often inconsistent, data sources. This is typical in situations where obtaining a complete and reliable national database is extremely difficult. To cope with limited data throughout the construction process of the disaggregated microsam, a macrosam must first be constructed. The macrosam provides the main macroeconomic characteristics and magnitudes of the economy and sets the basic data framework for further development of the microsam. It is highly aggregated and consists of only one activity, commodity, factor, and household account, capturing the basic macroeconomic features such as total intermediate demand, value-added, factor payments, foreign trade, tax and savings characteristics, domestic supply and demand, and all domestic and international monetary transfers.

---

[86] The difference of one account occurs because the activity account for tourism does not require a respective commodity account, because all its domestic production is exported and none of it enters the domestic commodity market (see Table 4.3 for a complete list of accounts).

The second step for achieving a consistent and balanced microsam is the construction of a preliminary SAM that is typically inconsistent and unbalanced, and will be referred to as the protosam. The protosam incorporates all available raw data, which are eventually adjusted to match various macroeconomic control totals. For those submatrices within the SAM for which an accurate disaggregation of the data is not available, estimates are made.

The accounts of the microsam have to be balanced (each row being equal to its respective column), while also achieving the aggregate control totals from the macrosam (for example, total imports or total exports that are represented by the sum of several cells within a row or column, but not necessarily all their cells, that would add up to a column or row total). The resulting microsam will be used as the initial database for the CGE modeling exercise. A cross-entropy approach to SAM estimation is used for the balancing process leading from the protosam to the balanced microsam.[87] The protosam provides a "prior" for the parameter estimation using the cross-entropy method. Although inconsistent, it is a starting point and contains useful information, which is used along with the various macroeconomic constraints to estimate the new microsam.

The section on price equations describes the construction of the Tanzanian macrosam for 1992 as well as the data sources used, and provides explicit documentation of all data entries. The section on the microsam documents the data sources and disaggregation criteria applied to the microsam, presents the cross-entropy technique used for the balancing process, and discusses figures and indicators of the final microsam.

Constructing a SAM under the data insufficiencies described is a challenge. Earlier work on SAMs for Tanzania by Rutayisire and Vos (1991) and Sarris (1994a) is based on 1976 national accounts data applying the 1976 input-output table for Tanzania, which is unfortunately the most recent input-output table available until the end of 1999.[88] However, the CGE analysis of structural adjustment measures, trade liberalization, and elements of the macroeconomic transformation Tanzania experienced in the early and mid-1990s requires a more recent database. Recently processed national accounts data for 1992 meet this requirement, although the preparation of an input-output table for 1992 is still in progress. Consequently, the 1992 SAM for Tanzania applies the basic structure of the 1976 input-output table and incorporates substantial adjustments as provided by other sources of information. Subsequent analysis will have to apply the more recent 1992 input-output table for Tanzania published by the Bureau of Statistics in Dar es Salaam, which was unavailable at the time the current exercise was carried

---

[87] The latest discussion on the cross-entropy approach is led by Golan and others (Golan and Judge 1996; Golan, Judge, and Miller 1996; Golan 1998), but can be best related to the present context in Robinson, Cattaneo, and El-Said (1998, 2000).

[88] Both versions are financial SAMs that include the domestic financial structure of the economy. Because the CGE analysis in this study focuses on real variables and aggregates of the economy, the nature of the SAM constructed here is nonfinancial and allows only limited comparison with the 1976 version.

out. Under the given circumstances, the construction of the current 1992 SAM for Tanzania is evaluated as a successful exercise that incorporates all data currently available and applies an extremely powerful method for the final balancing process, the cross-entropy approach. Furthermore, the 1992 Tanzanian SAM has to be seen in the context of other SAMs built for Africa and each country study's contribution to a broader and deeper knowledge of how to deal with insufficient raw data to construct a comprehensive and consistent database and a more detailed understanding of the features of SAMs specific to Africa.[89]

A Macrosam for 1992

The initial Tanzanian macrosam for 1992 contains 31 nonzero entries, balancing the entire economy at a gross output level of TSh 2,759,506 million and a total domestic absorption of TSh 2,940,773 million. The difference results from Tanzania's high trade deficit in 1992 of TSh 387,681 million, or 243 percent of total export earnings.

As in many developing countries with insufficient data processing and publishing capacity, data from various sources are often inconsistent. Adjusting data from these different sources is necessary to gain a consistent economywide database. This adjustment process needs to fulfill certain criteria. The decision about the core data source, which determines the macrosam's control totals to which all other data will be reconciled and balanced, is the most important. For the present macrosam, the *Revised National Accounts of Tanzania 1987–1996* (URT 1997)[90] provides the control totals for the macrosam.

This latest version of the *National Accounts of Tanzania* (URT 1997) incorporates a variety of other surveys conducted in recent years and some new economic features.[91] Besides various household expenditure categories, the most important new feature is the estimate for informal sector activities. Formal GDP at factor costs (f.c.) is current TSh 935,247 million; informal—or nonmonetary—GDP at f.c. is estimated at current TSh 340,668 million, or 36.4 percent of total GDP at f.c. The informal GDP component considers agriculture, construction, and owner-occupied dwellings, and therefore not only provides general information on the informal sector share in total GDP, whose magnitude as estimated by different authors ranges from 30 to more than 60 percent, but also allows the explicit specification of own-household consumption.

---

[89] Under the Macroeconomic Reform and Regional Integration in Southern Africa research project of the Trade and Macroeconomics Division of the International Food Policy Research Institute, SAMs are constructed for Malawi, Mozambique, Tanzania, Zambia, and Zimbabwe. SAMs for other countries such as Madagascar, Botswana, Uganda, and Ghana are in process or in planning for construction.

[90] Prepared by the Planning Commission at the President's Office, in cooperation with the Bureau of Statistics in 1997.

[91] These surveys include the Household Budget Survey 1991/92, the 1991 Informal Sector Survey, several agricultural surveys, and the 1994 Survey of Construction, Trade, and Transport.

A second important data source is an unpublished supplementary data set that the Bureau of Statistics used to prepare the *Revised National Accounts 1987–1996*.[92] Listing 79 economic sectors, this data set provides sector-specific information on gross output, intermediate demand, imports, tariffs, sales taxes, exports, private consumption, government consumption, investment, and changes in inventory, which are used as control totals for the Tanzanian macrosam and as a source of information for the disaggregated microsam.

Table 4.1 depicts a schematic diagram that introduces the different features and functionality of the macrosam. The macrosam specifies two government accounts: government recurrent and government investment. The former deals with the government's recurrent budget activities and the latter with the government's development (or investment) budget activities. In the case of the Tanzanian SAM, the development budget includes all government expenditures related to gross fixed capital formation. Keeping two separate accounts guarantees more flexibility for upcoming modeling purposes in which the government might boost the national level of infrastructure through increased investment spending. Two additional tax collection accounts are specified: domestic taxes and tariffs, which capture the entire national tax scheme at the macroeconomic level.[93] Table 4.2 presents the Tanzanian macrosam for 1992 in millions of current TSh, which is used as the macroeconomic point of reference for constructing the 1992 Tanzanian microsam. Appendix B provides detailed cell by cell documentation of the 31 nonzero entries of the 1992 macrosam, including data sources used and data manipulation undertaken.

The Microsam

This section describes the disaggregation of the microsam, the choice of data sources, the data manipulation carried out, and the estimation process for balancing the microsam. The documentation follows the previous section on the macrosam. The same numbering and notation is used for the description of the protosam and microsam entries, although in most cases it is not a single-cell entry any more, but a vector or matrix of entries depending on the disaggregation of the respective macrosam accounts. All crucial calculations, distributions, and data adjustments to estimate the protosam are documented. The cross-entropy approach for estimating the final microsam from the basis of the constructed protosam is discussed, including the implementation in the GAMS program.

For construction of the microsam, the activity and commodity accounts of the macrosam are disaggregated into 56 and 55 sectors, respectively. Three additional

---

[92] This data set was made available through staff members of the National Accounts Section of the Bureau of Statistics in Dar es Salaam.

[93] These two tax accounts are pure auxiliary accounts for the collection of different taxes within the economy that are then transferred to the government. In the commodity account column, they enable the distinction between sales taxes and tariffs, which otherwise would have to be combined into one payment from "commodities" to "government recurrent."

Table 4.1—Macroeconomic social accounting matrix

	Activities	Commodities	Factors	Households	Enterprises	Domestic taxes	Tariffs	Government recurrent	Government investment	Rest of the world	Capital account	Total
Activities		Domestic supply		Own household consumption								Total sales
Commodities	Intermediate demand			Final household consumption				Final government consumption	Government investment	Exports free on board	Private investment	Domestic demand
Factors	Value-added				Operating surplus							Value-added
Households			Value-added labor							Remittances from abroad		Household income
Enterprises			Value-added capital					Government transfers				Enterprise income
Domestic taxes	Indirect taxes	Sales tax		Income taxes	Corporate taxes							Domestic taxes subtotal
Tariffs		Import tariffs										Import tariffs
Government recurrent						Indirect and sales taxes	Import tariffs			Aid-related grants		Recurrent government receipts
Government investment								Government investment deficit		Aid-related loans		Financing government investment
Rest of the world		Imports cost, investment, freight	Factor payment abroad					Interest payment to the rest of the world				Payments to the rest of the world
Capital account				Household savings	Enterprise savings			Government savings		Net capital inflow		Total savings
Total	Gross output	Domestic absorption	Value-added	Household expenditure	Enterprise expenditure	Domestic tax subtotal	Import tariffs	Government recurrent expenditure	Government investment expenditure	Foreign exchange available	Total private investment	

Source: Author.

50

Table 4.2—1992 macrosam for Tanzania (millions of 1992 TSh)

	Activities	Commodities	Factors	Households	Enterprises	Domestic taxes	Tariffs	Government recurrent	Government investment	Rest of the world	Capital account	Total
Activities		2,320,484 (cell 4)								165,682 (cell 26)		2,759,506
Commodities	1,276,427 (cell 1)			913,213 (cell 12)				279,080 (cell 20)	52,521 (cell 25)		419,532 (cell 31)	2,940,773
Factors	1,456,047 (cell 2)											1,456,047
Households			841,879 (cell 8)		368,663 (cell 15)					96,755 (cell 27)		1,307,296
Enterprises			550,669 (cell 9)					27,620 (cell 21)				578,289
Domestic taxes	27,032 (cell 3)	43,475 (cell 5)										70,507
Tariffs		23,451 (cell 6)										23,451
Government recurrent				16,656 (cell 13)	65,054 (cell 16)	70,507 (cell 18)	23,451 (cell 19)			172,671 (cell 28)		348,339
Government investment								34,957 (cell 22)		17,564 (cell 29)		52,521
Rest of the world		553,363 (cell 7)	63,499 (cell 10)					24,250 (cell 23)				641,112
Capital account				104,087 (cell 14)	144,572 (cell 17)			–17,568 (cell 24)		188,440 (cell 30)		419,532
Total	2,759,506	2,940,773	1,456,047	1,307,296	578,289	70,507	23,451	348,339	52,521	641,112	419,532	

Source: Author.
Note: Cell numbers in parentheses refer to numbering in Appendix B.

commodity accounts are created to capture different marketing margins for exports, imports, and domestically produced and consumed goods. Because the analytical focus of the underlying study is on agriculture, 21 activities are agricultural. The disaggregation of activities and commodities is based on the 72-sector listing given by the *Revised National Accounts of Tanzania 1976–1990* (URT 1995d), which is the same disaggregation used for the 1976 input-output table. In addition, a category for tourism is created to capture this fast-growing sector of the Tanzanian economy.[94] Because the entire gross output of this sector is supposed to be exported, no commodity account for tourism needed to be created.

The microsam distinguishes six typical export crop activities (cotton, sisal, tea, coffee, tobacco, and cashew nuts); five cereals (maize, wheat, paddy, sorghum, and other cereals); pulses; two drought-resistant staple crops, namely, cassava and other roots); oil seeds; sugar; other horticulture; other crops; livestock; fishing; and forestry and hunting. The nonagricultural sectors are mining; 22 manufacturing sectors; electricity; water; construction; and 9 service categories, including commerce; transport and communication; and public administration.[95]

The factor disaggregation of the microsam follows the breakdown of labor categories in the Labor Force Survey 1990/91 (URT 1993). The following five labor categories are chosen: professionals (administrators/managers, professionals, associate professionals), white collar (clerks/cashiers, services/shops), blue collar (craft workers, machine operators), unskilled labor, and agricultural labor. Additional factors of production are land and capital.

The disaggregation of households follows the Household Budget Survey 1991/92 (URT 1996a), which provides detailed consumption data for urban farm, urban nonfarm, rural farm, and rural nonfarm households. Because this categorization captures the desired distinction between rural and urban populations and has been applied in many other data sources, it was chosen for this study. All other institutional accounts of the microsam follow the macrosam. Table 4.3 lists in detail all microsam accounts: activities, commodities, and institutions. Appendix C provides a detailed cell by cell description of the construction of the microsam, the sources used, and the data manipulation undertaken.

Given the limitations and inconsistencies of the available data for the SAM balancing procedure, the commodity columns and rows of the generated protosam show high deviations, making it difficult for the solver of the balancing program to find an optimal solution. To cope with this problem and to provide the solver with a better starting point, several adjustments are made. The input-output matrix is cleared of unreasonable entries, some negligible exports and imports are netted out from their respective counter flows, and activity columns or commodity rows are scaled up or down according to their sectoral

---

[94] Tourism has been growing at about 20 percent annually since the mid-1990s and has become one of the largest foreign-currency-earning sectors.

[95] For a detailed listing of the applied sector disaggregation, refer to Table 4.3.

Table 4.3—Accounts of the 1992 microsam for Tanzania

Account	Code	Description	Account	Code	Description
		Agriculture sectors (activities)			
1	ACOTT	Cotton	2	ASISA	Sisal
3	ATEA	Tea	4	ACOFF	Coffee
5	ATOBA	Tobacco	6	ACASH	Cashew nuts
7	AMAIZ	Maize	8	AWHEA	Wheat
9	APADD	Paddy	10	ASORG	Sorghum
11	AOCER	Other cereals	12	ABEAN	Beans
13	ACASS	Cassava	14	AROOT	Other roots and tubers
15	AOILS	Oil seeds	16	ASUGA	Sugar
17	AOHOR	Other horticulture	18	AOCRO	Other crops
19	ALIVE	Livestock	20	AFISH	Fishery
21	AFOHU	Forestry and hunting			
		Nonagriculture sectors (activities)			
22	AMINE	Mining	23	AMEAT	Meat and dairy products
24	AFOOD	Processed food	25	AGRAI	Grain mill products
26	ABEVT	Beverages	27	ATEXT	Textiles not elsewhere specified
28	AWEAR	Wearing apparel	29	ALEAT	Leather products
30	AWOOD	Wood and wood products	31	APAPE	Paper and printing
32	ACHEM	Other Chemicals	33	AFERT	Fertilizer and pesticides
34	AFUEL	Petroleum refineries	35	ARUBB	Rubber products
36	APLAS	Plastic products	37	AGLAS	Glass products
38	ACEME	Cement, clay, etc.	39	AIRON	Iron and steel
40	AFMPR	Manual of metal products	41	AMAEQ	Machinery equipment
42	AELEQ	Electrical equipment	43	ATREQ	Transport equipment
44	AOMAN	Other manufactures	45	AELEC	Electricity
46	AWATE	Water	47	ACNST	Construction
48	ATRAD	Wholesale and retail	49	AHORE	Hotels and restaurants
50	ATR_C	Transport and commodities	51	AFI_I	Financial institutions
52	AREAL	Real estate	53	ABUSI	Business services
54	APUBA	Public administration	55	AOSER	Other services
56	ATOUR	Tourism			

(continued)

Table 4.3—Continued

Account	Code	Description	Account	Code	Description

The same sector disaggregation as activities applies to the respective commodity accounts—except for Tourism (ATOUR). In addition, three marketing margin accounts are specified under commodities.

Account	Code	Description	Account	Code	Description
		Marketing margins			
112	CCOME	Export marketing margin	113	CCOMD	Domestic marketing margin
114	CCOMI	Import marketing margin			
		Factors of production			
115	UPRO	Professional labor	116	UWCO	White collar labor
117	UBCO	Blue collar labor	118	UNSK	Unskilled labor
119	RURA	Agricultural labor	120	LAND	Land
121	CAPITAL	Capital			
		Households			
122	HHUFA	Urban farmers	123	HHUNF	Urban nonfarmers
124	HHRFA	Rural farmers	125	HHRNF	Rural nonfarmers
		Other institutional accounts			
126	ENTR	Enterprises	127	ITAX	Domestic indirect taxes
128	TTAX	Tariffs	129	GOVR	Government recurrent
130	GOVI	Government investment	131	WORLD	Rest of the world
132	KACCOU	Capital account	133	DST	Change in inventory

Source: Author.

excess demand or excess supply values. After this adjustment subroutine, the obtained protosam is balanced through the cross-entropy balancing procedure described in the next section.

For detailed information on the microsam entries, refer to Appendix Table D.1. The new macrosam, which is recalculated after balancing the microsam using the cross-entropy estimation method, is presented below, after the description of the cross-entropy approach.

Balancing the SAM Using a Cross-Entropy Approach.[96] The microsam entries presented in the previous section are not only the result of sectoral data information and relative spreads within the various account subgroups, but also the result of the final balancing procedure of the SAM. A cross-entropy approach to SAM

---

[96] For a more detailed discussion of the cross-entropy approach to SAM estimation, see Robinson, Cattaneo, and El-Said (2000).

estimation is used for the balancing process leading from the unbalanced protosam to the balanced microsam. Because of limited data availability and consistency, the cross-entropy approach serves as an appropriate tool for estimating a balanced and consistent database, starting from an unbalanced database that contains all available information.

The SAM used so far is defined as a matrix T of monetary flows $T_{i,j}$ (a payment from account j to account i), representing receipts and expenditures of all economic agents. Following the convention of double-entry bookkeeping, total receipts and total expenditures of a particular agent i have to be equal, that is, respective row and column sums are balanced:

$$y_i = \sum_j T_{i,j} = \sum_j T_{j,i} \tag{1}$$

Dividing every cell entry of the flow matrix T by its respective column total generates a matrix A of column coefficients:

$$A_{i,j} = \frac{T_{i,j}}{y_j} \text{ with } \sum_i A_{i,j} = 1 \ \forall \ i \tag{2}$$

In matrix notation it follows that:

$$y = A \, y \tag{3}$$

Balancing a SAM is an underdetermined estimation problem using information from many sources and various years. Starting from an unbalanced matrix, the cross-entropy estimation procedure generates a balanced matrix with the least possible changes in the cells of the original unbalanced matrix. The cross-entropy approach[97] allows the incorporation of errors in variables, inequality constraints, and prior knowledge about any part of the SAM, not just row and column sums. These features of the cross-entropy estimation technique allow great flexibility in incorporating specific information and implementing certain limits to which the estimation results are restricted. The general cross-entropy approach[98] is described by the following optimization problem:

---

[97] Following information theory developed by Shannon (1948) and further developed by Theil (1967), the expectation of separate information values can be described as the expected information of data points: $-I(p{:}q) = -\sum_{i-1}^{n} \frac{p_i \ln p_i}{q_i}$, where q and p are prior and posterior probabilities regarding a set of events E_i and $-I(p{:}q)$ are the Kullback-Leibler (1951) measure of the cross-entropy distance between the two probability distributions. The cross-entropy approach minimizes the cross-entropy distance between the probability distributions that are consistent with the information in the data and the prior.

[98] As formulated by Golan, Judge, and Robinson (1994) to update an input-output table by solving for a new coefficient matrix A that minimizes the entropy difference between the underlying prior $\overline{A}$ and the new matrix A.

$$\min \sum_i \sum_j A_{i,j} \cdot \ln \left(\frac{A_{i,j}}{\overline{A}_{i,j}} \right) \tag{4}$$

s.t.: $\quad \sum_j A_{i,j} y_j = y_i \quad$ and $\quad \sum_j A_{i,j} = 1 \ \forall \ i$

where $\overline{A}$ is a coefficient matrix representing any (perhaps inconsistent and unbalanced) prior that was chosen as a starting point of the cross-entropy balancing process to achieve the desired new coefficient matrix A.[99] The described problem is set up to minimize the entropy difference between the two coefficient matrices, which becomes more obvious by rearranging it to

$$\min \sum_i \sum_j A_{i,j} \cdot (\ln A_{i,j} - \ln \overline{A}_{i,j}) \tag{5}$$

Additional equality and inequality constraints can be formulated as linear "adding-up" constraints on various elements of the SAM. For an aggregator matrix G, which has ones for those microsam entries that correspond to a certain macrosam aggregate and zeros otherwise, the formulation for k such aggregation constraints is given by

$$\sum_i \sum_j G_{i,j}^{(k)} \cdot T_{i,j} = \gamma^{(k)} \tag{6}$$

where $\gamma^{(k)}$ is the value of the aggregate and the T_{ij}'s are the microsam flows.
Measurement errors in variables can be incorporated into the system through

$$y = \overline{x} + e \tag{7}$$

where y is a vector of row sums and $\overline{x}$ is the initially known vector of column sums measured with error. The error e is defined as a weighted average of known constants

$$e_i = \sum_w W_{i,w} \cdot \overline{v}_{i,w} \tag{8}$$

where w is a set of weights W, v are constants, and weights are subject to

$$\sum_w W_{i,w} = 1 \text{ with } 0 \le W_{i,w} \le 1 \tag{9}$$

---

[99] This means that the prior $\overline{A}$ does not need to satisfy the model $y = \overline{A} \ y$, but the sum of its column coefficients is one, that is, $\sum_i \overline{A}_{i,j} = 1 \ \forall \ j$.

For the purposes of the Tanzania microsam, a symmetric distribution around zero given lower and upper bounds is chosen, using three weights.[100] Consequently, the optimization problem of minimizing the entropy difference now contains a term for the weights W

$$\min \left(\sum_i \sum_j A_{i,j} \cdot (\ln A_{i,j} - \ln \overline{A}_{i,j}) + \sum_i \sum_w W_{i,w} \cdot \ln W_{i,w} \right) \tag{10}$$

The explicit application of the cross-entropy estimation procedure on the Tanzania microsam contains a set of additional constraints that constrain various sums over submatrices of the SAM to their respective macroeconomic control totals. First, within activities, the sum over all factor payments is fixed to their aggregate value as specified in the macrosam. As a result, total GDP at f.c. is constrained to its original value. Sectoral production may change within specified lower and upper limits, which are imposed through the error specification, allowing shifts in relative sector shares of production in the economy.

Second, the foreign trade entries are constrained to their macroeconomic totals, although the relative commodity composition of imports and exports may change. Third, total final household, government, and investment demands are bound to their macroeconomic totals as reported in the *Revised National Accounts of Tanzania 1987–96* as well as to total own-household consumption.

Finally, total income taxes, sales taxes, other indirect taxes, tariffs, and total remittances to households from abroad are fixed at their macroeconomic totals. Some single-cell entries are locked to their initial values if the data source applied is reliable, such as government investment demand and factor payments abroad.

The 1992 Macrosam and Microsam after the Balancing Procedure. The distribution of macroeconomic data according to the sector disaggregation of the microsam and the cross-entropy estimation procedure to balance the protosam leads to the final Tanzanian microsam for 1992. Appendix Table D.1 presents the Tanzanian microsam 1992. Appendix Table E.1 presents the sector-specific structure of the economy. After obtaining the final microsam, it is aggregated to obtain the final macrosam, allowing comparison between initial and final macroeconomic structure and indicating the changes that occurred during the balancing procedure. Table 4.4 presents the obtained values of the new macrosam, including their respective changes from the initial macrosam.

For the cross-entropy balancing procedure certain macroeconomic control totals are imposed as constraints. In other words, some cell entries and some

---

[100] Note that if the error distribution is symmetrically centered around zero and all weights are equal—as their initial prior values—the respective error equals zero.

Table 4.4—New macrosam for 1992 (millions of 1992 TSh)

	Activities	Commodities	Factors	Households	Enterprises	Domestic taxes	Tariffs	Government recurrent	Government investment	Rest of the world	Capital account	Total
Activities		**2,440,513** +120,029		273,340						165,682		2,879,535
Commodities	**1,396,456** +120,029	**211,682** new		913,213				279,080	52,521		419,532	3,272,484
Factors	1,456,047											1,456,047
Households			**884,150** +42,272		**275,629** −93,033					**126,875** +30,120		1,286,655
Enterprises			**508,398** −42,272					27,620				536,018
Domestic taxes	27,032	43,475										70,507
Tariffs		23,451										23,451
Government recurrent				16,656	65,054	70,507	23,451			172,671		348,339
Government investment								34,957		17,564		52,521
Rest of the world		553,363	63,499					24,250				641,112
Capital account				**83,446** −20,642	**195,335** +50,762			(17,568)		**158,320** −30,120		419,532
Total	2,879,535	3,272,484	1,456,047	1,286,655	536,018	70,507	23,451	348,339	52,521	641,112	419,532	

Source: Author.

submatrix totals of the proposed microsam are fixed at their initial levels. In particular, this is true for

- total value-added;
- the three tax aggregates (other indirect taxes, sales taxes, and tariffs);
- the trade flows (total exports and imports);
- all aggregate final demand categories (household, government, government investment, and private investment demands as well as own-household consumption);
- total factor payments abroad;
- corporate and total individual income taxes;
- government transfers to enterprises and abroad;
- transfers from abroad to the government (recurrent and investment accounts).

Consequently, the respective cells of the new macrosam do not show any changes compared with the initial macrosam. Other cells are implicitly fixed. As the government investment demand and the related inflow from abroad are fixed, the balancing flow from government recurrent to government investment cannot change either. The government deficit is therefore the last unconstrained cell of the government expenditure column, but because the totals of all government revenue sources are fixed, the government deficit is implicitly constrained.

Total intermediate demand (commodities, activities) remains unrestricted for the balancing process, because it has to adjust to total value-added, which is increased to match total final consumption of the national accounts data. The macroeconomic total for intermediate demand increases by TSh 120,029 million, including TSh 18,213 million for total marketing margins for exports. The net change accounts for 8 percent of the original value, and the resulting change in total gross output accounts for 4.3 percent. According to the mechanism of the macrosam in which domestic supply equals gross output minus exports and own-household consumption—which are both fixed—the change in the total domestic supply value is the same as the reported increase of total intermediate demand.

The new entry in the new macrosam (commodities, commodities) represents total import and domestic marketing margin values. In the protosam TSh 226,911 million are distributed from final demand for retail and wholesale trade (CTRAD) to the two marketing margin accounts for domestic products and imports. The final figure of TSh 211,682 million corresponds to a decrease of 6.7 percent.

The initially chosen distribution of total value-added into capital value-added paid to enterprises and noncapital value-added paid directly to households changed by TSh 42,272 million, a 5 percent change from the initial factor payments to households. Total household savings are adjusted from TSh 104,087 million to TSh 83,446 million, whereas enterprise savings increase from TSh 144,572 million to TSh 195,335 million. Households receive TSh 93,033 million less value-added capital distributed through enterprises and TSh 30,120 million more remittances from abroad. Consequently, the payments to the capital account from abroad decrease by the latter amount.

Description of the CGE Model

This section provides a detailed specification of the applied CGE model, reporting on all variables, parameters, and equations used.[101] Different blocks of equations are introduced, following the conceptual functionality of the CGE approach. First, the price equations that define the underlying price system of the model are presented. These constitute the core of any CGE model because they solve for relative prices, including the exchange rate. Second, the quantity equations are presented, which describe production and value-added generation, followed by the block of income equations that describe the distribution of factor income to institutions. Third, the expenditure equations that characterize the budget constraints of the various actors of the model are described. Finally, the equation block of system constraints is presented, which defines the market clearing conditions and their related macroeconomic closures of the model. Table 4.5 presents a complete list of parameters and variables applied in the Tanzanian CGE model equations.

Price Equations

The price equations of the CGE model are as follows:

$$PM_{cm} = (pwm_{cm} \cdot (1 + tm_{cm}) \cdot EXR + mrm_{cm} \cdot PC_{CTRAD}) \cdot (1 + TVC_{cm}) \tag{11}$$

$$PE_{ae} = PWE_{ae} \cdot (1 - te_{ae}) \cdot EXR - mre_{ae} \cdot PC_{CTRAD} \tag{12}$$

$$PDC_{comm} = \sum_{activ} m_{activ,comm} \cdot (1 + TVA_{activ}) \cdot PDA_{activ} + mrd_{comm} \cdot PC_{CTRAD} \tag{13}$$

$$PQ_{comm} \cdot Q_{comm} = PDC_{comm} \cdot DC_{comm} + PM_{comm} \cdot M_{comm} \tag{14}$$

$$PX_{activ} \cdot X_{activ} = PDA_{activ} \cdot DA_{activ} + PE_{activ} \cdot E_{activ} \tag{15}$$

$$PC_{comm} = PQ_{comm} \cdot (1 + tc_{comm}) \tag{16}$$

$$PV_{activ} = PX_{activ} \cdot (1 - tx_{activ}) + TVCRED_{activ} - \sum_{comm} a_{comm,activ} \cdot PC_{comm} \tag{17}$$

$$PK_{activ} = \sum_{comm} PC_{comm} \cdot b_{comm,activ} \tag{18}$$

$$PINDCON = \prod_{comm} (PC_{comm})^{pwtc_{comm}} \tag{19}$$

---

[101] The section provides a full description of all relevant model equations to allow the reader unfamiliar with this type of model to understand its functionality and specific characteristics. Every equation is formulated and described, and comments are made regarding the function of the respective equation within the model framework. The reader who is familiar with the basic functionality of a CGE model of the applied type may proceed to the section dealing with the country-specific features of the Tanzanian CGE model. Although the model presentation in this section is strongly oriented toward the order of the model equations, Chapter 3 in Devarajan, Lewis, and Robinson (1994) and the model description in Bautista and Robinson (1996) provided valuable insights.

Table 4.5—Parameters and variables of the Tanzanian CGE model

Parameters (in lower case)

$a_{comm,\ activ}$	Input-output coefficients
ac_{comm}	Import aggregation (CES) shift parameter
$ad2_{activ}$	CES production function shift parameter
at_{activ}	Export transformation (CET) shift parameter
$\alpha_{activ,f}$	CES production function share parameter
$b_{comm,activ}$	Capital composition matrix
$\beta^h_{activ,\ hh}$	Marginal own-household consumption
$\beta^m_{comm,\ hh}$	Marginal market household consumption
δ_{comm}	Import aggregation (CES) share parameter
$econ_{activ}$	Export demand constant
η_{activ}	Export demand price elasticity
γ_{activ}	Export transformation (CET) share parameter
$\gamma^h_{activ,\ hh}$	Minimum own-household consumption
$\gamma^m_{comm,\ hh}$	Minimum market household consumption
$gishr_{comm}$	Government investment shares
$gles_{comm}$	Government consumption shares
$gshr^{gin}$	Initial share of government investment
$gshr^{gre}$	Initial share of government recurrent
$kshr_{activ}$	Shares of investment by sector of destination
$m_{activ,\ comm}$	Make matrix coefficients
mrd_{comm}	Marketing margin coefficient (domestics)
mre_{comm}	Marketing margin coefficient (exports)
mrm_{comm}	Marketing margin coefficient (imports)
$pwse_{activ}$	World price of export substitutes (in US$)
pwm_{comm}	World price of imports (in US$)
$pwtc_{comm}$	Nontraded consumer price weights
ρ^C_{comm}	Import aggregation (CES) exponent
ρ^P_{activ}	CES production function exponent
ρ^T_{activ}	Export transformation (CET) exponent
$sremit_{hh}$	Share of remittance to households
$strans2_{hh}$	Government transfer shares (drought)
tc_{comm}	Consumption tax rates
te_{activ}	Tax (+) or subsidy (–) rates on exports
th_{hh}	Household tax rate
tm_{comm}	Tariff rates on imports
tx_{activ}	Indirect producer tax rates
$wfdist0_{activ,\ f}$	Initial factor price sectoral proportionality ratios
$ymap_{f,\ hh}$	Income distribution matrix

(continued)

Table 4.5—Continued

Variables (in upper case)

CD_{comm}	Market household consumption by commodity
$CD^h_{activ,\ hh}$	$CD2_{activ}$ by household
$CD^m_{comm,\ hh}$	CD_{comm} by household
$CD2_{activ}$	Own-household consumption per activity
$CONTAX$	Consumption tax revenue
DA_{activ}	Domestic activity sales
DC_{comm}	Domestic commodity sales
DK_{activ}	Volume of investment by sector of destination
DST_{comm}	Inventory investment by sector
E_{activ}	Exports
$ENTSAV$	Enterprise savings
$ENTTAX$	Corporate taxes
ESR	Enterprise savings rate
ETR	Enterprise tax rate
$EXPTAX$	Export tax revenue
EXR	Exchange rate (TSh per US$)
$FAIDEQV$	Monetary equivalent of food aid
$FBOR$	Government foreign borrowing (recurrent)
$FBOR2$	Government foreign borrowing (investment)
$FDSC_{activ,\ f}$	Factor demand by sector
$FOODAID_{comm}$	Physical food aid influx
$FSAV$	Net foreign savings
FS_f	Factor supply
$FSAG_f$	Factor supply aggregate agriculture
$FXDINV$	Fixed capital investment
$GDTOT$	Total government consumption (recurrent)
GD_{comm}	Government demand (recurrent)
GI_{comm}	Government demand (investment)
$GININV$	Total government consumption (investment)
$GINREV$	Government investment revenue
$GOVGIN$	Government investment deficit
$GOVSAV$	Government savings
$GOVTE$	Government transfers to enterprises
$GOVTH2$	Government transfers to households (drought)
GR	Government revenue
$HHSAV$	Household savings
$HHTAX$	Individual income taxes
ID_{comm}	Final demand for productive investment

(continued)

$$con_{aed} \cdot \left(\frac{pwe_{aed}}{pwse_{aed}} \right)^{-\eta_{aed}}$$

$$(27)$$

$$ac_{cm} \cdot \left(\delta_{cm} \cdot M_{cm}^{-\rho_{cm}^C} + (1 - \delta_{cm}) \cdot DC_{cm}^{-\rho_{cm}^C} \right)^{-1/\rho_{cm}^C}$$

$$(28)$$

$$= DC_{cm} \cdot \left(\frac{PDC_{cm}}{PM_{cm}} \cdot \frac{\delta_{cm}}{1 - \delta_{cm}} \right)^{\frac{1}{1+\rho_{cm}^C}}$$

$$(29)$$

Production in value-added terms is defined as a (nested) CES function of mary factors (equation 20), and the profit maximization condition is derived m the first-order conditions (equation 21). Note that total intermediate demand r a certain commodity—this is not total intermediate demand by a certain sector production—is calculated by applying the input-output matrix coefficients to ross production ($X_{activ} \cdot a_{comm, activ}$ in equation 22), but intermediate demand does not ppear in the production function. This classical formulation is possible, because he intermediate demand branch of the nested production function is a linear com- bination of inputs, and its top level is a linear combination of total value-added and total intermediate demand. The generation of value-added is the only component of the production function that is specified as a CES function allowing for substitution between its factors.[107]

The CET transformation of exports and domestic supply defines real output for exportable goods (equation 25). The relevant export supply is derived as the explicit first-order condition of equation (25) in equilibrium, assuming that the ratio of the marginal rates of substitution of domestic supply and exports equals their price ratio (equation 26). This specification of export supply works under the small-country assumption, in which the national export volume has no influ- ence on world market prices. In the opposite case, where national exports do influence world market prices, the economy faces a downward sloping demand curve, and its respective export supply function can be expressed by equation (27).[108] In the Tanzanian CGE model, all export sectors follow the small-country assumption, facing exogenously determined (fixed) world market prices and not downward sloping world demand curves.

---

[107] As the derivatives of the nested production function for all intermediates are their constant input-output coeffi- cients, they can be summarized and incorporated into the net price equation for value-added (equation 17). The intermediate demand component of the nested production function is expressed as an inverse demand function for intermediate inputs using input-output table coefficients. Consequently, the formulation of the net price equation and the inverse intermediate demand function spares the explicit formulation of the "full" nested production func- tion. Johansen (1960) presented the first application of this model specification.

[108] Note, however, that producers are price takers in both cases, and if world demand is downward sloping, domes- tic producers do not act as monopolists.

Table 4.5—Continued

Variables (in upper case)

IDS	Total final demand for investment
$INDTAX$	Indirect tax revenue
INT_{comm}	Intermediate uses
$INVEST$	Total investment
MPS_{hh}	Marginal propensity to save by household
M_{comm}	Imports
PC_{comm}	Consumption price of composite goods
PDA_{activ}	Domestic activity goods price
PDC_{comm}	Domestic commodity goods price
PE_{activ}	Domestic price of exports
$PINDCON$	Nontraded consumer price index
PK_{activ}	Price of capital goods by sector of destination
PM_{comm}	Domestic price of imports
PQ_{comm}	Price of composite good (net of tc_{comm})
PV_{activ}	Value-added price
PWE_{activ}	World price of exports
PX_{activ}	Average output price
Q_{comm}	Composite goods supply
$REMIT$	Remittances to households
$REMFAC_f$	Factor payments abroad
$SAVING$	Total savings
$TARIFF$	Tariff revenue
$TRADM_{CTRAD}$	Total demand for trade and marketing services
TVA_{activ}	Value-added tax rates on activities
TVC_{comm}	Value-added tax rates on commodities
$TVCRED_{activ}$	Value-added tax rebate wedges
$VATAX$	Value-added tax revenue
$WFDIST_{activ,f}$	Factor price sectoral proportionality ratios
$WFAGDIST_f$	Factor price sectoral proportionality ratios for agricultural sectors
WF_f	Average factor price
X_{activ}	Domestic output
$YFCTR_f$	Factor income
YH_{hh}	Household income
YH_{hh}^{disp}	Disposable household income
$YH2_{hh}$	Monetary equivalent of own-household consumption

Source: Author.

Note: CES is constant elasticity of substitution.
CET is constant elasticity of transformation.

Equation (11) defines the domestic price of imports (for $cm \in comm$) as a function of the exogenous world price, exchange rate, tariff, and marketing margin. The import marketing margin is a commodity-specific fraction, mrm_{cm}, of the consumer price for trade, PC_{CTRAD}, per unit of the imported commodity. In other words, each unit of a specific commodity is associated with a certain fraction of one unit of the commodity transport, rather than its transport share being defined as a markup on the respective commodity price itself. The marketing margin term is added because PM_{cm} reflects the domestic border price equivalent of imports, which enters the price equation of the composite good, Q, the final consumption good.[102] Correspondingly, equation (12) defines the domestic price of exports (for $ae \in activ$), but the marketing margin term for exports is subtracted because PE_{ae} reflects the producer price of exports[103] and does not contain the marketing margin.

In equation (13) the price of a domestically supplied commodity, PDC_{comm}, is defined by the weighted prices of the activities ($\sum_{activ} m_{activ, comm} \cdot PDA_{activ}$) that are bought into this commodity market and its domestic marketing margin. The column coefficient matrix, $m_{activ, comm}$, is the make matrix that identifies the linear combination of activities creating a particular commodity. In equation (14) the composite commodity price, PQ_{comm}, is defined as the weighted average of its respective domestic and import commodity prices. Correspondingly, equation (15) defines the producer price, PX_{activ}, as the weighted average of the domestic activity price and the domestic export price. The final consumption price, PC_{comm}, is defined in equation (16) as the composite commodity price plus indirect consumption taxes. Equation (17) defines the value-added price (PV_{activ}) as the producer price net of indirect taxes and the value of total intermediate demand.[104] In equation (18) PK_{activ}, the price of the capital investment good by destination, is defined as a linear combination of the relevant consumer prices.[105] Finally, equation (19) defines the cost of living index $PINDCON$, the numeraire

---

[102] As later explained in the quantity equation section, Q is defined as a CES Armington composition of domestically supplied and imported commodities at market level and, therefore, both components have to contain their respective marketing margins.

[103] In the sense of a farmgate or factory gate price, as opposed to the free on board (F.O.B.) price at which the commodity is exported and that includes the marketing margin.

[104] Total intermediate demand ($\sum_{comm} a_{comm, activ} \cdot PC_{comm}$) is a linear combination of consumer prices PC_{comm} with respect to the column coefficients of the input-output coefficient matrix $a_{comm, activ}$.

[105] In the Tanzanian model all PK_{activ} are equal regardless of the sector of destination of capital investment, because the available data do not allow the construction of a capital investment matrix considering both sector of origin and sector of destination (therefore, $b_{comm, activ}$ consists of capital composition vectors—the matrix columns— which are the same for each sector of destination of capital investment). However, as the static CGE model generates savings, investment, and demand for capital goods within one period (assuming a fixed economywide capital stock), the heterogeneity of capital is of less importance. Investment is just a demand category and has no impact on the supply side of the model, because the demanded capital goods are not installed during the one period time frame (Devarajan, Lewis, and Robinson 1994, pp. 3–7).

---

of the model, as the geometric average of con[...] share weights.[106]

Quantity Equations

Equations 20–29 introduce the quantity equations of [...] production, foreign trade, and market supply decisions t[...] general behavior: (1) production technology is describ[...] function; (2) a CET function combines exports and do[...] output of exportable goods, and the export supply func[...] respective first-order condition; and (3) a CES import subs[...] the composite commodity as a combination of imports an[...] generates the import demand function by its first-order cond[...]

$$X_{activ} = ad2_{activ} \cdot \left(\sum_f \alpha2_{activ, f} \cdot FDSC_{activ, f}^{-\rho^P_{activ}} \right)^{-1/\rho^P_{activ}}$$

$$WF_f \cdot WFDIST_{activ, f} = PV_{activ} \cdot ad2_{activ} \cdot \left(\sum_f \alpha2_{activ, f} \cdot FDSC_{activ, f}^{-\rho^P_{activ}} \right)^{-1/\rho^P_{activ} - }$$
$$\cdot \; \alpha2_{activ, f} \cdot FDSC_{activ, f}^{-\rho^P_{activ} - 1}$$

$$INT_{comm} = \sum_{activ} X_{activ} \cdot a_{comm, activ}$$

$$TRADM_{CTRAD} = \sum_{ae} E_{ae} \cdot mre_{ae} + \sum_{cm} M_{cm} \cdot mrm_{cm} + \sum_{comm} DC_{comm} \cdot mrd_{cm}$$

$$DC_{comm} = \sum_{activ} m_{activ, comm} \cdot (DA_{activ} - CD2_{activ})$$

$$X_{ae} = at_{ae} \cdot (\delta_{ae} \cdot E_{ae}^{\rho^T_{ae}} + (1 - \delta_{ae}) \cdot DA_{ae}^{\rho^T_{ae}})^{1/\rho^T_{ae}}$$

(26)

$$E_{ae} = DA_{ae} \cdot \left(\frac{PE_{ae}}{PDA_{ae}} \cdot \frac{(1 - \gamma_{ae})}{\gamma_{ae}} \right)^{\frac{1}{\rho^T_{ae} - 1}}$$

---

[106] Note that the model solution expresses the endogenous price variables in relative terms with respect to the numeraire. According to the focus of analysis, the choice of the numeraire is crucial. The welfare analysis of this research makes the specification of an aggregate consumer price index or cost of living index as numeraire a convenient choice. A more production-oriented analysis might use a producer price index. A common numeraire is the GDP deflator defined as nominal GDP over real GDP. Alternatively, single prices can be used as numeraire(s), for example, the exchange rate or a particular wage of the economy. However, the use of the cost of living index causes nominal income to be a direct measure of utility, because all prices of the model (including wages) are expressed in real consumer good weights. For the underlying theory dealing with indirect utility functions, see Phlips (1974).

The domestic commodity supply, DC_{comm}, is defined according to its price equation (13) as the sum over the make matrix column coefficients multiplied by their respective domestic supply, DA_{activ}, net of own-household consumption (equation 24). The composite good, Q_{comm}, is defined as a CES aggregation function of the domestic commodity supply and imports (equation 28). Finally, an import demand function (equation 29) can be derived from the CES composite good equation just as the export supply function (equation 26) was derived from the CET transformation function (equation 25). Equation (23) sums export, import, and domestic marketing margins for all relevant commodities to an aggregate variable ($TRADM_{CTRAD}$).

Income Equations

The income equation block specifies the factor payments of the economy and their distribution to households and other institutions, as well as tax payments, savings, remittances, and other foreign payments.

$$YFCTR = \sum_{activ} WFDIST_{activ, f} \cdot WF_f \cdot FDSC_{activ, f} \tag{30}$$

$$\begin{aligned} YH_{hh} = \sum_{f \neq capital} ymap_{f, hh} \cdot YFCTR_f \\ + ymap_{capital, hh} \cdot (YFCTR_{capital} - ENTSAV - ENTTAX) \\ + sremit_{hh} \cdot REMIT \cdot EXR + strans2_{hh} \cdot GOVTH2 \end{aligned} \tag{31}$$

$$YH2_{hh} = \sum_{activ} PDA_{activ} \cdot CD2_{activ, hh} \tag{32}$$

$$TARIFF = \sum_{cm} (tm_{cm} \cdot M_{cm} \cdot pwm_{cm}) \cdot EXR \tag{33}$$

$$CONTAX = \sum_{comm} tc_{comm} \cdot PQ_{comm} \cdot Q_{comm} \tag{34}$$

$$INDTAX = \sum_{activ} tx_{activ} \cdot PX_{activ} \cdot X_{activ} \tag{35}$$

$$\begin{aligned} VATAX = \sum_{activ} TVA_{activ} \cdot PDA_{activ} \cdot (DA_{activ} - CD2_{activ}) \\ + \sum_{cm} M_{cm} \cdot [pwm_{cm} \cdot EXR \cdot (1 + tm_{cm}) + mrm_{cm} \cdot PC_{CTRAD}] \\ \cdot TVC_{cm} - \sum_{activ} TVCRED_{activ} \cdot X_{activ} \end{aligned} \tag{36}$$

$$HHTAX = \sum_{hh} th_{hh} \cdot (YH_{hh} - YH2_{hh}) \tag{37}$$

$$ENTTAX = ETR \cdot YFCTR_{capital} \tag{38}$$

$$HHSAV = \sum_{hh} MPS_{hh} \cdot (YH_{hh} - YH2_{hh}) \cdot (1 - th_{hh}) \tag{39}$$

$$ENTSAV = ESR \cdot (YFCTR_{capital} - ENTTAX) \tag{40}$$

$$GR = TARIFF + CONTAX + INDTAX + HHTAX + ENTTAX + VATAX \\ + FBOR \cdot EXR + FBOR2 \cdot EXR + EXPTAX + FAIDEQV \tag{41}$$

$$GINREV = FBOR2 \cdot EXR + GOVGIN \tag{42}$$

$$SAVING = HHSAV + ENTSAV + GOVSAV + FSAV \cdot EXR \tag{43}$$

Equation (30) defines factor payments for each primary factor as the sum over all sector payments regarding the intersectoral average factor wage (WF_f), sectoral factor demand ($FDSC_{activ,f}$), and a sector-specific factor price proportionality ratio ($WFDIST_{activ,f}$). An undistorted economy would show all $WFDIST_{activ,f}$ equal to one, because the marginal factor return in each economic activity would be equal (assuming perfect factor mobility). However, experience from developing countries indicates a substantial deviation of factor payments among sectors that can be captured by the ratio of the sector-specific factor payment and the average factor return across the economy.

After its generation, value-added is distributed to households using a distribution matrix of fixed coefficients defined over factors and households ($ymap_{f,hh}$ in equation 31). As value-added capital is supposed to be distributed through enterprises, the receipts of households are net of enterprise savings and corporate taxes. Because the model contains own-household consumption, a separate household income has to be generated (equation 32) that is entirely spent on home consumption. Note that $YH2_{hh}$ is not additional income, but the amount of YH_{hh} spent on own-household consumption, and thus represents the nonmonetary income part of the household budget. This nonmonetary income for own-household consumption is defined as the sum over constant sectoral shares of the respective gross output.[109]

Equations (33) to (38) describe total tax collection within the model that sums to government revenue net of foreign borrowing (equation 41). Tariffs are collected on the border price equivalent of imports (equation 33), sales taxes are paid on final and intermediate consumption of the composite good (equation 34),

---

[109] The section on the country-specific features of the applied model presents a detailed explanation of the functional interdependency of income generation and expenditure regarding own-household consumption.

and other indirect taxes—associated with the production process—are levied on gross output (equation 35). VAT on domestic supply—net of own-household consumption—and imports is specified as a European-style destination VAT with a rebate mechanism (equation 36), which is described in more detail in the section on the country-specific features of the model.[110] Household taxes are a fixed fraction of monetary income (equation 37) and enterprises pay a variable rate on capital income (equation 38), which might be fixed depending on the applied macroeconomic closure of the model.

Domestic savings depend on (1) household-specific marginal propensities to save that are applied to the household's monetary income net of income taxes (equation 39) and (2) enterprise savings that are paid as a flexible rate on capital income net of corporate taxes (equation 40). Total savings is defined as the sum over household and enterprise savings, flexible government savings, and foreign savings in local currency (equation 43).

Expenditure Equations

The system of expenditure equations describes household, government, and investment demand for marketed commodities, as well as own-household consumption demand for activities.

$$
\begin{aligned}
CD^m_{comm,\,hh} \cdot PC_{comm} &= PC_{comm} \cdot \gamma^m_{comm,\,hh} \\
&+ \beta^m_{comm,\,hh} \cdot \left(YH^{disp}_{hh} - \sum_{comm} PC_{comm} \cdot \gamma^m_{comm,\,hh} - \sum_{activ} PDA_{activ} \cdot \gamma^h_{activ,\,hh} \right) \\
&with\ CD_{comm} = \sum_{hh} CD^m_{comm,\,hh}
\end{aligned}
\tag{44}
$$

$$
\begin{aligned}
CD^h_{activ,\,hh} \cdot PDA_{activ} &= PDA_{activ} \cdot \gamma^h_{activ,\,hh} \\
&+ \beta^h_{activ,\,hh} \cdot \left(YH^{disp}_{hh} - \sum_{comm} PC_{comm} \cdot \gamma^m_{comm,\,hh} - \sum_{activ} PDA_{activ} \cdot \gamma^h_{activ,\,hh} \right) \\
&with\ CD2_{activ} = \sum_{hh} CD^h_{activ,\,hh}
\end{aligned}
\tag{45}
$$

$$
GD_{comm} \cdot PC_{comm} = gles_{comm} \cdot (GDTOT + gshr^{gre} \cdot (FAIDEQV - GOVTH2))
\tag{46}
$$

$$
GI_{comm} \cdot PC_{comm} = gishr_{comm} \cdot (GININV + gshr^{gin} \cdot (FAIDEQV - GOVTH2))
\tag{47}
$$

$$
GR = \sum_{comm} PC_{comm} \cdot (GD_{comm} + GI_{comm}) + GOVSAV + GOVTE + GOVTH2
\tag{48}
$$

---

[110] "European-style" refers to the destination principle of VAT, which means that goods sold in a country pick up the VAT, that is, exports are exempt and imports are taxable. This is sometimes referred to as consumption VAT in contrast to income VAT, which applies the origin principle (see Shoup 1990).

$$GINREV = GININV \tag{49}$$

$$FXDINV = INVEST - \sum_{comm} DST_{comm} \cdot PC_{comm} \tag{50}$$

$$PK_{activ} \cdot DK_{activ} = kshr_{activ} \cdot FXDINV \tag{51}$$

$$ID_{comm} = \sum_{activ} DK_{activ} \cdot b_{comm, \, activ} \tag{52}$$

$$IDS = \sum_{comm} ID_{comm} \tag{53}$$

Equations (44) and (45) define the value of total final and own-household demand as two combined LESs applied to the households' disposable income. Final sectoral government demand is defined as constant shares of fixed total real government expenditure (equation 46) and sectoral government investment as constant shares of the government development budget (equation 47). Total government revenue has to equal the sum of all government expenditures on commodities plus government savings and transfers to enterprises (equation 48). Moreover, total government investment must equal the revenue of the development budget (equation 49). Gross fixed capital formation equals total nominal investment net of the nominal value of fixed real changes in inventory (equation 50). As the model is driven by savings, total nominal investment ($INVEST$) adjusts for changes in economywide savings to fulfill the saving-investment clearing condition (equation 57). The value of final capital demand by destination ($PK_{activ} \cdot DK_{activ}$) is defined as a sector-specific share of total gross fixed capital formation $FXDINV$ (equation 51). Note that PK_{activ} is a sector-specific price for a sector-specific capital investment good DK_{activ}. As discussed earlier, the composition of this sector-specific capital investment for each economic activity is captured in the capital composition matrix, $b_{comm, \, activ}$, which, when applied to DK_{activ} leads to real capital investment by origin, ID_{comm}, as defined in equation (52). To fix the economywide real investment, the sum over all final demand for productive investment categories is defined (equation 53).

Market-Clearing Conditions and Initial Macroeconomic Model Closures

After describing the supply and demand side of the model, the price system, and the income-generation and distribution process, the market-clearing conditions have to be specified.

$$Q_{comm} + FOODAID_{comm} = INT_{comm} + CD_{comm} + TRADM_{comm} + GD_{comm}$$
$$+ GI_{comm} + ID_{comm} + DST_{comm} \tag{54}$$

$$FS_f = \sum_{activ} FDSC_{activ,f} \qquad (55)$$

$$\sum_{cm} pwm_{cm} \cdot M_{cm} + \sum_{comm} PC_{comm} \cdot FOODAID_{comm} \cdot EXR = \sum_{ae} pwm_{ae} \cdot E_{ae}$$
$$+ FSAV + FBOR + FBOR2 + FAIDEQV \cdot EXR + REMIT$$
$$- \sum_f REMFAC_f \qquad (56)$$

$$SAVING = INVEST \qquad (57)$$

Equation (54) represents the physical balance of all commodity markets, where total composite commodity supply (including food aid) equals the sum over intermediate demand and all final demand categories.[111] All factor markets are balanced according to equation (55). The balance of payments equation requires total payments for imports to equal total receipts for exports plus foreign savings and borrowing (equation 56). The latter two are usually fixed in the applied general equilibrium approach, which leaves the exchange rate as the adjusting variable. The last equation of the model represents the saving-investment balance, which is determined by total savings as defined in equation (43) and aggregate nominal investment as specified in equation (50). Fixing aggregate real investment, IDS, determines the investment side and consequently forces total savings to adjust through enterprise savings, which are determined by the enterprise savings rate, ESR. All other saving components are either fixed ($FSAV$), determined by fixed rates ($HHSAV$), or equilibrate other functions of the model ($GOVSAV$). The model is driven by investment, and savings adjust accordingly.[112]

The latter option is one of the macroeconomic closures of the applied CGE framework. Table 4.6 presents all other initial macroeconomic closures of the model as specified in the base run.[113]

The foreign exchange market closures fix foreign savings, $FSAV$; foreign borrowing regarding recurrent and investment budget of the government, $FBOR$ and $FBOR2$; remittances from abroad, $REMIT$; and factor payments abroad, $REMFAC_f$, at their initial base run values. This leaves the exchange rate, EXR, as the equilibrating variable of the foreign exchange market.[114] The government closures fix total final government consumption, $GDTOT$; the government investment budget deficit, $GOVGIN$; government transfers to enterprises, $GOVTE$; the enterprise tax rate, ETR; and the inflow of

---

[111] Note that the element $TRADM_{comm}$ is zero for all commodities except the trade sector, $CTRAD$, for which it is the sum over all marketing margins.

[112] Alternatively, the model functions in a rather neoclassical way if ESR is fixed as well and, thus, total savings are determined through the given equilibrium conditions. In this case, aggregate investment has to adjust by freeing real investment, IDS, instead of holding it fixed.

[113] Note that reruns of the model base and experiment specifications for policy analysis will show different closure settings according to their analytical focus.

[114] Note that the most common alternative to this closure specification is the fixing of the exchange rate, EXR, and the freeing of foreign savings, $FSAV$, at the same time. The comparison of the two scenarios allows for the isolation of net exchange rate effects as part of simulation results.

Table 4.6—Initial macroeconomic model closures

Foreign exchange market closure:
$\overline{FSAV}, \overline{FBOR}, \overline{FBOR2}, \overline{REMIT}, \overline{REMFAC}_f$

Saving-investment closure:
$\overline{MPS}_{hh}, \overline{IDS}, \overline{DST}$

Government closure:
$\overline{GDTOT}, \overline{GOVGIN}, \overline{GOVTE}, \overline{ETR}, \overline{FOODAID}_{comm}$

Factor markets closure:
$\overline{FS}_{capital}, \overline{WFDIST}_{activ, capital}, \overline{FS}_{lab}, \overline{WFDIST}_{activ, lab}, \overline{FDSC}_{activ, land}, \overline{WF}_{land}$

Source: Author.
Note: Overlined variables are fixed at their initial database values.

food aid, $FOODAID_{comm}$. This leaves government savings, $GOVSAV$; total government revenue, GR; and the total investment budget, $GINREV$, to adjust endogenously. Finally, the factor markets are constrained by macroeconomic closures in various ways. Total factor supply of capital and all labor categories, $FS_{capital}$ and FS_{lab}, are fixed along with their sectoral factor price proportionality ratios, $WFDIST_{activ, f}$. Consequently, the respective factor wages, WF_f, serve as the adjusting variable of the model. In the case of land, the sectoral factor demand, $FDSC_{activ, land}$, and the average return to land are fixed, which locks up the use of land per sector within the modeling horizon. To enable different returns to land, the closure specification allows for changes in the sector-specific proportionality ratios, $WFDIST_{activ, land}$.

Country-Specific Features of the Tanzanian CGE Model

Motivated by the specific analytical focus of the Tanzania study and by country-specific characteristics of the Tanzanian economy, the applied CGE model incorporates some special features. The following subsections describe the following model features in detail:
- incorporation of own-household consumption
- treatment of a VAT variable
- introduction of a food aid variable
- integration of marketing margin coefficients
- employment of factor market segmentation for aggregate agriculture.

Own-Household Consumption. Although there is a declining trend in the share of agricultural production in total GDP, about 85 percent of the national workforce is still engaged in agriculture, most of whom are small-scale farmers. Consequently, a large share of agricultural food production is not channeled through commodity markets but is consumed by producers directly. This part of production counts as informal sector activities because they are not monitored as part of official GDP. However, the most recent national accounts data on Tanzania for 1996 report on nonmonetary GDP categories and thus indicate the national magnitude of nonmarketed production. In addition, the Household Budget Survey 1991/92 (URT 1996a) provides consumption data on different own-produced food categories for the four household groups considered. Matching this production and consumption data allows for an explicit specification of own-household consumption (OHC) in the model as opposed to final household demand.

The OHC incorporated in the model has two important characteristics. First, the model values OHC at different prices compared with marketed goods, because nonmarketed goods do not require any transportation and marketing and thus do not include any marketing margins, that is, households consume OHC at farmgate prices, not at consumer prices. Second, OHC shows higher consumption minimums than marketed goods and, therefore, shows much less price elasticity than marketed consumption.

Equations (44) and (45) show how these OHC characteristics are incorporated into the model.[115] $CD^m_{comm, hh}$ represents final marketed consumption per household, defined as an LES formulation with fixed minimum consumption levels, $\gamma^m_{comm, hh}$, and fixed marginal consumption shares, $\beta^m_{comm, hh}$, for each commodity. A similar specification applies to $CD^h_{activ, hh}$, the OHC of nonmarketed produce (activities). The two expenditure systems are linked through the marginal consumption shares, $\beta^m_{comm, hh}$ and $\beta^h_{activ, hh}$, which together add up to one. This means that fixed marginal shares regarding both kinds of consumption are spent from disposable income, YH^{disp}_{hh}, net of the fixed minimum expenditures on final and OHC. Final consumption per household adds up to total final demand, $CD_{comm} = \sum_{hh} CD^m_{comm, hh}$, and enters the material balance defined by equation (44). Own consumption per household adds up to total OHC for each activity, $CD2_{activ} = \sum_{hh} CD^h_{activ, hh}$, and is netted out from domestic production to obtain domestic supply entering the commodity markets (see equation 24). As indicated by equation (32), total expenditure on own consumption per household is added up to a second—nonmonetary—income category, $YH2_{hh}$, which is netted out from total income, YH_{hh}, for calculations of household taxes and savings.[116]

VAT. Because Tanzania introduced a VAT in 1998, the formulation of a VAT is incorporated into the model. This feature permits analysis of alternative tax scenarios on the basis of the 1992 database, the most recent complete national data set available. Like most other African countries that have already imposed

---

[115] The disposable income spent on final and own-household consumption as in equations (44) and (45) is defined as $YH^{disp}_{hh} = (1 - MPS_{hh}) \cdot (YH_{hh} - YH2_{hh}) \cdot (1 - th_{hh}) + YH2_{hh}$.

[116] Note that disposable income, YH^{disp}_{hh}, is net of taxes and savings, but includes the nonmonetary income that is spent on OHC.

VATs, Tanzania applied a European-style VAT with a rebate mechanism, including zero-rating and exemptions (URT 1996c).[117] Zero-rating, as announced in the First Schedule of the VAT Bill in March 1997, applies primarily to exports. Consequently, the VAT is generally applied to domestic supply and imports only, which defines a "destination" VAT. The Second Schedule of the VAT Bill regulates the exempt supplies and imports that, while not taxed, are not entitled to a rebate on their input purchases. For domestic supplies the VAT is implemented as a wedge, TVA_{act}, between the domestic activity goods price and the domestic commodity goods price as specified in equation (13) defining PDC_{comm}. As TVA_{activ} is levied on domestic activity supply prices, PDA_{activ}, but imports are defined as commodities, a second VAT wedge, TVC_{comm}, has to be applied to the domestic import prices as shown in equation (11). To achieve the same effective rate for domestic supplies and imports, the two tax rates are related as follows:

$$TVC_{comm} \cdot PDC = \sum_{activ} m_{activ, comm} \cdot TVA_{activ} \cdot PDA_{activ} \tag{58}$$

All sectors but those exempt from the VAT are entitled to a rebate.[118] Thus, a sector-specific VAT credit per unit of output (see equation 17), $TVCRED_{activ}$, is computed for all activities, except those that are exempt:

$$TVCRED_{activ} = \frac{\sum_{comm} a_{comm, activ} \cdot PQ_{comm} \cdot \dfrac{TVC_{comm}}{1 + TVC_{comm}} + \sum_{comm} b_{comm, activ} \cdot DK_{activ} \cdot PQ_{comm} \cdot \dfrac{TVC_{comm}}{1 + TVC_{comm}}}{X_{activ}} \tag{59}$$

Intuitively, equation 59 expresses the VAT credit a particular activity receives as rebate per unit of its output being equal to the sum of VAT paid on all intermediate inputs and all capital investment demanded by this activity. As seen from equation (17), the rebate, $TVCRED_{activ}$, is incorporated in the price system as a wedge between the value-added price, PV_{activ}, and the producer price, PX_{activ}.

Food Aid Injections. A food aid variable is added to the model, operating as complementary market supply through an exogenous commodity injection from abroad. This formulation enables the simulation of drought-related distortions in domestic food markets, which is of particular interest given the weather and

---

[117] Zero-rating applies a rate of zero to the supplies of a sector and entitles it to a rebate of the input tax paid on its purchases; that is, the sector is completely relieved of tax. If a sector is exempt from VAT, no tax is charged on its supply, but it is not entitled to a rebate of the VAT paid on its inputs.

[118] All sectors levied with a VAT and all zero-rated sectors are entitled to a rebate. Only the exempt sectors are not entitled to a rebate.

harvest conditions experienced recently. In normal weather years Tanzania is self-sufficient in most food crops. However, weather conditions such as those of the 1996/97 cropping season may result in a dramatically reduced harvest and, consequently, severe undersupply in domestic food markets. The general food deficit estimated by the government in September 1997 amounted to 776,000 tonnes (FAO 1998a).[119] To model the interaction of crop failure and food aid from abroad, a food aid variable, $FOODAID_{comm}$, is incorporated into the CGE model specification. Any level of crop failure can be simulated individually for each sector by decreasing the general productivity parameter, $ad2_{activ}$, of the CES production function (equation 20). To compensate for the resulting losses in production, foreign food aid for domestic commodity markets is modeled as physical unit injections into the material balance equations of the concerned markets (equation 54). That concludes the matter for the affected commodity markets—their supplies are increased by the inflow of food aid that turns up in the system. Nevertheless, for the sake of proper national bookkeeping, the inflow of food aid is added as an expenditure item on the left-hand side of the balance of payments equation (equation 56). Accordingly, the monetary equivalent of total food aid injections, $FAIDEQV$, is defined as

$$FAIDEQV = \sum_{comm} PC_{comm} \cdot FOODAID_{comm} \qquad (60)$$

is added to the right-hand side of the balance of payments equation to make it a neutral transaction in terms of net flows when appearing on both sides of the balance of payment equation.

The aid inflow is not neutral regarding government transactions, because the government receives the physical food aid and then supplies it to the domestic markets, generating additional revenue. Consequently, the government has to spend the additional revenue on final and investment demand, assuming no aid-inflow-induced changes in government savings or transfers. To keep these supplementary government expenditures as distributionally neutral as possible, $FAIDEQV$ is split between final and investment demand according to their initial shares in total government expenditure on commodities, $gshr^{gre}$ and $gshr^{gin}$, as indicated by equations (46) and (47).

Marketing Margins. The data presentation of the national accounts for Tanzania follows the convention of reporting transportation and other marketing costs separately. Consequently, the original data show a large final demand for $CTRAD$,[120] and the

---

[119] As reported by the FAO (1998a), the extent of the food deficit was due to the complete failure of the 1996/97 Vuli crop (the short-rains minor cropping season) and a reduced Masika harvest (the main long-rains season).

[120] The data reveal 10.6 percent of total final household demand and 11.6 percent of all final demand categories.

demand for all other commodities is net of their transportation and marketing costs.[121] Within the construction of the Tanzanian SAM for 1992, final demand for *CTRAD* is spread over all other consumption categories according to sector-specific marketing margins that are adopted from the national accounts of Mozambique.[122] Although no comprehensive direct information on marketing margins for Tanzania is available, the particular market characteristics, largely determined by geographical conditions, require their consideration. As in many African countries, transport facilities and infrastructure as well as related communication opportunities are extremely poor, increasing the costs of the marketing process. This is especially true for Tanzania, because it occupies a large territory with extremely scattered and widespread urban areas, the major destinations for marketed produce.[123] The major cropping area for maize, the dominant food staple in Tanzania, is the southern highlands, including the regions of Iringa, Mbeya, Rukwa, and Ruvuma, but the main national demand of marketed consumption is in the Dar es Salaam region, about 1,000 kilometers away. Altogether, the marketing costs for certain products are even likely to exceed their production costs. These circumstances explain the importance of incorporating an analytical feature into the CGE framework that captures marketing costs that depend on the country's infrastructure conditions.

Three wedges are implemented in the price equations (11), (12), and (13), representing marketing margins per unit of marketed imports, exports, and domestic supply. Each wedge is defined as a sector-specific fraction of the commodity trade, mrm_{cm}, mre_{ae}, and mrd_{comm}, associated with one unit of the considered marketed commodity multiplied by the consumer price of trade services, PC_{CTRAD}. Consequently, the costs for transportation and marketing associated with a particular good do not change with the relevant price of that good, but with the commodity price of trade services, *CTRAD*. As PM_{cm} and PE_{ae} are the domestic market prices of internationally traded goods, the national marketing costs have to be added to the border price equivalent of the imports and subtracted from the border price equivalent of the exports.[124] The marketing margin wedge for domestic supply, mrd_{comm}, is embedded in the domestic commodity good price PDC_{comm} and thus applies when activities are transformed into commodities and enter the domestic commodity markets. Total demand for *CTRAD*

---

[121] For a purchase in any commodity market, this means that a consumer buys a good at its place of production and buys the corresponding trade and transportation service separately to deliver the item to its commodity market.

[122] Not only do no national accounts information on marketing margins exist in Tanzania, but hardly any research is conducted or literature published on this particular feature. This is not due to a lack of interest or potential research capacity, but results from the difficulties in administering, realizing, and financing a countrywide multisector project on the identification of sectoral marketing margins.

[123] Mwanza and the Lake Victoria region in the northwest; the northern Kilimanjaro area, including Moshi and Arusha; the coast of Dar es Salaam; and Mbeya in the south exemplify the widespread geographical distribution of urban areas.

[124] Consider the respective origin and destination of the goods in question: (1) imports have to be delivered from the port of entry to the domestic markets, where price PM_{cm} is relevant; (2) exports have to be delivered from their place of production, where PE_{ae} is relevant, to the port of departure, where border price equivalents of world market prices apply.

regarding transportation and marketing of other goods adds up to $TRADM_{CTRAD}$ as defined by equation (23) and enters the market-clearing equation (54) for $CTRAD$.[125] The incorporation of marketing margins into the model allows investigation of the effect of the quality of infrastructure on marketing behavior, commodity prices, production, and consumption patterns and, therefore, income-generating and welfare issues.

Factor Market Segmentation for Aggregate Agriculture. The model allows for the segmentation of factor markets into agricultural and nonagricultural submarkets. The underlying idea is to constrain factor mobility between agricultural and nonagricultural sectors and, thus, to a large extent, between rural and urban areas. Because the model does not contain any kind of migration mechanism, it is desirable to forestall implicit migration through labor market behavior. This is especially advisable because the modeling horizon in a CGE framework—the period from the initial equilibrium to the equilibrium of the solution of the model exercise—is undetermined and does not indicate the possible extent of migration. To strictly avoid factor mobility between different groups of sectors, new labor categories could be introduced that would apply only to each of these groups respectively. For modeling convenience, a different technique is applied in the Tanzanian CGE as described in the following: to restrict factor mobility between agriculture and nonagriculture, a separate factor supply variable for aggregate agriculture, $FSAG_f$, is introduced in the model, defined as

$$FSAG_f = \sum_{aag} FDSC_{aag,f} \tag{61}$$

Equation (61) represents additional factor market equilibriums for aggregate agriculture, where $FDSC_{aag,f}$ is the factor demand per agricultural sector. Furthermore, a factor price differential for all agricultural sectors, $WFAGDIST_f$, is added to the model, which redefines the agricultural factor price proportionality ratios as

$$WFDIST_{aag,f} = WFAGDIST_f \cdot wfdist0_{aag,f} \tag{62}$$

where *aag* represents the subset of all agricultural activities and $wfdist0_{aag,f}$ is the initial base run value of $WFDIST_{aagf}$. The corresponding model closure fixes total factor supply of aggregate agriculture, $FSAG_f$, for each factor and frees the agricultural factor price proportionality ratios, $WFDIST_{aag,f}$, which then can be uniformly adjusted by $WFAGDIST_f$ according to equation (62). Consequently, the separated factor markets for aggregate agriculture and nonagriculture have two independent schemes of distortion capturing intersectoral differentials in factor returns.

---

[125] Note that $TRADM_{comm}$ is zero for all commodities but $CTRAD$.

CHAPTER 5

The Effects of Macroeconomic Policies on Growth, Equity, and Intersectoral Shifts

This chapter analyzes (1) trade liberalization and industrial protection to quantify the bias to date against agriculture under general equilibrium conditions and to compare it to earlier analysis in a partial equilibrium framework; (2) exchange rate devaluation—one of the core policies of Tanzania's structural adjustment efforts—in the context of the economy's import dependency; and (3) the behavior of Tanzania's commodity markets in relation to its country-specific economic conditions and in consideration of some typical policy scenarios.

Trade Liberalization, Industrial Protection, and the Bias against Agriculture

An extensive discussion of the policy bias against agriculture took place after World War II, when developing countries sought rapid industrialization of their economies. Import substituting industrialization (ISI) became the most common development strategy. Under ISI, the government inhibits foreign trade through (1) high import tariffs on manufactured goods and export taxes on agricultural goods; (2) import quotas for competitive imports, and (3) overvaluation of the exchange rate. These trade policy measures discriminate between "good" imports (raw materials and machinery) and "bad" imports (goods that could be produced domestically). Consequently, relative prices of industrial products increase compared with agriculture produce, which leads to deteriorating domestic terms of trade of agriculture.[126] This environment increases relative factor payments of manufacturing sectors and causes labor migration from agriculture to nonagriculture sectors (rural-urban migration),

---

[126] The agricultural terms of trade represent the ratio of a weighted price index of agricultural goods over the weighted price index of nonagriculture goods. The index can be constructed using various prices and quantity weights, depending on the focus of the analysis.

thereby increasing urbanization. In the medium term, this particular urbanization process, which involves a push out of agriculture, may increase poverty, because it is not based on a pull from rapidly growing industry. The rural population suffers from relatively low wages and relatively high prices for nonagricultural products that are not locally produced, and urban centers are not able to absorb the rapidly growing workforce. Besides the ISI-related trade policy measures, other direct measures that affect agricultural productivity and performance are implemented, including (1) marketing boards and other types of monopolies; (2) centrally administered producer and consumer prices, causing an implicit taxation of agriculture; and (3) input subsidies, causing competitive advantages for the concerned industrial sectors. While these direct measures were applied to nearly all sectors, they were applied in a biased manner that extracted resources from agriculture.

The term urban bias, coined by Lipton (1977), became common during the ISI period in relation to policy discrimination against agriculture. The term draws on the importance of the social and economic conflict between rural and urban classes as a major obstacle to overall economic growth and development. As a reaction to the shortcomings of industrial-led development, price reforms became the key policy instrument, and the motto "getting prices right" reflected the efforts to work against the existing urban bias.[127]

Motivation and Construction of Bias Measures in a CGE Framework

Research on the bias against agriculture focuses on nominal and effective protection rates of the implemented policy measures. Most studies reveal that the effective rate of protection is higher than the nominal imposed trade taxes, and that economywide costs of intervention are higher than expected. Besides the direct effects of policy interventions like price control and taxation, indirect effects occur through implicit exchange rate performance and are identified as significant, and sometimes even larger, than their underlying direct effects. Krueger (1992) and Schiff and Valdes (1992),[128] who examined 18 countries for a comparative World Bank study from 1987 to 1990, particularly support these findings, as does an eight-country study by Bautista and Valdes (1993).[129] However, all these studies apply a partial equilibrium framework focusing on sector-specific policy measures and their sector-specific effects, although the policy bias under observation is an economywide and, hence, general equilibrium issue.

The partial equilibrium approach assumes perfect substitutability between domestically produced and traded goods, meaning that a good is either tradable or not without the existence of different degrees of tradability. In a general equilibrium

---

[127] Inappropriate domestic policies were identified as the major cause of the agricultural crises in Sub-Saharan Africa in the Berg report (World Bank 1981).

[128] The studies follow a methodology developed in Krueger, Schiff, and Valdes (1988).

[129] The Bautista and Valdes (1993) study, which covers 1981 to 1990, was carried out at the Trade and Macroeconomics Division of the International Food Policy Research Institute, Washington, D.C.

framework, different degrees of tradability are expressed by differing elasticities of substitution between import goods and domestic products or elasticities of transformation between goods produced for export or domestic use. In the perfect substitutability framework, no cross-hauling (two-way trade) can be observed, and the law of one price (LOP)[130] applies to traded goods and, therefore, changes in their world prices completely translate into changes in the domestic price system regardless of their trade shares.[131]

As pointed out above, a general equilibrium approach considers different degrees of tradability (imperfect substitutability) through its CES-CET structure and the related elasticities of substitution and transformation.[132] In this framework, changes in world prices of traded goods are only partially transmitted to their respective domestic prices. Furthermore, intersectoral price effects through quantitative repercussions are captured in a CGE framework, because it simultaneously allows for substitution between different commodities in demand, which, in turn, further lowers the final price transmission.[133] The domestic price transmission mechanism of the CGE approach is illustrated in Figure 5.1.

Figure 5.1—Domestic price transmission mechanism

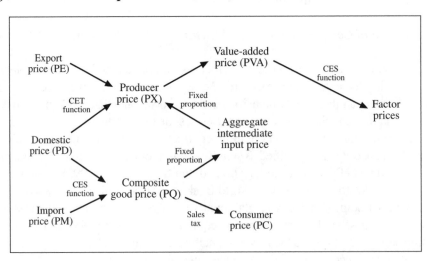

Source: Author.

---

[130] The controversial history of the discussion of empirical testing of the LOP, beginning with an article by Isard (1977), can be found in Ceglowski (1994), Baffes (1991), and Ardeni (1989).

[131] The usefulness of imperfect substitution depends especially on the degree of sector aggregation. A highly disaggregated multisector model may be sufficiently described with perfect substitution, because if sectors basically coincide with commodities, a particular good or sector is either traded or not. In a more aggregated framework (with, for instance, less than 100 sectors), each sector comprises several commodities of which some may be traded and others may not. In the latter case, it is more favorable to employ imperfect substitution.

[132] For the values of all sectoral CES and CET elasticities, refer to Table 5.5.

[133] For the variety of price transmission elasticities and their substantial difference between industrial and developing countries, see Mundlak and Larson (1992).

Bautista et al. (2001) became the first to develop agricultural terms of trade measures to assess the bias against agriculture in a general equilibrium framework.[134] With respect to gross output, X, and its value-added price, PVA, the agricultural terms of trade are defined as the ratio of the weighted price indices of aggregate agriculture over aggregate nonagriculture:

$$AG_X^{TOT} \frac{\sum\limits_{aag} PVA_{aag} \cdot s_{aag}^X}{\sum\limits_{aagn} PVA_{aagn} \cdot s_{aagn}^X} \qquad (63)$$

where

$$s_{aag}^X = \frac{X_{aag}}{\sum\limits_{aag} X_{aag}} \quad \text{and} \quad s_{aagn}^X \frac{X_{aagn}}{\sum\limits_{aagn} X_{aagn}} \qquad (64)$$

are the gross output shares of a specific activity aag ($aagn$) relative to the agricultural (nonagricultural) aggregate, which sum up to one for all aag ($aagn$). Thus, the two weighted price indices for agricultural and nonagricultural sectors are defined by:

$$P_{VA}^{AG} = \sum\limits_{aag} PVA_{aag} \cdot s_{aag}^X \quad \text{and} \quad P_{VA}^{AGN} = \sum\limits_{aagn} PVA_{aagn} \cdot s_{aagn}^X \qquad (65)$$

The presented measure of agricultural terms of trade in relation to value-added prices and gross output (AG_{VA}^{TOT}) represents a measure of resource pull for a production-oriented analysis in a CGE framework. Nevertheless, several other terms of trade measures can be constructed similarly using other domestic prices and their respective weights. Four other agricultural terms of trade will be referred to as the following:

AG_M^{TOT} with $\quad PM \& M \quad$ (domestic market price and quantity of imports),
AG_E^{TOT} with $\quad PE \& E \quad$ (domestic market price and quantity of exports),
AG_Q^{TOT} with $\quad PQ \& Q \quad$ (composite good price and quantity), and
AG_X^{TOT} with $\quad PX \& X \quad$ (producer price and gross output).

Note that the two trade-related measures AG_M^{TOT} and AG_E^{TOT} are constructed with respect to their traded quantities only. These are the appropriate measures in a CGE framework with imperfect substitutability, but for comparison with a partial

---

[134] See Bautista et al. (2001) for a detailed discussion of partial equilibrium measures applied in Krueger, Schiff, and Valdes (1988) and the newly constructed agricultural terms of trade measures used under the CGE framework. Figure 5.1 is taken from the Krueger, Schiff, and Valdes paper, and the following discussion draws heavily upon it.

equilibrium approach they are somewhat controversial. Because partial equilibrium assumes perfect substitutability, world market prices are fully transmitted into the domestic price system (including PQ, PX, and PVA) and not only into domestic import and export prices (PM and PE). Consequently, they affect total production X. For this reason, control measures for AG_M^{TOT} and AG_E^{TOT} are constructed using gross output, X, for their relative weights instead of imports, M, and exports, E.[135] Results of the analysis will be reported for the trade weight measures, but cross-checks are reported when significant deviations occur between the two versions.

The model features the following factor market specifications and closures for this experiment series:

- Labor and capital are segmented between agriculture and nonagriculture and no migration between different labor markets is allowed.
- The capital market in nonagriculture and the land market (only agriculture) operate with fixed sectoral factor demand, that is, no factor movements among sectors.
- All labor markets and the capital market in agriculture operate with fixed total factor supply, but factors are free to move among sectors of their respective segment (agriculture or nonagriculture).

Despite the factor market behavior and the macroeconomic closure rules, the model is also driven by individual production and consumption behavior. Such behavior depends on a number of parameters to be specified in the initialization process of the model construction. Most of these parameters are set endogenously so that the base solution to the model exactly replicates the values in the SAM, that is, the model is "calibrated" to the SAM. The remaining parameters—a set of demand, supply, and substitution elasticities—are set exogenously.

Table 5.5 (shown later in this chapter) presents the CES and CET trade elasticities dealing with the sectoral structure of the economy. Appendix G provides sensitivity analysis on these substitution elasticities and reveals that the qualitative results for a devaluation experiment remain robust for variations of the elasticity values from 75 to 175 percent of their applied values.

Because no better information was available at the time of this study, income elasticities for all households and all marketed commodities are close to 1, and those for OHC items are around 0.9 for all household types (except for other food items, which carry an income elasticity of about 1.25 for all household types).[136] However, a recent World Bank study by Delgado and Minot (2000) provides income elasticities for urban and rural households on nine major food and nine nonfood commodities that range from 0.38 (for maize) to 1.98 (for transport and communication). Applying these elasticities to the current study, and comparing the

---

[135] However, even if AG_M^{TOT} and AG_E^{TOT} apply the gross output value X as their relative weights, they are constructed considering traded goods only and represent the bias against traded agriculture. To examine the average bias against total agriculture, the measures could be constructed considering all sectors of the economy whether they are traded or not.

[136] Choosing all elasticities equal to one, the LES demand system would behave like a Cobb-Douglas function, that is, featuring fixed expenditure shares.

results of a 50 percent reduction in the trade balance (devaluation experiment) with the results of the same experiment with the original elasticity specification, reveals extremely small differences. Deflated total household expenditures, for example, decrease by 7 to 16 percent for the four household types using the original elasticities; applying the alternative set of elasticities, the results change only marginally, showing deviations of between 0.1 to 2.0 percent.

The parameters of the LES demand system (subsistence minimums and marginal budget shares) are derived using income elasticities, average budget shares, and the so-called Frisch parameter (Frisch 1959) for each socioeconomic group. Applying this method establishes a functional relationship between the Frisch parameter and the own-price elasticity of demand for each commodity (Dervis, de Melo, and Robinson 1982). To test for the model's sensitivity with respect to own-price elasticities of demand, the Frisch parameter was varied from –4.8 to –1.6 for all household types while simulating the same devaluation (50 percent reduction of the trade balance) as before. Comparing the results of this experiment series shows that the effect of varying the Frisch parameter in the given range, and thereby implicitly varying the own-price elasticity of demand, is only marginal; for example, the above-mentioned household expenditures deviate by less than 1 percent.

The model does not require the exogenous specification of supply elasticities, but one can compute arc elasticities for every simulation. However, these elasticities depend a great deal on the nature of the respective simulation and are general equilibrium elasticities. They may differ substantially from partial equilibrium elasticities because they are the result of all sectoral price and quantity changes in the new equilibrium after inducing a policy experiment. In other words, the condition of all other things being equal of partial equilibrium does not apply.

The Policy Bias Experiments

Four experiment series are conducted with the Tanzanian model to analyze the policy bias "against" agriculture caused by the existing indirect tax system: tariffs, production taxes, and consumption taxes. Each experiment series consists of the same cumulative experiments—described in detail in the following section—but they represent different economic scenarios:

- Experiment series one is conducted from the initial indirect tax scheme with flexible exchange rate.
- Experiment series two is also conducted from the initial indirect tax scheme, but with a fixed exchange rate.
- Experiment series three is conducted from a synthetic indirect tax scheme with a flexible exchange rate.
- Experiment series four is conducted from a synthetic indirect tax scheme as well, but with a fixed exchange rate.

As noted earlier, some empirical studies reveal a much lower urban bias than typically assumed and some taxes favor rather than disfavor agriculture. Whether or not the overall effect of the entire distorting indirect tax scheme is positive or negative for agriculture cannot be determined a priori. This is the reason for putting the policy bias "against" agriculture in quotation marks, because the policy bias may actually "favor" agriculture. The interpretation of the experiment results will focus special attention on this question.

Experiment Series One: Initial Base with Flexible Exchange Rate. To measure the bias against agriculture for the Tanzanian base year of 1992, the standard bias experiments are applied as specified in Bautista et al. (2001). The entire distorting indirect tax system is removed, one tax at a time, to separate the individual effects of different taxes and to analyze their cumulative effects on agricultural performance.[137] First, trade taxes are removed, which in 1992 were only tariffs, because export taxes had been suspended in 1982.[138] As this step of the experiment series represents the removal of the criticized industrial protection, only tariffs on industrial products are set to zero (tm_{cagn}) in the first experiment of the series. Tariffs on agricultural imports are removed in the last experiment of the series to show the overall impact of the existing trade regime. Then indirect taxes of production for all activities (tx_{activ}) are eliminated, followed by the removal of all commodity sales taxes (tc_{comm}).[139] Finally, all remaining indirect taxes are set at zero, which in the current analysis are only the tariffs on agricultural imports. The loss in revenue is compensated for by a nondistorting increase in the corporate tax rate, yielding the base value of government revenue, a standard approach in public finance models. The foreign exchange market closure for the experiment series assumes a fixed trade balance and allows the exchange rate to adjust freely to the imposed policy shocks.

Experiment Series Two: Initial Base with Fixed Exchange Rate. In experiment series one, the results rely not only on commodity price changes (and their related quantity changes), but also on the induced change in the real exchange rate. In a general equilibrium approach, changes in the exchange rate, in turn, cause changes in other prices. To isolate the exchange rate effects within the results of the described experiment series, an identical second series of experiments is carried out in which the exchange rate is fixed and adjustments in foreign trade are captured through changes in the trade balance. This second series of experiments represents direct price effects, and the difference between this result and the first experiment series with a flexible exchange rate indicates the separate exchange rate effect.

Experiment Series Three: Synthetic Base with Flexible Exchange Rate. Harmonization of the tariff system has been a major goal of Tanzania's structural adjustment

---

[137] Bautista et al. (1999) first create an undistorted base by removing all existing taxes in the model. Then they impose synthetic tariffs and export taxes to measure their potential bias effects. Unlike Bautista et al. (1999), the current experiment series starts from the distorted base and removes all existing taxes step by step.

[138] Export taxes were only reintroduced under the 1996/97 budget at a very low level of 2 percent.

[139] Effective indirect taxes on production are mainly on tobacco (13 percent), forestry and hunting (6 percent), mining (17 percent), and hotels and restaurants (6 percent). Effective sales tax rates range from 0 to 10 percent across agricultural and nonagricultural sectors.

efforts since 1990. A diverse system with 20 tariff rates was reduced to 4 nonzero rates ranging from 5 to 50 percent, and since then has been further adjusted. However high the nominal tariff rates for most imports might be, the effective tax collection on imports with a nonzero tariff is only 4.8 percent in the 1992 database. This is due to extensive tax exemptions, as well as illegal tax evasion and the generally poor administration of tax collection. However, the government of Tanzania has made serious efforts to improve revenue collection by introducing the Tanzanian Revenue Authority in June 1996.[140] To simulate the actually desired tax environment, a synthetic base is created with a 20 percent tariff on all merchandised nonagricultural imports and a zero tariff rate for all other sectors. Furthermore, an export tax of 2 percent on traditional export goods is imposed to analyze the potential effects of its reintroduction in 1996 within the 1992 data framework. Production and commodity taxes remain the same as in the first and second experiment series.

The sequence of experiments is the same as in series one and two, except that the export taxes are removed and no remaining agriculture import tariffs have to be eliminated at the end of the series. The indirect tax scheme is removed in the following order: tm_{comm}, te_{activ}, tx_{activ}, and tc_{comm}. The third experiment series assumes the same foreign exchange market closure as the first, with a fixed trade balance and a flexible exchange rate.

Experiment Series Four: Synthetic Base with Fixed Exchange Rate. Experiment series four repeats the removal of all indirect taxes from the synthetic base under a flexible trade balance and a fixed exchange rate. This series again isolates from their pure price effects the exchange rate-related effects of the policy experiments in series three.

Results of the Agricultural Bias Experiments

Table 5.1 presents the results of the first experiment series that removes all existing indirect taxes from the initial base under a flexible exchange rate regime.[141] The columns of the table specify the different tax removals within the experiment series, and the rows indicate the agricultural terms of trade (in boldface) and their underlying price indices. The last row of the table shows the changes in the exchange rate. The numeraire of the model is the producer price index, because the agricultural bias analysis focuses on the effects on the production performance of agricultural versus nonagricultural sectors. Thus all prices in the model, including the exchange rate, are relative prices with respect to the producer price index.[142]

---

[140] Since it started operating in July 1996, the Tanzanian Revenue Authority is the ultimate authority for income tax, sales tax, and customs and excise. Among other control measures, the Tanzanian Revenue Authority monitors the preshipment inspection carried out by two private companies to diminish the excessive loss in revenue through inappropriate collection practices in the past.

[141] The results of all experiment series are presented in standardized tables, although some of the series do not contain all the experiments so that all tables can be read the same way and the results from all series are easy to compare.

[142] The weighted average of the agricultural and nonagricultural price indices in Table 5.1, P_X^{AG} and, P_X^{AGN} will be equal to one by construction.

Table 5.1—Policy bias experiments from initial base: Flexible exchange rate

Cumulative elimination (from left to right) of:

	tm_{cagn}	te_{activ}	tx_{activ}	tc_{comm}	tm_{cag}
AG_M^{TOT}	103.8	103.8	103.8	103.7	97.1
P_M^{AG}	101.2	101.2	101.4	101.5	95.2
P_M^{AGN}	97.5	97.5	97.7	97.9	98.0
AG_E^{TOT}	100.1	100.1	99.9	99.8	99.8
P_E^{AG}	101.5	101.5	101.2	101.0	101.2
P_E^{AGN}	101.4	101.4	101.2	101.2	101.3
AG_Q^{TOT}	100.8	100.8	100.6	98.9	98.6
P_Q^{AG}	100.1	100.1	100.1	98.9	98.7
P_Q^{AGN}	99.3	99.3	99.5	100.0	100.1
AG_X^{TOT}	100.2	100.2	99.7	97.4	97.2
P_X^{AG}	100.2	100.2	99.7	98.1	98.0
P_X^{AGN}	99.9	99.9	100.1	100.7	100.8
AG_{VA}^{TOT}	100.1	100.1	97.3	93.6	93.4
P_{VA}^{AG}	100.3	100.3	100.6	98.7	98.5
P_{VA}^{AGN}	100.2	100.2	103.4	105.4	105.5
Real exchange rate	1.013	1.013	1.013	1.014	1.015

Source: Author.

Notes: tm_{cagn} = tariffs on nonagriculture commodities; te_{activ} = export taxes on all activities; tx_{activ} = production taxes on all activities; tc_{comm} = consumption taxes on all commodities; and tm_{cag} = tariffs on agriculture commodities.

$AG_{M(E, Q, X, VA)}^{TOT}$ = agricultural terms of trade with respect to import (export, composite good, producer, and value-added) prices.

$P_{M(E, Q, X, VA)}^{AG}$ = weighted price index for aggregate agriculture with respect to import (export, composite good, producer, and value-added) prices.

$P_{M(E, Q, X, VA)}^{AGN}$ = weighted price index for aggregate nonagriculture with respect to import (export, composite good, producer, and value-added) prices.

Note that the individual experiments are cumulative and the effects reported for a certain experiment are cumulative effects that include all previous experiments' effects. To learn about the isolated effect of one of the experiments, its results have to be compared with its immediate predecessor.[143]

The agricultural terms of trade regarding import prices, *PM*, and export prices, *PE*, represent the closest point of reference for comparison with a similar partial

---

[143] For decomposition experiments like this, the order of the single experiments matters. The order chosen here follows an economic logic with respect to how the distorting tax scheme can be removed step by step, starting with trade taxes (trade liberalization) and followed by domestic taxes. However, the size of the incremental effects of each particular tax removal does not change significantly with a change of order, but depends on the magnitude of the removed tax rather than the existence or nonexistence of other taxes.

equilibrium analysis. Domestic import and export prices are determined by their respective world market prices, trade taxes, and the exchange rate:

$$PM_{cm} = pwm_{cm} \cdot (1 + tm_{cm}) \cdot EXR \tag{66}$$

$$PE_{ae} = PWE_{ae} \cdot (1 - te_{ae}) \cdot EXR \tag{67}$$

where pwm_{cm} and PWE_{ae} are world market prices for imported goods (cm) and exported goods (ae) and EXR is the exchange rate. The two price equations show that a change in nominal trade taxes is completely transmitted into a change in the related domestic import or export price.

Prior to the examination and decomposition of the obtained terms of trade values, a consideration of the development of the exchange rate is crucial. In experiment series one, the removal of all tariffs on industrial imports causes a depreciation of 1.3 percent. Throughout the remaining experiments, the exchange rate stays almost unchanged, because the elimination of domestic taxes has no immediate (direct) effect on the exchange rate. The removal of tariffs on nonagricultural goods causes agricultural prices to rise 1.2 percent and nonagricultural prices to fall 2.5 percent, implying an increase of 3.8 percent in agricultural terms of trade with respect to imports. Note that the agricultural price index increases in accordance with the depreciation, and the nonagricultural price index decreases in accordance with the elimination of industrial tariffs—counting for approximately 4 percent of the related imports—reduced by the depreciation effect. For the same experiment, AG_E^{TOT} remains almost constant, because both price indices are primarily affected by the exchange rate. For the domestic production price measures AG_X^{TOT} and AG_{VA}^{TOT} and their underlying price indices, no significant changes occur as tariffs and the exchange rate do not directly affect them. A small effect is observed for the composite good measure, because the underlying prices and quantities contain import elements, and are thus tariff and exchange rate sensitive. Table 5.1 shows no changes in its second column, labeled "te," because there are no export taxes in the initial base to be removed.

There are no significant changes in the trade-related measures regarding the removal of producer and consumer taxes, tx and tc, because the relevant prices are not directly influenced by these taxes, as can be seen from equations (66) and (67). The producer tax, tx, is embedded within the value-added price, PVA, as shown by its price equation:

$$PVA_{activ} = PX_{activ} \cdot (1 - tx_{activ}) - \sum_{comm} a_{comm, activ} \cdot PC_{comm} \tag{68}$$

where PC_{comm} is the commodity price, $a_{comm, activ}$ is the input-output coefficient matrix, and the subtracted term of the equation represents total intermediate demand costs for one unit of production. Consequently, the elimination of tx fully appears at the value-added level and only indirectly affects AG_Q^{TOT} and AG_X^{TOT}. AG_{VA}^{TOT} decreases by 2.8 percent mainly due to the 3.2 percent increase in the nonagricultural price index.

This result shows that most production taxes in the base are levied on nonagricultural sectors whose relative prices increase when tx is removed. In other words, in the initial base, nonagricultural sectors are disfavored through the existing producer tax and the value-added terms of trade of agriculture—the ultimate indicator for resource shifts of factors between aggregate agriculture and aggregate nonagriculture—deteriorate through the elimination of tx. Therefore, agriculture is (relatively) favored and protected by the initially existing production tax, meaning that there is a policy bias in favor of and not against agriculture.

The removal of the consumer tax, tc, causes a 1.7 percent decrease in AG_Q^{TOT}, because the composite good price, PQ, upon which this measure is based, directly depends on tc:

$$PQ_{comm} = \frac{PC_{comm}}{(1 + tc_{comm})} \qquad (69)$$

Due to the reversal of the agricultural and nonagricultural price indices, the value-added terms of trade decrease by an even more significant by 3.7 percent. The elimination of the remaining tariffs in agriculture reverses the result for the import-price-related measure AG_M^{TOT}. Agricultural import shares and total tariffs collected in agriculture may be relatively small, but the average tariff on imports in agriculture is substantially higher than for nonagriculture. As the measure considers only traded goods, the latter is the deciding factor for the measure's deterioration.

Table 5.2 summarizes the terms of trade measures of experiment series two to isolate the relative commodity price effects from the exchange rate effects.

A comparison of the results with those of the first experiment series in Table 5.1 shows no difference in the import-related measure AG_M^{TOT}.[144] As the exchange rate

Table 5.2—Policy bias experiments from initial base: Fixed exchange rate

Cumulative elimination (from left to right) of:	tm_{cagn}	te_{activ}	tx_{activ}	tc_{comm}	tm_{cag}
AG_M^{TOT}	103.8	103.8	103.7	103.7	97.1
AG_E^{TOT}	100.0	100.0	99.9	99.8	99.8
AG_Q^{TOT}	101.8	101.8	101.6	99.9	99.7
AG_X^{TOT}	101.1	101.1	100.6	98.3	98.2
AG_{VA}^{TOT}	101.3	101.3	98.5	94.8	94.6
Real exchange rate	1.000	1.000	1.000	1.000	1.000

Source: Author.
Note: For explanations of the experiment abbreviations refer, to Table 5.1.

---

[144] For complete information on the results of all four experiment series, including the terms of trade measures and their related price indices, refer to Appendix Tables F.1 through F.4.

effect no longer applies to either imported agriculture or imported nonagriculture goods, the price indices experience the same relative change, and their ratio remains the same. For AG_E^{TOT} the clean base value of 100 can be observed, because there is no longer a change in the exchange rate that would affect domestic export prices.[145] The only significant change from series one takes place with the elimination of the industrial protection. Consequently, the first experiment of Table 5.2 shows changes between 0.9 to 1.2 percent for the absorption and production measures AG_Q^{TOT}, AG_X^{TOT}, and AG_{VA}^{TOT} when compared with the results of Table 5.1. In the fixed exchange rate experiment with a flexible trade balance, the price shock causes larger quantity adjustments that reverberate undampened through the domestic price system. The additional effect on the terms of trade measures is of the same magnitude as the observed depreciation in experiment series one, except that it is slightly reduced though intersectoral repercussions. The differences of the three measures vary only marginally throughout the experiments in line with the minor exchange rate development in experiment series one.

Table 5.3 presents the results of experiment series three, which is based on the imposed synthetic base with a 20 percent tariff on merchandised import goods, a 2 percent tax on traditional exports, and a flexible exchange rate. The terms of trade measures are particularly compared with the results of Table 5.1, the initial base experiment series under a flexible exchange rate.

The elimination of a 20 percent tariff on all merchandised imports causes a 15.4 percent improvement in the import-related agricultural terms of trade. Recall that in a partial equilibrium framework with perfect substitutability, the relative price increase of agricultural tradable goods is completely transmitted to the domestic price system, and thus to the measures AG_Q^{TOT}, AG_X^{TOT}, and AG_{VA}^{TOT}, depending on the GDP share of tradables. In a CGE environment, in which imperfect

Table 5.3—Policy bias experiments from synthetic base: Flexible exchange rate

Cumulative elimination (from left to right) of:					
	tm_{cagn}	te_{activ}	tx_{activ}	tc_{comm}	tm_{cag}
AG_M^{TOT}	115.4	115.4	115.3	115.3	115.3
AG_E^{TOT}	100.2	102.2	102.0	101.9	101.9
AG_Q^{TOT}	104.2	105.1	104.8	103.1	103.1
AG_X^{TOT}	101.8	102.7	102.2	99.9	99.9
AG_{VA}^{TOT}	101.6	102.8	100.0	96.3	96.3
Real exchange rate	1.041	1.033	1.033	1.034	1.034

Source: Author.
Note: For explanations of the experiment abbreviations, refer to Table 5.1.

---

[145] The model assumes that Tanzania is a small country facing fixed world prices for its exports and imports.

substitutability of the Armington (1969) function is imposed—determining total supply of the composite good—the final effect on the production and consumption terms of trade is much lower. In addition, the effect is diminished through the induced exchange rate depreciation of 4.1 percent. In the end, it remains a 4.2, 1.8, and 1.6 percent improvement of AG_Q^{TOT}, AG_X^{TOT}, and AG_{VA}^{TOT}, respectively. These changes are remarkably lower than the 15.4 percent increase in AG_M^{TOT} that occurs after the removal of the 20 percent industrial protection. This result indicates an enormous deviation between sector-specific implemented nominal protection and economywide effective protection rates.[146]

The removal of the 2 percent export tax on traditional export goods offsets one-fifth of the initial depreciation, lowering all domestic export prices by 0.8 percent and leaving unchanged the relative price ratio AG_E^{TOT}. However, in accordance with equation (67), the elimination of *te* increases domestic export prices for traded agriculture and, therefore, the aggregate relative price of traded agriculture to traded nonagriculture (AG_E^{TOT}) by 2.0 percent. As in experiment series one, there is also an upward trend of the terms of trade measures for the *tx* and *tc* experiment, but due to the higher trade taxes, their actual level is also higher: 4.2 percentage points higher for AG_Q^{TOT}, 2.5 for AG_X^{TOT}, and 2.7 for AG_{VA}^{TOT} (Table 5.3 compared with Table 5.1). The overall deterioration of the agricultural terms of trade regarding value-added prices for experiment series three is 3.7 percent, compared with 6.4 percent in series one. Finally, to isolate the exchange rate effect included in the results of experiment series three, Table 5.4 presents the outcome of series four.

As in experiment series two, this scenario does not allow for a depreciation to counteract the price effects of the tax removals. After the elimination of the trade taxes, *tm* and *te*, the measures AG_Q^{TOT}, AG_X^{TOT}, and AG_{VA}^{TOT} show an additional 2.6,

Table 5.4—Policy bias experiments from synthetic base: Fixed exchange rate

Cumulative elimination (from left to right) of:				
	tm_{cagn}	te_{activ}	tx_{activ}	tc_{comm}	tm_{cag}
AG_M^{TOT}	115.3	115.3	115.2	115.2	115.2
AG_E^{TOT}	100.0	102.0	101.8	101.7	101.7
AG_Q^{TOT}	107.4	107.6	107.4	105.6	105.6
AG_X^{TOT}	104.7	105.1	104.5	102.2	102.2
AG_{VA}^{TOT}	105.5	106.0	103.1	99.2	99.2
Real exchange rate	1.000	1.000	1.000	1.000	1.000

Source: Author

Note: For explanations on the experiment abbreviations, refer to Table 5.1.

---

[146] This result, of course, cannot be directly compared with partial equilibrium findings. Due to its partial equilibrium nature, Krueger, Schiff, and Valdes (1988) analyze sector-specific (nominal) trade measures and their (effective) impact on this particular sector. Obviously, these sector-specific results are much larger than the results within a CGE approach, where the effects of sector-specific measures diminish due to this intersectoral and economywide analytical framework.

2.4, and 3.2 percent increase, respectively, which remains at these levels during the removal of tx and tc. In this experiment series the results are dominated by the positive effects on agriculture caused by the removal of the distorting indirect tax system. However, even considering the higher import and export taxes of the synthetic base, the value-added related measure AG_{VA}^{TOT} shows that agriculture is still slightly disfavored after the removal of all indirect taxes.

As mentioned earlier, the CGE framework with its intersectoral repercussions does not always allow for a decomposition of its results. To provide some additional information on the general economic effect of the four experiment series, three sets of tables are attached in Appendix F: (1) real value-added of a seven-sector disaggregation that indicates the factor resource pull caused by the experiments (Tables F.5 through F.8); (2) nominal GDP indices of all final demand categories, exports, and imports to show how these aggregates gain or lose (Tables F.9 through F.12); and (3) the percentage change of deflated household consumption as a measure of welfare shifts among different household groups (Tables F.13 through F.16).

For the experiment series with flexible exchange rates, the model closures lock up real investment, government expenditure, and the trade balance. Therefore, the experiments carried out can only affect private consumption, which makes real household consumption a clean welfare measure that shows pure composition effects.[147] As shown in Figure 5.2, experiment series one and three show almost no change in overall deflated household consumption, but due to their exchange rate rigidity, series two and four show a 1.4 and 3.1 percent increase respectively.[148]

In general, the removal of the trade taxes causes relatively few welfare effects, until the elimination of tx and tc causes more significant effects that are spread more unevenly among farm and nonfarm households. Regarding the trade tax experiments tm and te under the fixed exchange rate regimes, the farm households gain slightly more than the nonfarm households, but in the end are clearly disfavored compared with the nonfarm households. The spread in welfare losses and gains is wider for the experiment series with flexible exchange rates. However, farm households are not only disfavored compared with nonfarm households, but they absolutely lose through the elimination of the distorting indirect tax system.

---

[147] Changes in one or more of the three aggregates—government consumption, private investment, and trade balance—would lead to a distortion of the "clean" welfare measure of household consumption. First, if government expenditures were to change, the problem of how these changes affect the welfare of different household groups would arise, for example, how different household groups value national security. Second, the same argument applies to total private investment, which may be valued positively by everybody, but with different relative weights. Finally, an increase of the trade deficit (less exports and/or more imports and, therefore, higher total absorption and household consumption) may be valued positively by everybody because of the increase in total commodity availability. The increased deficit, however, has to be financed through larger foreign capital inflow, which ultimately must be paid back, implicitly placing a larger burden on subsequent periods or generations.

[148] For the series with fixed exchange rate, increased capital inflows are in line with a deterioration of the trade balance, which leads to stronger welfare gains.

Figure 5.2—Changes in deflated household consumption

a. Experiment series one

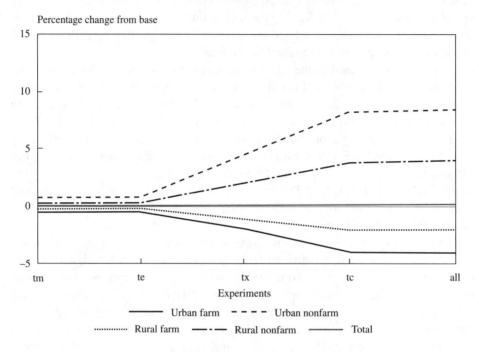

b. Experiment series two

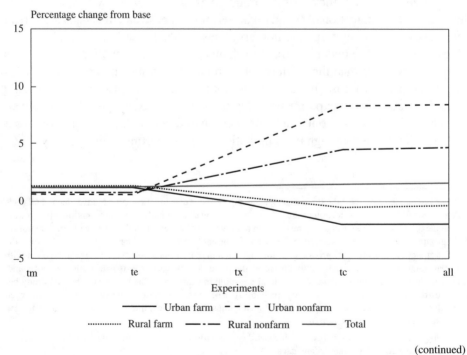

(continued)

Figure 5.2—Continued

c. Experiment series three

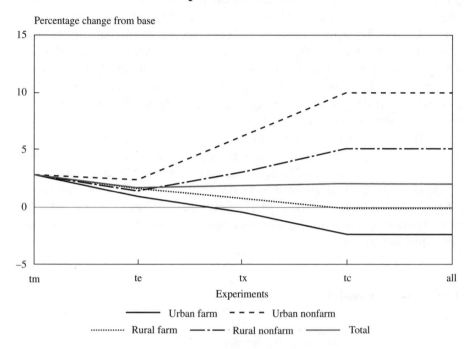

d. Experiment series four

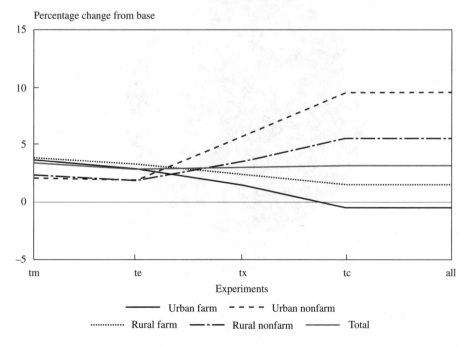

Source: Author.

To decompose and interpret the results of the agricultural bias analysis, two further structural aspects of the underlying economy are important. First, consider the composition of exports and imports, which is presented in Figures 5.3 and 5.4 for the seven-sector disaggregation of the initial database. As the trade-related terms of trade measures, AG_M^{TOT} and AG_E^{TOT}, depend on import and export shares, the trade composition provides information on the sectoral sensitivity of these measures. Second, the import content of all productive sectors—particularly export sectors—is an important feature, because the share of imports used in the production process is extremely relevant for a sector's response to trade tax experiments.

Figure 5.3 shows that agricultural exports do not play the sole dominating role in the 1992 database for Tanzania as they used to do in the 1980s, but that manufactures, especially textiles, are at least as important. As illustrated in Figure 5.4, imports are clearly dominated by heavy and light manufactures. For the effect of trade taxes on sectoral export performance, the measure of direct and indirect import content of production, as shown in Figure 5.5, is crucial for the intersectoral shifts of export shares.

Figure 5.3—Composition of merchandise exports

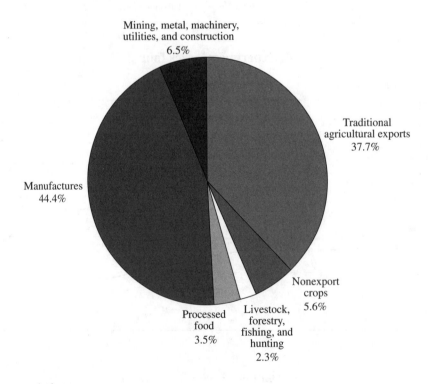

Source: Author.

Figure 5.4—Composition of merchandise imports

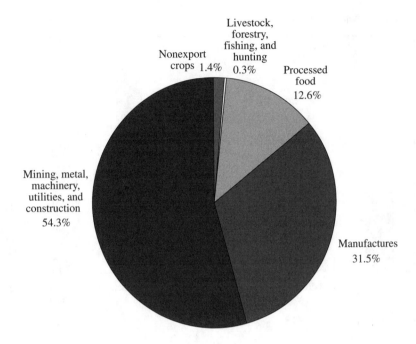

Source: Author.

Figure 5.5 shows a much higher measure of direct and indirect import content for the production of manufactures than for traditional agricultural exports.[149] Thus the implementation of a protective tariff aiming at import substitution and causing higher prices for imports disfavors the more import-dependent manufacturing sector compared with the relatively import-independent agricultural export sector. By contrast, the generally positive effect of the elimination of the import tariffs on relative agricultural prices is reduced, because agriculture gains relatively less from the induced decrease in import prices.

---

[149] Applied is an input-output import content indicator that measures the level of imports required for the production of one unit of output. It is a "direct" and "indirect" measure as described in Chenery, Robinson, and Syrquin (1986, pp. 213–8), which considers directly imported inputs (such as imported steel for car production) and indirectly imported inputs (such as imported coal used for domestic steel production that is then used for car production). Chenery, Robinson, and Syrquin develop a measure of the direct and indirect import content of exports and a similar measure for domestic final demand. The current study applies the measure to total output of a sector.

The original ICE is defined as: $ICE = eA^m R^d S^e$ where

e = unit row vector $(1, ..., 1)$,

A^m = matrix of intermediate import coefficients,

$R^d = (I - A^d)^{-1}$, the inverse of the matrix of domestic input-output coefficients, and

S^e = column vector of export shares.

Figure 5.5—Sectoral direct and indirect import content, 1992

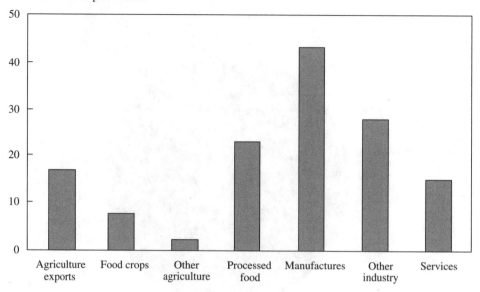

Measure of import content

Source: Author.

Conclusion

Measures of agricultural bias show remarkably different results when developed in an analytical CGE framework rather than a partial equilibrium/perfect substitutes framework. This is especially true for Tanzania in 1992 because some trade liberalization measures were already effective at this time, and the traditional dominance of agriculture in domestic production and foreign trade diminished throughout the structural adjustment process. The major findings and their related concluding remarks can be summarized as follows:

- The elimination of distorting trade taxes (tariffs and export taxes) does have a positive, but declining, effect on the agricultural terms of trade while moving from domestic trade price measures to consumption, production, and, finally, value-added price measures.
- The effect on production-related measures in a CGE framework, which ultimately determines sectoral production decisions and performance, is substantially lower than indicated by comparable partial equilibrium methods.
- The removal of domestic production and consumption taxes, tx and tc, which are mainly levied on the nonagricultural sectors, causes an opposite effect on the agricultural terms of trade. At a minimum, they even out the benefits from the trade tax elimination, but in most cases they overcompensate for them, causing an overall negative effect on agricultural production.
- Consequently, aggregate agriculture was protected rather than disfavored by the distorting domestic indirect tax scheme in place. This translates into a bias in favor of rather than against agriculture.

- Exchange rate effects do have a significant influence on the magnitude of the results. Under a fixed exchange rate regime, the results are heavily dampened, but their general direction remains the same.
- The declining agricultural terms of trade translate into an uneven spread of welfare gains and losses between farm and nonfarm households, respectively, thus increasing poverty. As farm households (rural and urban) rather than rural households are hurt by the tax scheme removal, the term agricultural bias seems more appropriate than urban bias.[150]
- Decomposition and interpretation of the results rely on structural features of the economy, such as sectoral shares in foreign trade and the import content of sectoral production, especially the import content of export-oriented sectors. These are the relatively high trade shares of nonagricultural sectors, such as textiles, and the relatively low trade shares of the traditional agricultural export sectors. Agriculture is not nearly as traded as in comparable Krueger, Schiff, and Valdes (1988) environments.

Exchange Rate Devaluation in an Import-Dependent Economy

A key element of most IMF/World Bank-guided structural adjustment programs is devaluation of the domestic currency to improve the trade balance, lower the balance of payment deficit, and restore overall economic equilibrium. On the one hand, a devaluation increases the relative domestic prices of imported commodities and urges consumers to substitute them with domestically produced goods.[151] On the other hand, the domestic prices of exports increase with devaluation, leading to an increase in competitiveness on world markets. Consequently, a devaluation should improve the trade balance by simultaneously increasing exports and decreasing imports.

Two major aspects concerning the economic effect of an exchange rate devaluation are considered below. The first aspect concerns the analysis of exchange rate fluctuations and their effect on relative domestic competitiveness between agriculture and nonagriculture. The analysis of the agricultural bias in the previous section showed that changes in trade taxes induce changes in the exchange rate, which are distinct from direct industrial protection, and are found to be substantial. This section analyzes exchange rate devaluation as a policy measure to promote trade, total production, and national welfare. Its effects are not only assessed with respect to agricultural versus nonagricultural production opportunities, but also regarding export versus nonexport production within agriculture, as well as income effects on agricultural and nonagricultural households in rural areas. The second aspect concerns the analytical focus on the

---

[150] Welfare gains and losses of farmers and nonfarmers have to be evaluated with respect to their unequal relative group size. The four different household categories applied in this analysis represent the following percentage shares of total population: urban farmers 12.4, urban nonfarmers 12.7, rural farmers 72.2, and rural nonfarmers 2.7 percent.

[151] Consequently, exchange rate devaluation complements measures to protect domestic "infant" industries through high tariff rates. Both measures support ISI development strategy to increase relative import prices and favor their domestic substitutes. However, the devaluation favors the competitiveness of exports on the world markets, while the ISI protection hurts exports and, in general, all tradables.

underlying import dependence of the different sectors and the effect on their economic performance under a devaluation scenario. The results show that the sectoral import content of production not only determines the general production and export opportunities of the respective sectors, but that intersectoral variation in import content determines relative sectoral performance.[152]

The Devaluation Experiment

We simulate a devaluation of the real exchange rate sufficient to eliminate the initial trade deficit by cutting the trade deficit in five steps of 20 percent increments. In this experiment series the exchange rate is the adjusting variable. The definition of a "sustainable" trade balance is a macroeconomic issue that is outside the scope of the static CGE framework. However, the model incorporates a functional relationship between the trade balance and the real exchange rate. The improvement in the trade balance leads to a cut in aggregate absorption. The model includes a simple macroeconomic closure whereby the absorption shares of final government consumption, government investment, and private investment are fixed at their initial values. This specification provides a simple model of the sharing of the burden of cuts in absorption among the macroeconomic aggregates.

Furthermore, the Tanzanian CGE model employs the following assumptions regarding the operation of factor markets in the case of the devaluation scenario:

- All factor markets are segmented between aggregate agriculture and aggregate nonagriculture.
- Land use by crop within agriculture is fixed, which limits supply responsiveness because only labor and capital are free to move across sectors within agriculture.[153]
- Capital used in nonagriculture is fixed by sector, which limits supply responsiveness.

These factor market specifications, which imply a short- to medium-term adjustment period, condition the simulation results. They imply that adjustment to a shock will lead to less quantity response and more price response as compared with full factor market mobility.

---

[152] The sectoral import content of production is measured by how much imports are directly and indirectly required for the production of one unit of output following the concept presented in the previous section.

[153] Fixed land use for tree crops (coffee, sisal, cashew) is more realistic than for cotton or food crops for which fixed production areas represent the short-term assumption of the model. Technically, one should prevent the model from overreacting in its supply response because of unrealistically large shifts in cropping areas. Maize, for example, the dominant food crop, will only reluctantly release resources to other agricultural sectors for other than economic reasons, such as individual food security behavior. Fixing sectoral demand for land controls this problem. Note that fixing the acreage per sector makes the sectoral factor price proportionality factor, *WFDIST*, the equilibrating variable of the land factor markets. Therefore, the different agricultural sectors pick up different rents on their land use according to their profitability. This is of particular importance because the relative income distribution among households depends on factor payments in fixed shares, that is, if land, for example, generates higher relative value-added, the income distribution will shift in favor of households with the high-income shares from the factor land. The same applies for the fixed sectoral capital utilization in nonagriculture mentioned in the next point.

Results of the Devaluation Experiments

The 1992 base year data for Tanzania show a substantial foreign trade deficit amounting to 25 percent of GDP at market prices. Total imports are more than three times total exports. Such a severe imbalance in a country's foreign trade and, consequently, in its domestic commodity markets, has a dramatic effect on overall economic structure. How different sectors are affected by the devaluation of the exchange rate depends mainly on their trade shares. The applied CGE framework is an appropriate tool to capture these effects, given the specification of CES substitution in demand between domestic supply and imports and CET transformation between domestic supply and exports. The results depend strongly on the parameter choice for the CES substitution and CET transformation elasticities. Table 5.5 shows output, absorption, and trade shares; trade ratios; and substitution elasticities. The table indicates the main sectoral structure of the Tanzanian economy in 1992. These structural features condition the economy's response to depreciation of the exchange rate.

Table 5.5—Sectoral structure of the Tanzanian economy based on 1992 SAM

	Composition (percent)				Ratios (percent)		Elasticities	
	X	VA	EX	IM	EX/X	IM/Q	SIGT	SIGC
Cotton	0.7	0.7	11.8	n.a.	83.1	n.a.	5.0	n.a.
Sisal	0.2	0.1	1.9	n.a.	53.7	n.a.	5.0	n.a.
Tea	0.2	0.2	1.4	n.a.	31.2	n.a.	5.0	n.a.
Coffee	0.3	0.4	3.1	n.a.	53.4	n.a.	5.0	n.a.
Tobacco	0.4	0.6	0.6	n.a.	6.8	n.a.	5.0	n.a.
Cashew nuts	0.3	0.5	1.9	n.a.	31.4	n.a.	5.0	n.a.
Maize	5.1	7.2	0.0	n.a.	0.0	n.a.	1.2	n.a.
Wheat	0.3	0.2	0.1	0.1	0.8	6.2	1.2	2.0
Paddy	1.4	1.6	n.a.	n.a.	n.a.	n.a.	n.a.	n.a.
Sorghum	0.4	0.6	0.0	n.a.	0.1	n.a.	1.2	n.a.
Other cereals	0.1	0.2	0.0	0.7	0.6	58.3	1.2	3.0
Beans	1.6	2.6	0.2	n.a.	0.6	n.a.	1.2	n.a.
Cassava	0.8	1.4	0.4	n.a.	2.5	n.a.	1.2	n.a.
Other roots	0.9	1.6	0.0	0.2	0.2	11.0	1.2	3.0
Oil seeds	0.9	1.4	0.6	0.0	3.3	0.8	1.2	3.0
Sugar	2.9	1.3	n.a.	n.a.	n.a.	n.a.	n.a.	n.a.
Other horticulture	3.0	5.1	0.7	0.0	1.3	0.3	1.2	3.0
Other crops	0.8	1.3	0.3	n.a.	2.1	n.a.	1.2	n.a.
Livestock	2.3	3.4	0.1	0.2	0.3	2.2	1.2	3.0
Fishery	1.7	2.5	1.0	n.a.	3.0	n.a.	1.2	n.a.
Forestry and hunting	2.5	4.4	0.2	0.1	0.4	0.8	1.2	3.0
Mining	2.1	3.5	1.1	2.3	2.8	18.4	1.3	1.5
Meat and dairy	1.8	2.0	0.5	0.3	1.5	2.7	1.3	1.5
Processed food	2.5	1.4	1.0	7.5	2.1	53.7	1.3	3.0
Grain milling	5.1	1.0	0.0	2.5	0.0	8.8	1.3	1.5
Beverages	3.8	3.0	0.3	0.6	0.4	2.8	1.3	1.5
Textiles and leather	2.5	1.2	14.2	4.2	28.7	29.7	1.3	1.0
Wood and paper	1.9	1.4	4.9	1.8	13.1	15.9	1.3	1.5

(continued)

Table 5.5—Continued

	Composition (per cent)				Ratios (per cent)		Elasticities	
	X	VA	EX	IM	EX/X	IM/Q	SIGT	SIGC
Chemicals	0.9	0.4	n.a.	12.5	n.a.	68.1	n.a.	0.8
Rubber	1.7	1.0	1.7	8.0	5.2	45.4	1.3	0.8
Iron and steel	1.9	0.7	2.6	8.7	6.9	47.2	1.3	0.8
Machinery equipment	1.0	0.9	n.a.	35.7	n.a.	75.7	n.a.	0.8
Electrical equipment	2.4	2.5	n.a.	n.a.	n.a.	n.a.	n.a.	n.a.
Construction	7.0	5.2	n.a.	n.a.	n.a.	n.a.	n.a.	n.a.
Trade	10.4	12.8	n.a.	n.a.	n.a.	n.a.	n.a.	n.a.
Tourism	0.9	0.7	17.9	n.a.	100.0	n.a.	0.5	n.a.
Hotels and restaurants	2.1	2.3	7.5	1.3	17.9	12.8	0.5	1.5
Transportation and communications	7.2	6.6	6.2	0.9	4.4	2.5	0.5	1.5
Financial institution	2.9	3.5	0.0	4.4	0.1	23.1	0.5	1.5
Real estate	2.6	4.4	n.a.	7.9	n.a.	37.7	n.a.	1.5
Public administration	10.3	6.8	0.1	n.a.	0.1	n.a.	0.5	n.a.
Other services	1.8	1.5	17.6	n.a.	50.7	n.a.	0.5	n.a.
Total average agriculture	27.0	37.3	24.3	1.4	4.7	1.3	n.a.	n.a.
Total average nonagriculture	73.0	62.7	75.7	98.6	5.3	21.8	n.a.	n.a.

Source: Author.

Note: n.a. = Not applicable.

X = Output, VA = Value-added, EX = Exports, IM = Imports, Q = Absorption, SIGT = Elasticity of transformation, and SIGC = Elasticity of substitution.

In Tanzania, neither sector-specific information nor time-series data for econometric estimation are available. In lieu of econometric estimation, sensitivity analysis concerning the devaluation experiment is reported in Appendix G. The sensitivity analysis shows that the results of a 25 percent devaluation experiment vary only moderately when trade elasticity values range from 75 to 175 percent of their initial values. Hence, the qualitative results are not affected, and policy conclusions are robust.

The relationship between the gradual reduction of the trade deficit and the equilibrium exchange rate is presented in Figure 5.6.

The relationship between elimination of the trade deficit and the depreciation of the exchange rate is nearly linear. A trade deficit reduction of 20 percent (US$273 million) can be achieved through an exchange rate devaluation of 9 percent, and the deficit can be eliminated entirely by devaluing 47 percent.[154] How much the exchange

---

[154] The results of this experiment series are path-independent, that is, the same results for the elimination of the foreign trade deficit—or any partial reduction of it—are obtained regardless of whether it is eliminated all at once or in any desired gradual series of reductions. Linearity is a rather unexpected functional relationship in this case because the sectoral elasticities of substitution and transformation are point elasticities. Hence, one would expect a gradual reduction of the trade deficit to become more and more difficult to achieve and to require gradually higher (supplementary) depreciation rates. This cannot be observed for this experiment series.

Figure 5.6—Exchange rate depreciation and trade balance

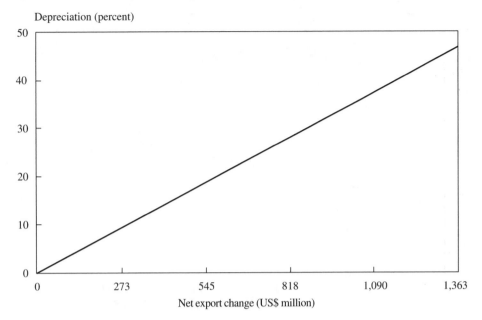

Source: Author.

rate has to change to achieve the assumed reduction of the trade balance depends on the specified elasticities of substitution and transformation, as well as the degree of responsiveness of sectoral production to changes in relative prices. The trade performance also depends on their differences across sectors, especially between agriculture and nonagriculture as well as export and nonexport agriculture. Total real exports and imports closely follow the real exchange rate depreciation. Figure 5.7 shows imports as more than three times the value of exports in the base. Imports decrease by approximately one-third, and exports increase by nearly 150 percent over the experiment series (Figure 5.8). In absolute real terms, imports and exports contribute roughly the same amount to the improvement in the trade balance.

The elimination of the trade balance can be also be thought of in nominal terms in the sense of how much both exports and imports contribute to eliminate the nominal finance gap in foreign trade. Looking at the development of foreign trade in nominal terms reveals that, due to the exchange rate effect, the total import value (expressed in local currency) does not decrease at all, and that nearly all the adjustment is achieved through the increasing total export value that more than triples (see Figures 5.9 and 5.10 for absolute values and percentage changes respectively).

The foreign trade pattern for the experiment series shows that for the economy as a whole, substantially reducing the total import value is difficult. This depends on a couple of partly interrelated facts: (1) as previously mentioned, if the elasticity of substitution is low, it is difficult to substitute imports through domestic products; (2) if the domestic share in the composite good combination is extremely low, even

Figure 5.7—Total real foreign trade

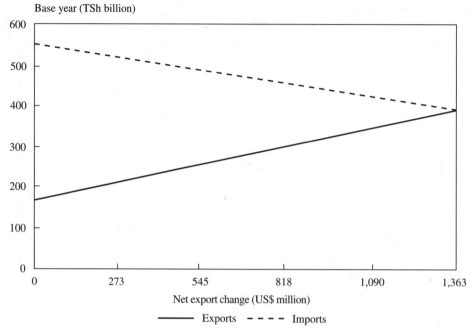

Base year (TSh billion)

Net export change (US$ million)

———— Exports   - - - - Imports

Source: Author.

Figure 5.8—Real foreign trade (percentage change)

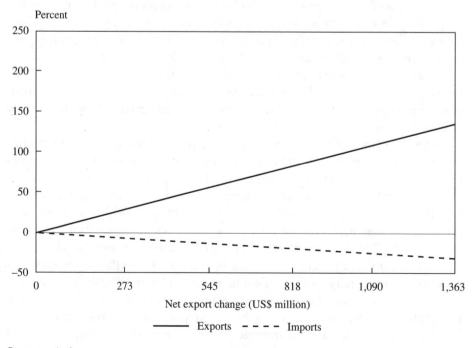

Percent

Net export change (US$ million)

———— Exports   - - - - Imports

Source: Author.

Figure 5.9—Total nominal foreign trade

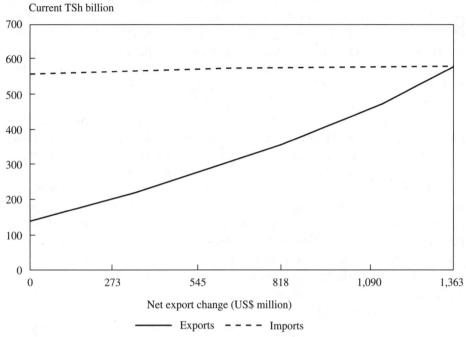

Source: Author.

Figure 5.10—Nominal foreign trade (percentage change)

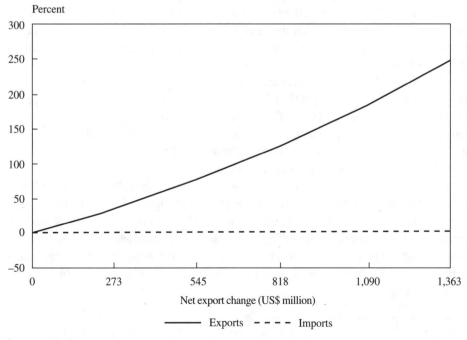

Source: Author.

103

a high substitution elasticity does not allow for large quantity changes; (3) if domestic production in general is import intensive,[155] substitution elasticities of imported intermediate goods (or their import components) are low, and import shares
of intermediates are high, total imports can only be reduced though the reduction of
production; and (4) if export-oriented production in particular is earmarked by the
characteristics listed under (3), it creates an even more difficult situation, because
each dollar of the desired increase in exports requires that a substantial fraction of
this dollar be devoted to an increase in imports.

Two conclusions result from these rigid substitution opportunities. First,
imports might not be substituted through domestic products, but rather decreased
without replacement. Consequently, cross-sectoral substitution mechanisms in
production and consumption functions are stimulated to replace with other commodities the commodity in short supply, causing higher prices and production
costs and lower consumer welfare. Second, depending on the degree of import
dependence of production—particularly export-oriented production—total imports can only be reduced through a relative decrease in total domestic production. This positive correlation between imports and gross output is often ig-
nored when domestic import prices are implicitly increased through tariff or
exchange rate policies aimed at import substitution and the promotion of domestic industrial production.

To explore the effect of depreciation on the sectoral composition, we aggregate the results from the 42-sector model to 7 aggregate sectors. While all sectoral
exports increase, Figure 5.11 shows that agricultural exports increase much more
than nonagricultural exports. Agriculture dramatically increases its share of total
exports, becoming the largest export sector (see Figure 5.12).

Given the increase in agricultural exports, relative price changes between agriculture and nonagriculture might be expected to improve the aggregate domestic
terms of trade in favor of agriculture. This expectation is only partly validated, as
shown in Figure 5.13.

Looking at two agricultural terms of trade measures, the terms of trade with
respect to producer prices (TOT_xd) and those with respect to value-added prices
(TOT_va) move differently. TOT_xd deteriorates monotonically (finally, by 3.6
percent), while TOT_va first improves and than deteriorates toward the end of the
experiment series, never falling below its initial value.

Three characteristics of Tanzania determine the results for the agricultural
terms of trade from devaluation: (1) trade shares in agriculture compared with
nonagriculture, (2) relative changes in intermediate input costs in agriculture and
nonagriculture, and (3) factor mobility and supply response of aggregate agriculture and nonagriculture. Although agricultural exports increase due to the devaluation, and agriculture becomes the largest export sector among the seven aggregates,
it is the relative importance of total agriculture as documented in Table 5.5 that

---

[155] In the sense of the direct and indirect input-output import content of production as explained in the section on
the results of the agricultural bias experiments.

Figure 5.11—Real export values

Current TSh billion

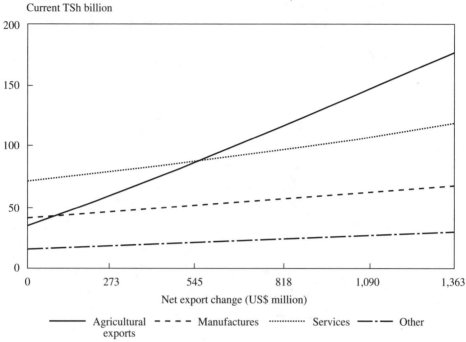

Net export change (US$ million)

——— Agricultural exports   – – – Manufactures   ·········· Services   —·— Other

Source: Author.

Figure 5.12—Composition of exports

Percent of total exports

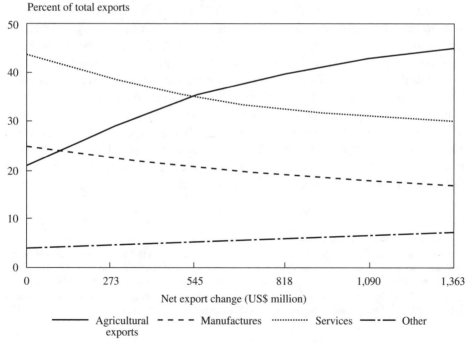

Net export change (US$ million)

——— Agricultural exports   – – – Manufactures   ·········· Services   —·— Other

Source: Author.

Figure 5.13—Agricultural terms of trade with fixed sectoral capital demand

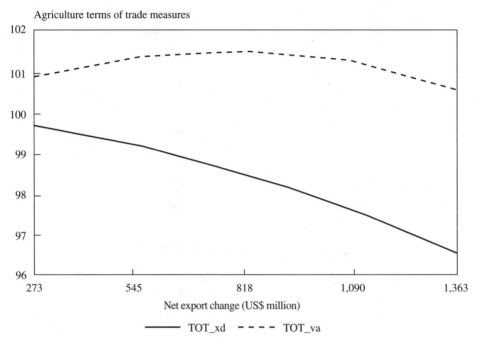

Source: Author.

mainly determines the development of the agricultural terms of trade. Agriculture represents only 27 percent of total output (37.3 percent in value-added terms) and constitutes only 24.3 percent of total exports in 1992.[156] Consequently, although the devaluation is extremely favorable for export agriculture, it is also favorable to exporting nonagriculture and unfavorable for nonexporting agriculture.

The different behavior of the producer price and value-added price measures (*TOT_xd* and *TOT_va*) is due to relative changes in intermediate input prices that constitute the wedge between value-added and producer prices. With devaluation, labor migrates to export agriculture, and the relative wages in agriculture correspond to wages in nonagriculture (*TOT_va* remains constant). The change in intermediate input prices, due to the devaluation, causes agricultural producer prices to fall compared with nonagriculture (*TOT_xd* decreases).[157]

---

[156] Although these are still large shares, the relative importance of agriculture in Tanzania decreased significantly in recent years. Agriculture used to contribute 50 percent to GDP and 80 percent to total foreign exchange earnings. In comparison, nonagriculture is much more important today and dominates the economywide effects.

[157] Graphically, the agricultural terms of trade with respect to value-added prices remain almost constant, while the agricultural terms of trade with respect to producer prices deteriorate.

Typically, one would expect the two measures to develop along the same lines as in Figure 5.14, which shows the results of a comparative experiment with capital mobility among nonagricultural sectors.[158]

To understand why the results are so different in the case of fixed sectoral capital demand, one must look at the underlying components of the terms of trade measures. Tables 5.5 and 5.6 present the development of agricultural and nonagricultural price indices and their related agricultural terms of trade for the alternative model closures.

For the comparative experiment series under free capital mobility among nonagricultural sectors, TOT_va decreases continuously by more than 10 percent, caused by a corresponding deterioration of its underlying agricultural price index (P_{VA}^{AG}), while its nonagricultural price index (P_{VA}^{AGN}) remains almost constant. The agricultural price index in the current analysis (P_{VA}^{AG}) develops similarly to the comparative experiment series, but the respective nonagricultural price index

Figure 5.14—Agricultural terms of trade with mobile sectoral capital demand

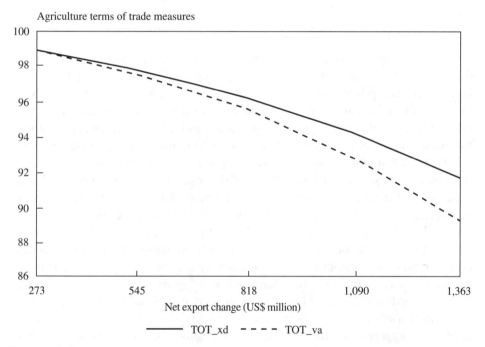

Agriculture terms of trade measures

Net export change (US$ million)

——— TOT_xd   - - - - TOT_va

Source: Author.

---

[158] The current experiment runs under factor markets segmentation between aggregate agriculture and nonagriculture (for capital and all labor categories) and, in addition, fixed sectoral capital factor demand—capital cannot move from one sector to another within aggregate nonagriculture. This is a rather short- to medium-term model closure that is considered appropriate in the case of a currency devaluation aiming at immediate changes in production and foreign trade.

Table 5.6—Agricultural terms of trade (TOT) (value-added) and price indices under mobile versus fixed sectoral capital demand in nonagriculture

		Net export change as a percentage of initial trade deficit				
	Base	20	40	60	80	100
Sectorally *mobile* capital						
TOT_va	100.0	98.9	97.4	95.4	92.8	89.3
P_{VA}^{AG}	100.0	98.5	96.8	94.9	92.5	89.7
P_{VA}^{AGN}	100.0	99.6	99.4	99.4	99.8	100.4
Sectorally *fixed* capital						
TOT_va	100.0	100.9	101.3	101.5	101.3	100.6
P_{VA}^{AG}	100.0	98.9	97.7	96.2	94.6	92.8
P_{VA}^{AGN}	100.0	98.1	96.4	94.8	93.5	92.3

Source: Author.

(P_{VA}^{AGN}) shows quite different behavior. It does not remain constant, but follows the agricultural price index, deteriorating even slightly more, causing a small increase in the agricultural terms of trade, *TOT_va*. The explanation for this is twofold: (1) capital cannot move into the export-oriented, nonagricultural sectors, which expand as the exchange rate depreciates; and (2) due to fixed capital stocks, the expansion of domestic production of capital-intensive intermediate inputs and substitutes for imported intermediates is limited.[159] The increasing demand for intermediates and the restricted ability of domestic production to respond leads to substantial increases of prices for intermediates. Consequently, the cost share of intermediate inputs in total production costs increases and their value-added share falls. The gap between value-added and producer prices widens.

In terms of producer prices, however, the devaluation has a strong negative effect on nonexport agriculture, which more than offsets the positive policy impacts on export agriculture. To isolate and quantify these two countervailing effects, the agricultural terms of trade measures are calculated separately for export agriculture (*exTOT_xd*, *exTOT_va*) and nonexport agriculture (*neTOT_xd*, *neTOT_va*) aggregates. The experiment results show different movements for the agricultural subaggregates (Figure 5.15).

The producer-price-related measure for export agriculture increases by 38.4 percent and decreases by 7.2 percent for nonexport agriculture. As shown in Figure 5.16, the latter overcompensates for the strong first effect due to the high share of nonexport

---

[159] Refer to Table 5.7 for a detailed presentation of sectoral value-added shares. The current analysis shows that the sectoral performance of production, and thus structural economic changes, largely depends on sector-specific labor and capital intensities.

Figure 5.15—Export versus nonexport agricultural terms of trade

Percentage change from base

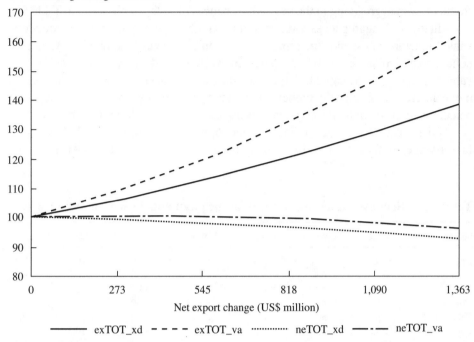

Net export change (US$ million)

——— exTOT_xd – – – – exTOT_va ·············· neTOT_xd —··— neTOT_va

Source: Author.

Figure 5.16—Export versus nonexport agricultural price indices

Percentage change from base

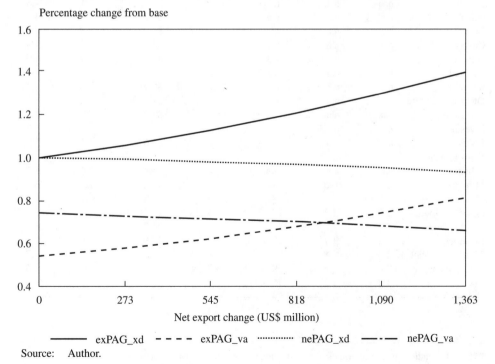

Net export change (US$ million)

——— exPAG_xd – – – – exPAG_va ·············· nePAG_xd —··— nePAG_va

Source: Author.

agriculture in total agriculture. With respect to value-added prices, the effect on the export-oriented agricultural terms of trade is even higher and on nonexport agriculture slightly lower, aggregating to the negligible changes of *TOT_va* observed in Table 5.6.

In the base, aggregate export agriculture pays 54.3 percent of its total production value to factors and spends the remaining part on intermediate demand.[160] Aggregate nonexport agriculture is much less input intensive, paying 74.5 percent of its production value to labor, land, and capital. Throughout the experiment series, the two price indices move differently, ending with higher value-added payments by export agriculture (81.1 percent) and lower value-added payments by nonexport agriculture (66.4 percent).

One expects a resource pull from nonexport to export agriculture led by higher factor wages in factors more intensively used in export agriculture (see Table 5.7

Table 5.7—Sectoral structure of total factor payments based on 1992 SAM

Sector	UPRO	UWCO	UBCO	UNSK	RURA	Land	Capital
Cotton	n.a.	n.a.	n.a.	n.a.	81.9	10.8	7.3
Sisal	n.a.	n.a.	n.a.	n.a.	82.0	10.8	7.2
Tea	n.a.	n.a.	n.a.	n.a.	83.0	10.2	6.8
Coffee	n.a.	n.a.	n.a.	n.a.	83.0	10.2	6.8
Tobacco	n.a.	n.a.	n.a.	n.a.	82.0	10.7	7.2
Cashew nuts	n.a.	n.a.	n.a.	n.a.	82.1	10.7	7.2
Maize	n.a.	n.a.	n.a.	n.a.	91.9	4.6	3.5
Wheat	n.a.	n.a.	n.a.	n.a.	84.8	9.1	6.1
Paddy	n.a.	n.a.	n.a.	n.a.	91.4	5.1	3.5
Sorghum	n.a.	n.a.	n.a.	n.a.	88.1	7.1	4.8
Other cereals	n.a.	n.a.	n.a.	n.a.	88.2	7.1	4.7
Beans	n.a.	n.a.	n.a.	n.a.	87.7	7.3	5.1
Cassava	n.a.	n.a.	n.a.	n.a.	88.0	7.2	4.9
Other roots	n.a.	n.a.	n.a.	n.a.	87.9	7.2	4.9
Oil seeds	n.a.	n.a.	n.a.	n.a.	87.9	7.2	4.9
Sugar	n.a.	n.a.	n.a.	n.a.	88.9	6.8	4.3
Other horticulture	n.a.	n.a.	n.a.	n.a.	87.2	7.4	5.3
Other crops	n.a.	n.a.	n.a.	n.a.	87.9	7.2	4.9
Livestock	n.a.	n.a.	n.a.	n.a.	85.4	8.5	6.0
Fishery	n.a.	n.a.	n.a.	n.a.	85.6	8.5	5.9
Forestry and hunting	n.a.	n.a.	n.a.	n.a.	85.4	8.6	6.1
Mining	1.3	0.5	69.1	3.1	n.a.	n.a.	26.1
Meat and dairy	2.3	1.7	18.7	2.4	27.8	n.a.	47.1
Processed food	2.2	1.7	19.1	2.3	27.2	n.a.	47.6
Grain milling	2.2	1.7	20.3	2.3	24.8	n.a.	48.7
Beverages	2.2	1.7	19.6	2.6	25.9	n.a.	48.0
Textiles and leather	3.5	2.8	29.2	3.8	n.a.	n.a.	60.7
Wood and paper	3.6	2.8	29.1	3.9	n.a.	n.a.	60.6
Chemicals	1.9	1.5	15.6	2.0	n.a.	n.a.	79.0

(continued)

---

[160] Including indirect taxes occurring in the production process that are paid by activities.

Table 5.7—Continued

Sector	UPRO	UWCO	UBCO	UNSK	RURA	Land	Capital
Rubber	1.9	1.5	15.7	2.0	n.a.	n.a.	78.9
Iron and steel	1.9	1.5	15.7	2.0	n.a.	n.a.	78.9
Machinery equipment	1.9	1.5	15.6	2.0	n.a.	n.a.	79.0
Electrical equipment	4.1	5.4	16.3	1.5	n.a.	n.a.	72.8
Construction	2.5	1.0	22.7	4.0	n.a.	n.a.	69.8
Trade	14.2	9.2	1.7	12.9	n.a.	n.a.	62.1
Tourism	20.2	12.2	2.3	17.5	n.a.	n.a.	47.7
Hotels and restaurants	20.8	12.7	2.4	18.1	n.a.	n.a.	46.0
Transportation and communications	10.6	11.0	20.3	7.8	n.a.	n.a.	50.3
Financial institutions	13.3	8.2	2.0	1.5	n.a.	n.a.	75.0
Real estate	13.4	8.2	2.0	1.5	n.a.	n.a.	75.0
Public administration	32.9	8.4	6.9	4.2	n.a.	n.a.	47.7
Other services	56.0	18.3	13.5	7.3	n.a.	n.a.	5.0
Total average agriculture	27.0	37.3	24.3	1.4	4.7	1.3	n.a.
Total average nonagriculture	73.0	62.7	75.7	98.6	5.3	21.8	n.a.

Source: Author.
Note: n.a. = Not applicable.
UPRO = Professional labor, UWCO = White collar labor, UBCO = Blue collar labor, UNSK = Unskilled labor, RURA = Agricultural labor.

on sectoral factor shares and Figure 5.17 for value-added developments in export and nonexport agriculture).

Assuming that Tanzanian factor markets are segmented between aggregate agriculture and aggregate nonagriculture, which prevents factor mobility between these two segments of the economy, the actual resource pull is limited.[161] Reduced factor mobility causes the gaps in factor returns to widen. However, in the long term, devaluation will cause significant resource pulls, including labor migration and capital movements between agricultural and nonagricultural sectors. Consequently, in the long run, structural changes in the economy will be observed not only within agriculture, which turns from food cropping to export cropping, but also between agriculture and nonagriculture. In the current short-term analysis, the wages of rural labor employed in agriculture increase by 151 percent throughout

---

[161] In the underlying model, the factor wage, WF_f, is not defined over activities, but is equal throughout all economic sectors, corresponding with all sectoral marginal revenues being equal. To match the more realistic approach of distorted factor markets in which one factor can generate different marginal products in different sectors, a sectoral proportionality multiplier ($WFAGDIST$ in equation 62 in Chapter 4) is applied, which can change for all agricultural sectors uniformly.

Figure 5.17—Export versus nonexport agricultural value-added

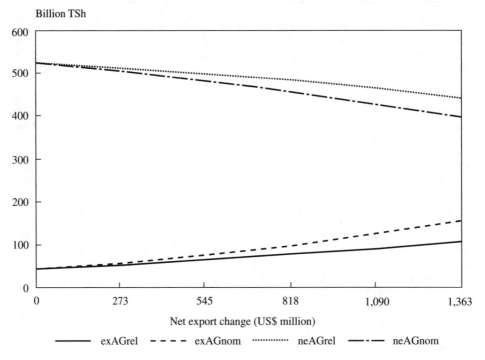

Billion TSh

Net export change (US$ million)

——— exAGrel   - - - - exAGnom   ·············· neAGrel   —·— neAGnom

Source: Author.

depreciation, but this is true for all agriculture sectors uniformly. In the end, the resource pull is determined by the demand for primary factors, sectoral value-added, producer prices, and export prices.[162]

Figures 5.18 and 5.19 illustrate the physical labor and capital shifts between export agriculture and nonexport agriculture. Their respective totals remain constant due to the factor market segmentation between agriculture and nonagriculture. Export agriculture more than triples its labor and capital use, pulling these resources away from nonexport agriculture. This is not true for the third value-added generating factor of production, land, whose quantities per activity are fixed. As the model does not allow for a change in land use within one equilibrating run, it is the scarcest and most constraining factor of agricultural production and, hence, gains all the remaining factor returns. Consequently, the return to land in export agriculture increases dramatically through a more factor-intensive production on a constant area of cultivation, while nonexport agriculture experiences a 20 percent decline in its aggregate return to land (see Figure 5.20).

---

[162] Refer to price and quantity equations of the model in the section on the macrosam for 1992 in Chapter 4 and the domestic price transmission mechanism presented in Figure 5.1 above to understand the underlying model mechanism that determines the resource pull through the demand function for primary factors, which depends on sectoral value-added. This is determined by producer prices, which in turn depend on export prices.

Figure 5.18—Export versus nonexport agricultural labor demand

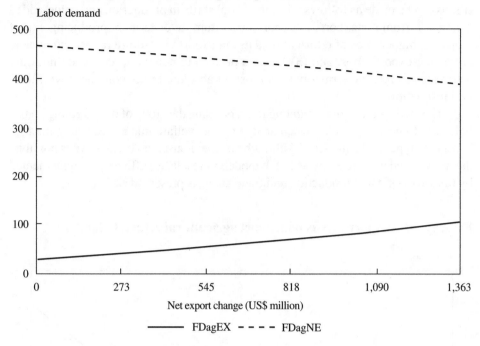

Source: Author.

Figure 5.19—Export versus nonexport agricultural capital demand

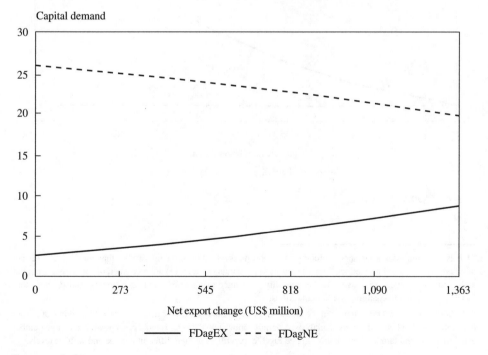

Source: Author.

113

With regard to welfare and equity effects of depreciation, several general propositions can be made as follows: (1) substantial shifts in production and value-added generation from nonexports to export agriculture favor farmers producing export crops, (2) higher rates of return to land use in export agriculture favor land owners producing export crops, and (3) farmers producing nonexport crops are not only disfavored in relative terms, but also lose in absolute terms compared with their initial situation.[163]

However, the differences among farmers within the group of rural farming households has to be kept in mind when analyzing the welfare impact regarding the four household types in the model.[164] Although no other household breakdown is possible, the income and welfare analysis of the modeling results is sufficiently supplemented by the sector-oriented production and trade analysis presented earlier.

Figure 5.20—Export versus nonexport agricultural return to land

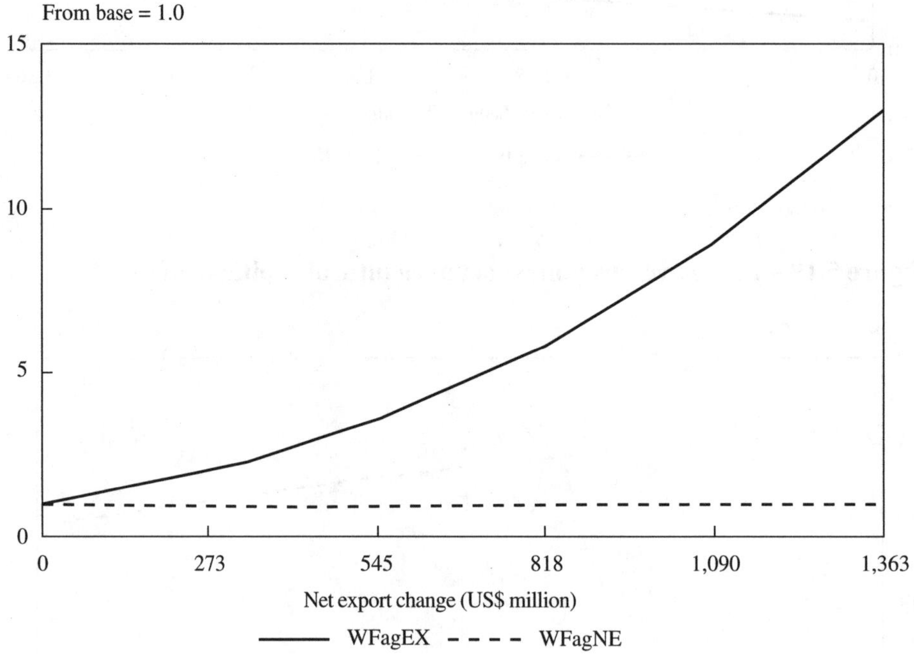

From base = 1.0

Net export change (US$ million)

——— WFagEX - - - - WFagNE

Source: Author.

---

[163] This may suggest that farmers producing for export markets (1) have medium rather than small farms, (2) are more educated and/or knowledgeable with respect to farm management, (3) are wealthier, (4) operate more input and capital intensively, (5) have a higher liquidity to finance expenditures and investments, and (6) are more flexible in reacting to changing market conditions.

[164] Data preparation and presentation of the Household Budget Survey 1991/92 determined the breakdown of household categories applied in the current analysis. A definite drawback of this household breakdown is the large number and variety of rural farming households lumped together regardless of their different income and welfare levels.

The characteristics of the Tanzanian economy that determine its response to a depreciation of the real exchange rate and, consequently, condition results and conclusions are the following:

- Due to low elasticities of substitution applied to Tanzania, substituting imports with domestic products is difficult.
- Due to low domestic shares in the composite good combinations, even high substitution elasticities do not permit large quantity changes.
- Not only absolute elasticity values, but also their relative size among sectors, matter.
- Because domestic production is import intensive, substitution elasticities of imported intermediate goods (or their import components) are low, and import shares of intermediates are high, total imports can only be reduced though a decline in production.
- Export-oriented production is in sectors that require significant imports (direct and indirect).[165] Each dollar of the desired increase of exports requires that a substantial fraction of this dollar be devoted to an increase in imports. This import dependence of export-oriented production makes reducing the Tanzanian trade deficit through policies that expand exports much more difficult.

Conclusion

The experiment series in this section reflects on one of the primary goals of IMF/World Bank-guided structural adjustment programs in Tanzania: depreciation of the exchange rate. The applied CGE modeling framework supports the analysis of sectoral implications of structural adjustment in the particular context of the Tanzanian economy. Considering the general structure of Tanzania's production and foreign trade in 1992 and the import dependence of production in particular, the simulation results from the depreciation of the exchange rate suggest the following conclusions:

- Due to low substitutability between imports and domestic produce, some intermediate and final imports cannot be replaced by domestic goods. Consequently, total domestic supply must decrease when imports are cut back in response to depreciation of the exchange rate.
- Total GDP decreases due to the reduced availability of imported intermediates.
- As a result of diminishing GDP, decreasing imports, and increasing exports, domestic supply (absorption) and, thus, overall welfare, must decrease.
- A devaluation is more likely to boost Tanzanian agriculture than industrial sectors because of high factor movements between export and

---

[165] Refer to the section on trade liberalization, industrial protection, and the bias against agriculture for a discussion of the direct and indirect import content of production and sector-specific values of the Tanzanian economy.

nonexport agriculture that are caused by increasing export opportunities in the context of devaluation.

- A devaluation widens the gap between export and nonexport agriculture because of the induced resource shifts in factor markets.
- A devaluation disfavors nonexport-oriented producers relative to export-oriented producers because of the induced changes in relative prices (terms of trade).
- A devaluation disfavors nonexport-oriented producers absolutely compared with their preadjustment situation because of worsening production opportunities.
- Land owners engaged in export-oriented agriculture gain most from the devaluation, because land suitable for export crops gains the relatively largest returns.

Macroeconomic policies, like a devaluation of the exchange rate, cause substantial structural changes with both losers and winners.

Commodity Market Behavior in the Context of an African Economy: Devaluation under Decreasing Marketing Margins

Like most other African countries, in the late 1980s and 1990s Tanzania undertook structural adjustment programs, consisting of substantial changes in its macroeconomic policies. Many African economies operate under significantly different conditions and additional constraints compared with economies in other regions and other stages of economic development. In the section on the microsam in Chapter 4, special features of the Tanzanian CGE model are presented that seek to capture the country-specific characteristics of the economy. The distinct structures of rural and urban households, agricultural and nonagricultural production, and foreign trade are important in determining how the economy reacts to macroeconomic shocks. Tanzania is also characterized by extremely high transportation and marketing costs. This section analyzes the impact of devaluation under different marketing margin scenarios on domestic commodity markets, sectoral production, income generation, and foreign trade.

Expanding on the previous devaluation experiments, this section assesses the effect of different marketing margin scenarios on sectoral and macroeconomic performance. Transportation and other marketing costs in developing countries are known to be relatively high compared with more industrial economies. This is documented in a broad, empirically based literature on transportation cost analysis, as well as more theoretically focused modeling literature (see, for instance, Lyon and Thomson 1993). Several aspects are crucial to the phenomenon that in African countries marketing costs are high relative to initial (farmgate) producer prices. These aspects are (1) weak infrastructure in telecommunication systems, hampering the exchange of information and ultimately market transactions; (2) insufficient road and railway infrastructure, which restricts some areas' access to regional and national markets; (3) irregular energy supply (especially gasoline) in remote areas; and (4) high costs to purchase, maintain, and repair transport equipment relative to the value of transported goods and relative to the distance traveled. For example, a case study (Ashimogo 1995) of one of Tanzania's major maize-producing regions, the Sumbawanga District (Rukwa region), shows that, due to varying road conditions and associated variance in transport costs, some areas might be completely excluded from regional market participation.

The Marketing Margin Experiment

To incorporate marketing costs, three different marketing margins are included in the Tanzanian CGE model.[166] In the current experiment series, the marketing margins are gradually reduced in four consecutive steps of 12.5 percent decrements to 50 percent of their initial values. Assuming that high marketing costs are due mainly to inadequate infrastructure, the reduction of domestic trade margins can be seen as increasing economywide efficiency based on infrastructure investment. The Tanzanian CGE model does not incorporate a formal link between government expenditure on construction (road projects) and the price for trade services and/or the physical marketing margin coefficients, which are the two components of the marketing costs of each sector. Furthermore, as the general modeling approach is comparative static, investment appears as a component of final demand, but does not increase the effective capital stock of the economy. The results of infrastructure investment are implicitly modeled through the decrease of the marketing margin coefficients. The investment, including additional government spending on infrastructure development, is not explicitly modeled, but is assumed to be part of investment demand.

Further model closures chosen for this experiment series assume the segmentation of all factor markets between aggregate agriculture and nonagriculture, as well as mobile capital within nonagricultural sectors. As opposed to the previous devaluation experiment, the objective of infrastructure investment has a clear medium-term focus, for example, road projects are not completed overnight. Substantial improvement of the national infrastructure system has to be accomplished through medium-term investment programs. In accordance with the medium-term nature of the analysis, the model now allows for migration between rural labor (*RURA*), mainly employed in agriculture, and unskilled labor (*UNSK*) employed in nonagriculture. In other words, physical factor units can be transformed from rural agricultural to unskilled urban labor, indicating rural-urban migration and vice versa.[167]

---

[166] As described in Chapter 4, the model contains three different marketing margin coefficients for each good depending whether it is imported, exported, or domestically produced and supplied. The margins are sector-specific coefficients specifying demand for trade and transportation services, and their values are incorporated into the respective price equations, as shown in equations (1) to (3) in Chapter 4.

[167] Migration is modeled by simply linking the two labor markets. Labor can move freely from one market to the other according to wage incentives, while the sum of total factor supply in both markets is kept constant.

As a first step in the experiment series, a devaluation of the local currency is imposed through a 50 percent reduction of the trade balance.[168] The devaluation has been chosen as the underlying macroeconomic policy shock to demonstrate how the effects of this previously analyzed structural adjustment measure vary in combination with other—complementary—economic measures, such as enhanced infrastructure investment. In combination with the reduction of the marketing margins, this experimental design allows for the analysis of two interrelated issues. First, it can be used to assess how the macroeconomic policy goal of reducing the trade deficit (or devaluing the real exchange rate) affects sectoral and overall economic performance under different trade cost scenarios.[169] Second, the different experiment results can be compared with each other to isolate the net effect of the reductions of the marketing margins in the new macroeconomic setting with devaluation, because the change in the trade balance in the first experiment applies to all subsequent experiments as well.

Results of the Marketing Margin Experiment

The effects of the current experiment series are shown in Figures 5.21 and 5.22, which present the exchange rate and two agricultural terms of trade indices (producer price and value-added price).

A 50 percent reduction of the trade balance under the initial marketing margins induces a 19 percent depreciation of the exchange rate. Decreasing all sectoral marketing margin coefficients uniformly in steps of 12.5 percent decrements to 50 percent of their initial values reduces the required depreciation to 11.9 percent at the last step. Lowering marketing margins increases the responsiveness of the economy to a change in the real exchange rate, with import and export transactions becoming cheaper. Decreasing marketing costs lowers domestic import prices, PM_{cm}, and raises domestic export prices, PE_{ae}, making both imports and exports more attractive.[170] It is not just the exchange rate and the marketing margin coefficients that directly influence the domestic prices of tradable goods, but the final demand price for trade services, PC_{CTRAD}, as well. Calibrated at 1 in the base run of the model, it decreases throughout the experiment series in response to the decreasing demand for trade services. Both the decreasing physical demand due to the cut in marketing margins and the decreasing final demand price of trade services contribute to the lower required devaluation indicated in

---

[168] The Tanzanian CGE model permits a choice between (1) fixing the exchange rate at any desired level to simulate a particular exogenous devaluation and solving the model endogenously for the adjusting trade balance, or (2) fixing the trade balance at any desired level (which would indicate that the macroeconomic goal is the reduction of the existing trade deficit by a certain percentage) and equilibrating the model through the required depreciation of the exchange rate. The objectives of the two formulations differ slightly, but the modeling results for every particular data pair of exchange rate and trade balance are exactly the same regardless of which approach is applied.

[169] As the cut in trade balance is the same for all the experiments, the combined effects of the induced macroeconomic policy (devaluation) in combination with the respective marketing margin level can be measured by comparing each experiment result to the initial base.

[170] See equations (11) and (12) in Chapter 4.

Figure 5.21—Exchange rate depreciation under changing marketing margins

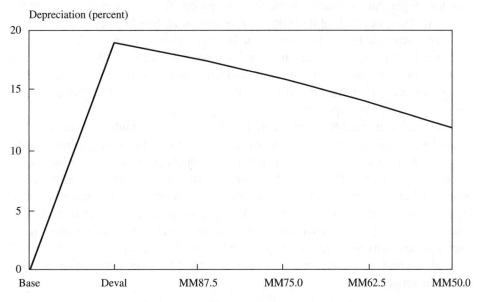

Depreciation (percent)

Devaluation under different marketing margin scenarios

Source: Author.

Figure 5.22—Agricultural terms of trade

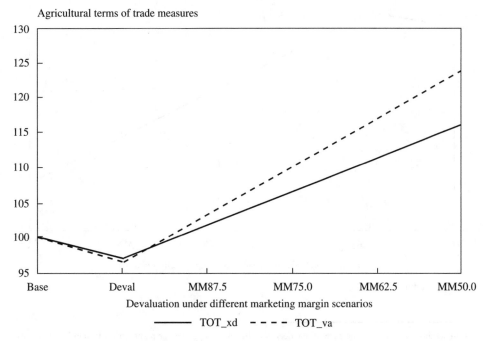

Agricultural terms of trade measures

Devaluation under different marketing margin scenarios

———— TOT_xd   – – – – TOT_va

Source: Author.

119

the experiment series. Although the response of PC_{CTRAD} is relatively small compared with the 50 percent decrease in marketing margin coefficients, its contribution to the change in domestic prices of tradable goods is significant (see Figure 5.23).

The required devaluation under the initial marketing margins first increases the price for trade services, because the 50 percent reduction of the trade balance requires a shift to production of some tradable goods, which requires marketing margin services. Then the price drops below its initial value and further decreases with each step of the experiment series, finally falling 7.7 percent.

The effect of a reduction in the trade balance on the agricultural terms of trade measures is consistent with the results from the earlier devaluation experiments. The measures deteriorate by 3.0 and 3.6 percent for producer price and value-added price, respectively. However, the first 12.5 percent reduction of all marketing margin coefficients offsets the negative effect caused by the devaluation.[171] The improvement in the agricultural terms of trade as the marketing margins decrease reflects the higher average marketing margin coefficients in agriculture compared with nonagriculture. The three quantity-weighted average coefficients for aggregate agriculture and nonagriculture, respectively, are presented in Table 5.8 as computed from the base run of the model.

Figure 5.23—Final demand price of trade services

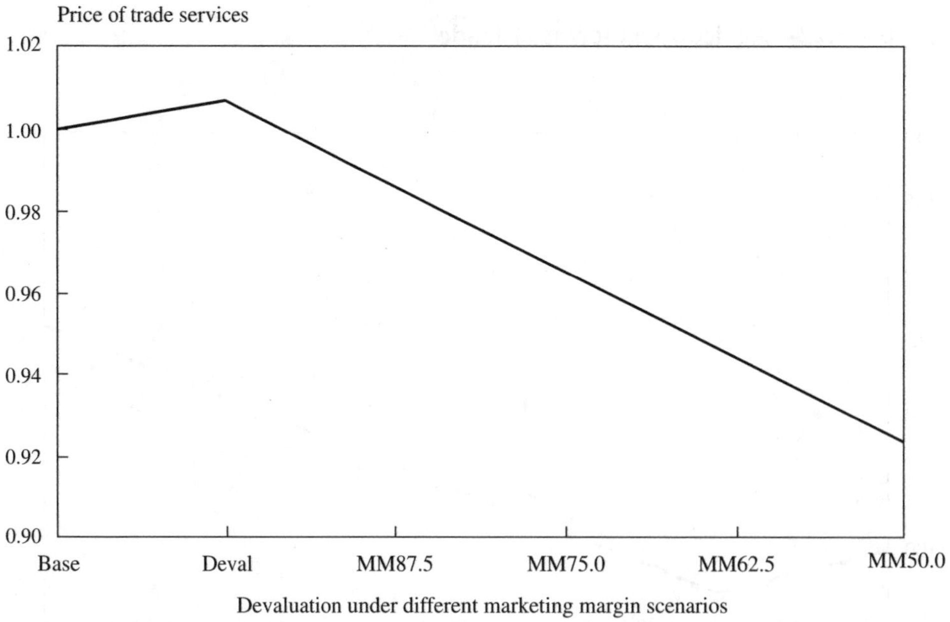

Devaluation under different marketing margin scenarios

Source: Author.

---

[171] Remarkably, the degree of the devaluation decreases by only 1.4 percentage points (from 19.0 to 17.6 percent), and therefore contributes only marginally to the positive influence on the agricultural terms of trade from lowering trade margins.

Table 5.8—Average marketing margin coefficients and respective total values for aggregate agriculture and nonagriculture

| | Average marketing margin coefficients per aggregate [a] | | | Total marketing margin values of aggregates (billion TSh) | | |
	Domestic sales	Exports	Imports	Domestic sales	Exports	Imports
Agriculture	0.25	0.48	0.26	141.7	6.5	0.5
Nonagriculture	0.10	0.32	0.13	102.0	11.8	58.4

Source: Base solution.

[a] The marketing margin coefficients represent fractions on the consumer price of *Trade and Transportation Services* that are associated with the domestic prices of the respective commodities.

The three average marketing margin coefficients are larger for agriculture than for nonagriculture. However, the relative effect of a uniform percentage reduction of all coefficients on agricultural performance depends also on the relative size of domestic sales, exports, and imports. Looking at the coefficients for imports, the average marketing margin rate for agricultural imports is twice as high as for nonagricultural imports. However, as the base year data show little agricultural imports, nominal marketing costs associated with agricultural imports are insignificant: TSh 0.5 billion compared with TSh 58.4 billion in nonagriculture. The high average coefficient for domestic absorption (0.25) applies to nearly all agricultural absorption (91.4 percent), generating nominal marketing costs of TSh 141.7 billion. The much lower average coefficient for nonagriculture (0.10), though applied to a higher value of nonagricultural absorption, ultimately applies to only 38.3 percent of total nonagricultural absorption, generating TSh 102 billion of marketing costs. Consequently, the positive effect of the reduction in marketing margins on the agricultural price index is much higher than for nonagriculture, and overall agricultural terms of trade improve (see Figure 5.22).

In terms of production, the initial devaluation under existing marketing margins primarily causes an increase in value-added of export agriculture and a decrease in value-added of nonexport agriculture, which accords with earlier devaluation results (see Figure 5.17). This gain and loss are of a similar magnitude, and thus offset each other in the aggregate—an indication that factors that are initially employed in agriculture only move within agriculture—which reflects the assumed factor market segmentation. When the marketing coefficients are gradually reduced, nominal value-added of nonexport agriculture at first reestablishes its old level and finally increases 28.2 percent compared with its base value.

By contrast, nominal value-added in export agriculture maintains the same level of improvement throughout the experiment series, as shown in Figure 5.24. Figure 5.25 presents the respective percentage changes from the base. Two factors contribute to the different performance of export and nonexport agriculture. First, although the average marketing coefficient of export agriculture is higher than the marketing coefficient for domestically marketed agriculture (0.48 compared with

121

Figure 5.24—Nominal changes in selected sectoral value-added

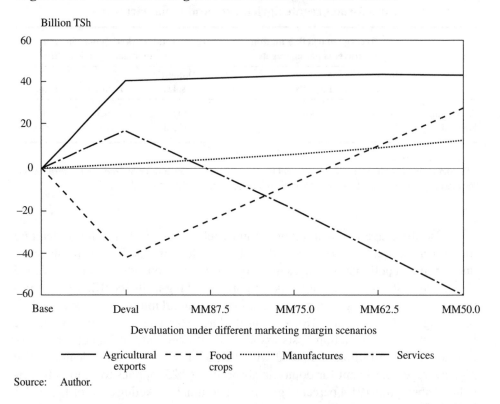

Devaluation under different marketing margin scenarios

——— Agricultural exports - - - - Food crops ·············· Manufactures —·—· Services

Source: Author.

0.25), the total value of marketing export agriculture is only a fraction of the respective value of domestically marketed agriculture (TSh 6.5 billion compared with
TSh 141.7 billion), which is due to the relative size of the two segments.[172] Second,
the coefficient for export agriculture (0.48) is also higher than the coefficient for
nonagriculture exports (0.32), indicating a potential competitive advantage for nonagricultural exports. The sectoral composition of total exports reveals that the share
of agricultural exports decreases by 10.8 percentage points, while exports of manufactures increase by 13.4 percentage points in reaction to the 50 percent reduction
of the marketing coefficients (see Figure 5.26). The competitive advantage mentioned is more than offset by something else, namely, the assumed factor market
segmentation between agriculture and nonagriculture. The decreasing demand for
trade services associated with the reduction of the marketing coefficients releases
resources from this sector and makes them available to other nonagricultural sectors. With devaluation, in which both export agriculture and export nonagriculture

---

[172] The marketing margin coefficients are weighted averages. Therefore, the lower coefficient for nonexport agriculture suggests that some large food-producing sectors have relatively low marketing costs that, in turn, indicates that
substantial parts of their commodities are consumed locally, and are thus not associated with high marketing costs.

Figure 5.25—Nominal changes in selected sectoral value-added

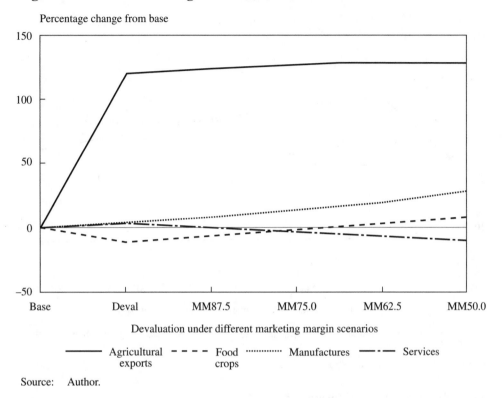

Percentage change from base

Devaluation under different marketing margin scenarios

——— Agricultural exports – – – Food crops ·········· Manufactures —·— Services

Source: Author.

compete with their respective nonexport sectors for resources to expand production, this additional factor supply creates a substantial competitive advantage for nonagricultural export goods.

The importance of the decreasing demand for trade services is also reflected in the sharp decrease of nominal value-added of the service sector (*nagserv*) in Figure 5.24, to which trade services contribute 75.8 percent. To assess the relevance of the trade services sector, note that trade services represent a large share in total GDP at f.c. (13.4 percent) and in nonagricultural GDP at f.c. (21.8 percent).

Figure 5.26 shows the sectoral composition of exports.[173] As the trade balance is fixed at 50 percent of its initial value in the first experiment, and the model equilibrates through adjusting the real exchange rate, the absolute difference between total imports and total exports cannot change, but the absolute values of total imports and exports can and do change, as shown in Figures 5.27 and 5.28. The effect of the initial devaluation follows earlier results. The absolute changes in total imports and exports are of the same magnitude, but they

---

[173] The changes in the composition of sectoral export performance are the same in real and nominal terms, because the relevant world market prices are exogenous and fixed.

Figure 5.26—Composition of exports

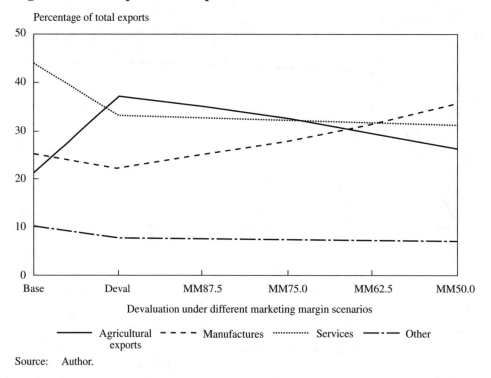

Source: Author.

Figure 5.27—Total real foreign trade

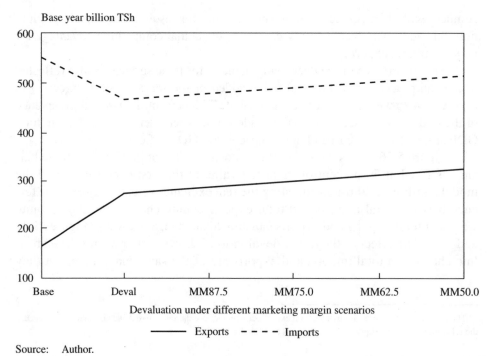

Source: Author.

Figure 5.28—Real foreign trade (percentage change)

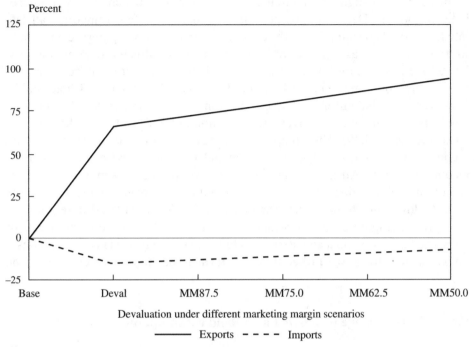

Source: Author.

represent different percentage changes from base values because of their different base levels: a 64.9 percent increase in exports, but only a 15.6 percent decrease in imports. Lowering the marketing costs favors foreign trade, and thus
requires less depreciation to achieve the same trade balance. The earlier devaluation experiment series shows that lower depreciation is associated with
lower export levels. Here this relationship is reversed. Although the real exchange rate appreciates with the gradual reduction of the marketing costs, real
total exports increase further, as do imports, because the directions of total import and export movements are strictly linked through the fixed trade balance.
Given the 50 percent reduction of the trade balance, total real exports further
increase, from 164.9 to 192.9 percent of their base value, which is associated
with an improvement in total real imports from 84.4 to 92.8 percent of their
base value. Consequently, although the absolute value of the trade deficit remains the same, it occurs at a higher level of foreign trade, and thus diminishes
relative to the total volume of foreign trade. The reduced need for cuts in imports (7.2 instead of 15.6 percent) indicates that it is less painful for the economy
as a whole to cope with the devaluation under a more cost-efficient transport
and marketing infrastructure.

The welfare effects associated with the experiment series are straightforward. The initial devaluation requires higher exports and fewer imports, which
forces domestic industries to produce more tradable goods. Because of segmented

and sticky factor markets, both requirements lead to higher marginal costs of production and a slight contraction of total GDP at f.c., which affects all households negatively. Decreasing output, higher exports, and fewer imports translate into lower final consumption in the economy and, therefore, aggregate household welfare must decrease. In general, farmers are more affected than nonfarmers, but among farmers, rural farmers are affected less than their urban counterparts, and among nonfarmers, urban households are hurt less than rural households. However, with the uniform relative reduction of marketing costs, farmers' welfare improves and partly recovers, whereas nonfarmers' welfare further deteriorates (see Figure 5.29). This complies with the assumption that trade services are produced by nonfarmers, and as the demand for trade services declines, their income decreases. All households together lose 10.2 percent in aggregate consumption (welfare) due to the devaluation, but they recover 4 percentage points with the lower marketing costs. The consumption levels of the different household groups (Figure 5.30) show that the economywide distributional effects of infrastructure investment and associated lower marketing costs favor farm households, which are poor, rather than nonfarm households, which tend to be

Figure 5.29—Change in deflated household consumption

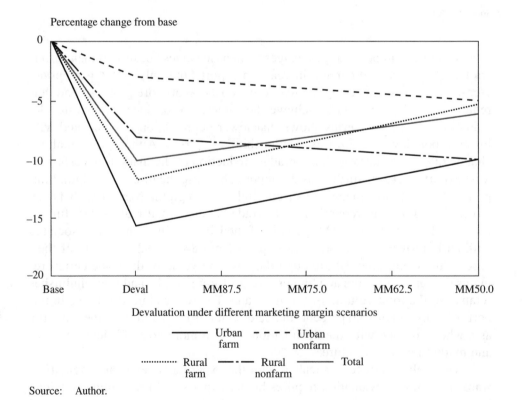

Source: Author.

Figure 5.30—Annual deflated average consumption in TSh per household

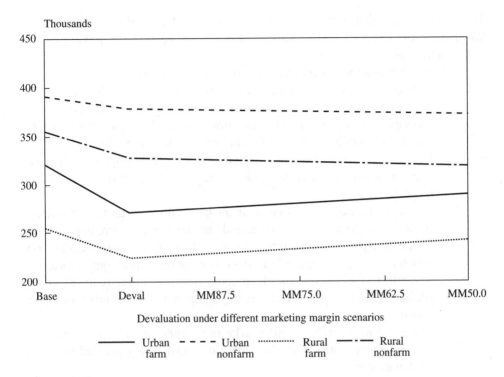

Devaluation under different marketing margin scenarios

——— Urban – – – – Urban ·········· Rural —·—· Rural
farm   nonfarm   farm   nonfarm

Source: Author.

wealthier.[174] Recall that a shortcoming of this household-specific welfare analysis is the disaggregation of households, which is based on the standard disaggregation applied to the Household Budget Survey 1991/92 and other surveys by the Bureau of Statistics. Unfortunately, it groups subsistence and small-scale farmers together with medium- to large-scale farmers in rural areas, regardless of their size, technology applied, activity diversification, and relative income generation. However, we can differentiate small-scale, nonexport producers from large-scale, export-oriented farmers. These results suggest that (1) export-oriented farmers gain through the devaluation, but lose in relative terms compared with nonexport farmers during the subsequent experiment series; and (2) nonexport farmers lose through the devaluation, but gain, and even overcompensate, their initial losses as a consequence of the uniformly lower marketing coefficients through a gain in their terms of trade that is driven by the increased productivity in transport and marketing services.

---

[174] Annual average household consumption by group is deflated by household-specific cost of living indices, which incorporate OHC and final household demand components.

Conclusions

The experiment series in this section compares the effect of devaluation with lower transport and marketing costs. The analysis suggests the following results and conclusions:

- An improved infrastructure, which allows for a more efficient transport and marketing system, releases scarce resources to other productive sectors.
- The decreasing demand by all sectors for transport and marketing services per unit of output releases resources to other productive sectors, which has an expansionary effect on the economy as a whole.
- Under higher cost-efficiency in transport and marketing, a much lower depreciation is required to achieve the same reduction in the current trade deficit.
- Given the marketing coefficients in the base data, their uniform reduction favors total agriculture in general and nonexport agriculture in particular.
- This effect partly compensates for the effect of the initial devaluation, which favors export agriculture but disfavors nonexport agriculture.
- The effect of a devaluation given better transport infrastructure is more equitable and less poverty enhancing compared with the effects of a devaluation alone.
- The existing transport and marketing structure primarily hampers nonexport agriculture, which is therefore particularly favored by lower marketing cost.
- Low income, rural, nonexport-oriented farm households benefit most from better infrastructure, because they often operate under extremely high transportation and marketing costs that exclude them from market participation.
- The improvement of transport and marketing infrastructure has a substantial effect on the structural and sectoral performance of the entire economy and, consequently, on the impact of other macroeconomic policies such as a devaluation.

CHAPTER 6

Results, Achievements, and Conclusions

This study analyzes the impact of stabilization and structural adjustment policies on Tanzania's macroeconomic performance, intersectoral shifts, and household welfare applying a CGE model based on a 1992 SAM. The results indicate that structural adjustment measures have a decisive effect on the overall performance and the sectoral structure of Tanzania's economy, and that macroeconomic policies matter. The analysis reveals that the applied CGE model is an appropriate analytical tool for addressing the study's objectives and adequately reflects the reality of Tanzania's economy, capturing the particular characteristics of the country and its regional context. This is particularly true when compared with partial equilibrium approaches, which lack the analytical depth of CGE modeling because they do not capture finite resource endowments, economywide interhousehold welfare effects, or endogenous income effects. In addition, they do not provide the kind of consistency checks inherent in a general equilibrium framework in which the accounts of all economic actors must add up and thus satisfy Walras's law (Hertel 1999). Additional sensitivity analysis in substitution and transformation elasticities, which are the core parameters of the applied CGE approach, indicates an acceptable robustness of the modeling results obtained.

Research Findings

Tanzania's Policy Bias against Agriculture

In many developing countries the domestic tax system is largely responsible for a policy bias against agriculture. Within the scope of the applied general equilibrium framework, agricultural bias measures are developed to quantify the existing bias against agriculture in Tanzania and to compare the results with earlier partial equilibrium findings. The CGE results reveal that partial equilibrium measures in the tradition of Krueger, Schiff, and Valdes (1988) overestimate the bias against agriculture because they (1) assume agriculture to be much more traded than it actually is, (2) neglect important indirect exchange rate effects of trade policies that work endogenously within the CGE approach, and (3) do not sufficiently capture the domestic price transmission mechanism that dampens the negative effect of the domestic tax scheme at the producer level. Furthermore, intersectoral linkages in domestic production and foreign trade, as well as the import content of sectoral production, influence the CGE results significantly and cannot be addressed appropriately within a partial equilibrium framework.

The substantial reduction of the bias against agriculture measured in the CGE framework for 1992, compared with earlier partial equilibrium results, reflects that in the case of Tanzania (1) agricultural production and trade shares have decreased compared with the 1980s, and (2) substantial changes in the tax system have taken place in the context of SAP policies that reduced the bias against agriculture. Consequently, by 1992, the bias against agriculture was almost eliminated, and agriculture was actually protected by some of the existing domestic taxes in place that levied a relatively higher tax burden on nonagricultural sectors. Finally, the analysis of the bias against agriculture showed that farm, not rural households in general, are particularly hurt and, therefore, the term agricultural bias is more appropriate than urban bias.

Devaluation under Import Dependency

The simulation of a devaluation of the exchange rate, a core element of structural adjustment policies, not only aims to quantify the effects on overall production and trade, but also to analyze intersectoral trade-offs and relative welfare shifts among households. The simulation results reveal Tanzania's high import dependency, which, on the one hand, is due to low substitutability between imports and domestic production and, on the other hand, is due to the high indirect import content of domestic production and exports. However, export agriculture is far less import dependent than nonagricultural exports and, hence, is relatively favored through a devaluation of the exchange rate. The devaluation reduces imports and leads to some contraction of total GDP. All exports rise, but agricultural exports increase at a higher rate compared with nonagricultural exports due to a lower import dependency of agricultural production. Consequently, lower imports in combination with increasing exports lead to a decrease in domestic supply, total absorption, and economywide welfare. Devaluation stimulates total agricultural production in Tanzania, in particular because of high labor mobility between export and nonexport agriculture. Increasing export opportunities cause substantial resource shifts into export agriculture and disfavor non-export-oriented farmers, both in relative terms compared with export-oriented farmers, and even in absolute terms compared with their preadjustment situation. Devaluation has a substantial effect on intersectoral shifts in production and interhousehold welfare patterns and, because of its diverse effects, considering both winners and losers is extremely important.

Complementary Measures Matter

A devaluation of the exchange rate shows very different results under alternative marketing margin scenarios. The improvement of existing infrastructure facilities in Tanzania would lead to substantial structural shifts and enhanced sectoral performance and, consequently, would result in more equitable income distribution, increasing overall welfare, and a dampening of the poverty effects that are otherwise observed. Investment in infrastructure that is directed at more cost-efficient transportation, communication, and marketing facilities is highly favorable for economic expansion in general and for nonexport agriculture in particular. Better infrastructure releases scarce resources from the trade and transportation sector to other productive sectors and provides transportation and marketing services at lower costs. Because of the higher domestic cost-efficiency, lower depreciation is required to achieve a targeted balance of trade improvement. Agriculture gains relative to nonagriculture because its mostly remote production locations require more effective transportation services. Nonexport agriculture gains most from improving infrastructure because high transport and marketing costs currently exclude nonexport agriculture from efficient market participation. A complementary measure, such as improving transport and marketing infrastructure, has a substantial influence on the entire economy's structural and sectoral performance and, consequently, on the final impact of macroeconomic policies, such as the exchange rate devaluation analyzed in this volume.

Methodological Developments

In terms of methodology, the Tanzania CGE model proved itself a useful simulation laboratory for analyzing structural adjustment. The CGE approach provides a good analytical framework, and it is flexible enough to incorporate both neoclassical model characteristics and structuralist model features appropriate for Tanzania, following Chenery's (1975) view of "neoclassical structuralism."

In general, the CGE model is a static, open-economy, single-country model with two-way trade and product differentiation specified as CES import aggregation and CET export transformation. Producers maximize profits with respect to their nested CES production function, and households maximize utility with respect to their linear expenditure systems. The model integrates macroeconomic features, market behavior, and microeconomic specifications of sectoral production and final consumption. It solves for relative prices across factor and commodity markets and guarantees an extremely high degree of intersectoral linkages that are appropriate for capturing all direct and indirect effects of structural adjustment measures. Other than its functional specification, a CGE model allows for explicit formulation of constraints, assumptions, and macroeconomic model closures to reflect market imperfections and model economic rigidities.

The Tanzania CGE model developed for this study incorporates several country-specific model features that reflect important aspects of economic reality in Tanzania. These features include (1) a segmented labor market, (2) fixed sectoral capital, (3) optional limited migration, (4) OHC of nonmarketed goods that complements the typical final household demand of marketed goods, (5) transport and marketing margins to capture the large wedges between producer and consumer prices, (6) a food aid variable to simulate food aid injections in the event of domestic

131

crop failures, and (7) a European-style VAT with a rebate mechanism introduced in July 1998. The country-specific advancements of the Tanzania CGE enabled the detailed analysis of structural adjustment policies carried out in this study.

Other than the development of the Tanzania CGE model, the preparation of the underlying database is a valuable contribution to policy analysis in Tanzania. The SAM that has been constructed for the CGE analysis has substantially improved on earlier versions because of its base year (1992 instead of 1976), the data sources used, and the cross-entropy estimation techniques applied. Because the share parameters used in the CGE model are calculated from the base year SAM, their reliability improved together with the increasing data quality and consistency of the underlying SAM. Furthermore, the advanced data estimation techniques allowed for a detailed sectoral disaggregation, which, in turn, enabled a more detailed analysis with a special focus on agriculture and its subsectors.

The study's simulation results are robust with respect to reasonable variations of the model's parameters. Although the results change with different parameter values, their general structure and interpretation remains the same. In particular, sensitivity analysis has been carried out to validate the robustness of the model's results with respect to the exogenous CES and CET substitution and transformation elasticities. The sensitivity analysis strongly indicates that the qualitative modeling results are only moderately sensitive to changes ranging from 75 to 175 percent of the initial elasticity values.

Further Model Developments and Future Research

The study leads to some suggestions for further research and advancements in both methodological and analytical aspects. A first advancement will be the application of the upcoming 1992 input-output table that is under construction at the National Accounts Section of the Bureau of Statistics in Dar es Salaam. The new input-output table will substantially improve the technology and sectoral production information of the underlying SAM database and, consequently, will provide a basis for improved analysis. Second, to carry out more poverty-focused analysis within the applied CGE framework, the household groups of the model have to be further subdivided. This will only be possible if the Tanzanian authorities decide to change the data preparation and presentation of the next household budget survey or if the raw data were available to create appropriate household categories.[175] In addition,

---

[175] The current Household Budget Survey distinguishes between farmers and nonfarmers in rural and urban areas and thus considers only four household groups. Even more difficult, the group of rural farmers comprises 67 percent of the entire population. Hence, they not only represent two-thirds of all Tanzanian households but also the vast majority of all poor households in Tanzania, which are mainly located in rural areas. In 1993, 52 percent of the rural population was below the relative poverty line of two-thirds of the national mean per capita income, while only 20 percent of the urban population was below this relative poverty measure. In absolute terms the difference was even more distinct, with 48 percent of all rural households but only 11 percent of all urban households living below the absolute poverty line in 1993 (World Bank 1996a).

132

the household budget survey should be designed as a real income-expenditure survey and not focus only on the expenditure pattern of households. It should also collect detailed information on formal and informal income. Moreover, data collection for the household budget survey should be more closely aligned with the commodity disaggregation of the national accounts and the input-output table to obtain a unified and consistent database comprising production, income distribution, and consumption. Once the underlying data fulfill these requirements, the model can incorporate a broader spectrum of poverty groups to accommodate more differentiated welfare and poverty analysis. This issue shows the limits of CGE modeling, which requires extensive data to capture broad economic interdependency. Third, future research should include more advanced estimation techniques for the response parameters of the CGE model, which can be estimated using a maximum entropy approach relying on historical data series and incorporating all CGE constraints at the outset (Arndt, Robinson, and Tarp 1999).

The country-specific specification of the Tanzanian CGE model accommodates a wide range of problem-oriented research, simulations, and forecasting. This is especially true for trade-related analysis, and could be used to provide analytical support for the next round of trade negotiations within the World Trade Organization. Other trade-related applications of the Tanzanian CGE could be to analyze intraregional trade issues. For this purpose a modified model version could incorporate the East African community, the Southern African Development Community countries, or any desired group of SSA countries as a separate region in order to analyze Tanzania's opportunities for enhanced intraregional trade and its potential benefits. The CGE framework can also be applied to issues in institutional economics, such as assessing efficiency losses associated with government actions (final demand for goods and services and/or supply of public administration). However, the incorporation of such features requires information on the relative efficiency of government and private entities, which raises problems of both data and theory. Another possible extension of the CGE model for Tanzania could exploit its microeconomic foundation and combine it with a village CGE model to analyze the effect of macroeconomic policies on a village economy and the agents involved.

APPENDIX A

Recent Economic Indicators and Policies

Table A.1—Country data for Tanzania: Economic and social indicators

Area	945,090	sq km
Land	886,040	sq km
Water	49,050	sq km
Total arable	400,000	sq km
Under cultivation	60,000	sq km
Irrigated land (1993 estimate)	1,500	sq km
Population (1998)	31.5	millions[a]
0–14 years	45	%
15–64 years	53	%
65 years and older	2	%
Density (1996)	34.7	per sq km
Growth rate (1978–95)	2.8	%
Urban population (1990–96)	24.9	%
Life expectancy at birth (1995)	50	years
Infant mortality	86	per 1,000 live births
Under 5 mortality	144	per 1,000 live births
Literacy/total population (1995 estimate)	67.8	%
Health		
Access to safe water (1990–96), shares of:		
Urban population	65.0	%
Rural population	45.0	%
Calorie intake per person	2,206	
Population per physician (1992)	21,496	
Population per hospital bed	981	
Household income (1990–96)		
Lowest quintile share	6.8	%
Highest quintile share	45.4	%
Gini coefficient	0.57	
GNP per capita (1997)	170	US$
Purchasing power parity (1997)	700	US$
GDP at market prices (1996)	5,837.8	million US$ (100.0%)
Gross domestic investment	18.0	% of GDP m.p.
Private consumption	83.4	% of GDP m.p.
General government consumption	13.2	% of GDP m.p.

(continued)

134

Table A.1—Continued

Exports of goods and nonfactor services	21.5	% of GDP m.p.
Imports of goods and nonfactor services	36.2	% of GDP m.p.
GDP at factor costs (1996)	5,374.3	million US$ (100.0%)
Agriculture	47.6	% of GDP f.c.
Industry	21.2	% of GDP f.c.
Services	31.2	% of GDP f.c.
Employment (1990/91)		
Total population	22,661,600	100.0% of total population
Younger than 10 years	7,061,360	31.2% of total population
Currently not economically active	4,305,313	19.0% of total population
Employed	10,889,205	48.1% of total population
of which:		
Agricultural sector	9,164,059	84.2% of total employed
Traditional	(9,086,122)	83.4% of total employed
Other	(77,937)	0.7% of total employed
Industry	1,270,531	11.7% of total employed
Services (mainly government)	454,615	4.2% of total employed
Unemployed	405,722	3.7% of total population
Consumer prices (end of 1997/98)	12.0	% annual change
Exchange rate (1998)	651	TSh / US$
Total debt committed (1997/98)	7,846.7	million US$
of which is undisbursed	1,467.0	million US$
Total debt service	36.4	% of exports of goods and nonfactor services

Sources: World Bank (1996b, 1998); BOT, *Economic Bulletin,* 1998, vol. 28, no.3; U.S. Central Intelligence Agency (1998); UNDP (1996); URT (1993); author's calculations.

[a] Estimated by a FAO/WFP mission to Tanzania for mid-November 1998 (FAO 1999).

Table A.2—Tanzania: Recent policy performance

Sector	Steps taken	Timing
External sector		
Trade policy	Abolished all trade restrictions except for petroleum products and goods restricted for health and security reasons	1993
	Reduced number of nonzero tariffs from seven to four, and top rate to 30 percent	June 1997
	Completed preliminary study of further reform of customs tariff structure	March 1998
External current payments	Removed limits on payments and transfers for current international transactions	1994
	Accepted the obligation of Article VIII of the Fund's Articles of Agreement	July 1996
International reserves	Increased gross international reserves	1995/96–1997/98

(continued)

External debt	Negotiated Paris Club flow rescheduling on Naples terms	January 1997
Regional initiatives	Endorsed the Common Market for eastern and southern Africa (COMESA)	1995
	Endorsed the road map for external trade liberalization proposed by the Cross-Border Initiative cosponsors, together with 12 other countries from the region	March 1995
	Endorsed the East African Monetary Affairs Committee	March 1998
Fiscal policies		
Overall	Achieved recurrent budget savings above 1 percent of GDP	1996/97–1997/98
Revenue	Established the Tanzanian Revenue Authority	July 1996
	Revised investment act to eliminate tax holidays	1996/97
	Harmonized duties between Zanzibar and mainland Tanzania on five major commodities	December 1996
	Implemented new preshipment inspection contract, with sealing of containers	January 1998
	Completed preparation for introduction of VAT on July 1, 1998	1997/98
	Adopted narrow definition of capital goods for customs purposes	June 1998
	Adopted effective and transparent monitoring system for bonded warehouse	June 1998
Expenditure	Introduced stringent expenditure control based on rigorous cash management system	From second half of 1995/96
	Fully protected social sectors in implementing cash budget	1997/98
	Revitalized development budget, reducing number of projects to a more manageable level	1996/97–1997/98
	Established sub-treasuries	1996/97–1997/98
Monetary policy and financial reform		
Overall	Liberalized interest rates and established competitive treasury bill auctions	1993
	Reduced rate of monetary expansion	1996/97–1997/98
Banking	Began licensing private banks	1993/94
	Split National Bank of Commerce into National Bank of Commerce (1997) and National Microfinance Bank	October 1997
	Issued invitation to bid on management contract for National Microfinance Bank	May 1998
Insurance	Implemented insurance sector liberalization	May 1998
Capital markets	Operationalized Dar es Salaam Stock Exchange	April 1998
Public sector reform		
Civil service reform	Reduced employment by 77,000, including removal of "ghost" workers from payroll, reducing the workforce to 273,000	1993/96; ongoing
	Introduced a pay reform program to reduce the number of salary scales and include most allowances in the basic wage; monetized most in kind benefits	June 1996

(continued)

Table A.2—Continued

	Restructured regional administration	1997/98
Parastatal reform	Removed more than one-half of parastatals from government control	1994–98
Sector policies		
Investment policy	Adopted new investment code	August 1997
Power	Established a system of direct payment to electricity parastatal Tanzania Electric Supply Company Ltd. from Ministry of Finance to cover bills for customers; electric company is not allowed to disconnect.	September 1997
Petroleum	Abolished monopoly on refined petroleum product import	April 1997
	Assigned collection of petroleum funds to Tanzanian Revenue Authority	1997/98
Mining	Revised legal framework and enacted new mining legislation	1997/98
Land policy	Adopted a new land policy to improve security of tenure and allocation of land	February 1995
Agriculture	Opened marketing and processing of traditional export crops to the private sector through legislation and accompanying regulations	1994
	Adopted agriculture and livestock policy, as well as cooperative development policy	1997
Water	Set up semiautonomous water boards in regional headquarters	1997/98
	Reviewed rural water policy	1997/98
Roads	Completed study in institutional arrangements for road management	March 1998
Social sectors		
Poverty reduction	Initiated implementation of National Poverty Eradication Strategy	June 1998
Education	Approved a new education and training policy	June 1995
	Adopted Basic Education Master Plan	February 1997
	Completed studies on issues in secondary education	June 1998
Health	Approved proposal for reform of the health sector	March 1995
	Introduced cost sharing at primary care facilities in nine districts	1997/98
Environment	Adopted national environmental policy	November 1997
	Endorsed the National Conservation Strategy for Sustainable Development	1996
Statistics	Published revised national accounts	May 1997
	Began publication of balance of payments data on basis of *Balance of Payments Manual* (5th ed.)	December 1997
	Began monthly publication of trade statistics based on customs data	January 1998

Source: URT, IMF, and World Bank (1999), <http://www.imf.org>.

Table A.3—Tanzania: Physiographic regions

Region	Description	Area in million ha
Coastal zone	Low altitude plains (below 750 m) on marine secondary and tertiary sediments	6.0
Eastern plateau and mountain blocks	Medium altitude plains (150–1,300 m) on Precambrian metamorphic rocks	21.1
Southern highlands	High altitude plateau (1,500–2,000 m) with volcanic and Precambrian metamorphic rock	6.7
Northern rift and volcanic highlands	Medium altitude plains (1,000–2,300 m) with volcanic and rift landforms	5.8
Central plateau	Medium altitude plains (1,000–1,300 m) on granite	32.7
Rukwa-Rusha rift	Medium altitude rift depression (800–1,200 m) with lake sediment	3.5
Inland sediments	Medium altitude plains (750–1,000 m) on Karoo sediments	6.7
Ufipa plateau	High altitude (1,500–2,200 m) on metamorphic, sedimentary, and granitic rock	1.8
Western highlands	Medium-to-high altitude (1,200–1,900 m) on volcanic or sedimentary rock	4.3

Source: World Bank (1994a, Table 2.1).

Table A.4—Tanzania's domestic tax policies during the 1990s

1992/93:
- Reductions in taxes on income, consumption, and customs duties to encourage compliance and generate additional revenue
- Unification of seven different excise rates to a uniform rate of 20 percent
- Reduction of the customs duty rates from seven to four
- Reduction of the maximum marginal customs duty rate from 60 to 30 percent
- Exemption of imported and local raw materials from sales tax
- Conversion of several specific rates to ad valorem rates
- Reduction of individual income tax rates from 20–75 percent to 5–30 percent

1993/94:
- Rise in sales tax on goods from 10 and 20 percent to 30 percent
- Rise in customs duty rates
- Introduction of a real estate tax
- Increase in taxes on petroleum products

1994/95:
- Strengthening of the import tax assessment procedures
- Limitation of bonded warehouses
- Elimination of virtually all discretionary exemptions
- Rise in maximum customs duty rate from 40 to 50 percent (although some rates are substantially reduced)
- Stabilization of sales taxes remain the same at 0, 5, 25, and 30 percent, but extension of tax base to other services at the minimum rate of 5 percent in preparation for the introduction of VAT (at this time planned to be introduced in January 1996)
- Rise of road toll from TSh 30 to TSh 35 per liter of petrol or diesel

1995/96:
- Revision of the income tax schedule, which effectively reduced the income tax rate of civil servants an average of 15 to 3 percent
- Reduction of sales tax on certain items from 30 to 5 percent
- Reduction of sales tax for imported raw materials from 30 to 20 percent
- Rise of customs duties and sales taxes to 10 percent on capital goods
- Increase of road toll from TSh 50 to TSh 60 per liter of petrol or diesel

Source: IMF (1996b).
Note: For a comprehensive summary of the Tanzanian tax system as of July 1996, see IMF 1996b.

Documentation of Macrosam Cell Entries

The notation for the cells of the macrosam cells is row, column. For example, "Commodities, Activities" represents an expenditure flow from the column "Activities" to the row "Commodities." Note that Tanzania's financial year ends on June 30; thus all data collected as financial year data have to be estimated for 1992 by computing the averages of 1991/92 and 1992/93 figures.

1. **(Commodities, Activities):** 1,276,427—Import-ridden intermediate demand. Total intermediate demand, including imports from unpublished Bureau of Statistics data sources adjusted by other indirect production taxes (Domestic Taxes, Activities).

2. **(Factors, Activities):** 1,456,047—Value-added at factor costs. Total value-added at factor costs as in Table 6(a) of URT (1997), adjusted accordingly to supplementary data to the *Revised National Accounts of Tanzania 1987–96*.

3. **(Domestic Taxes, Activities):** 27,032—Other indirect taxes. Other indirect taxes are calculated as a residual of total net taxes on products, as in Table 6(a) of URT (1997) and tariffs and sales taxes as provided by the supplementary data to the *Revised National Accounts of Tanzania 1987–96*.

4. **(Activities, Commodities):** 2,320,484—Domestic supply. Domestic supply is computed as the residual of the "Activities" column total (equal to gross output including informal-sector activities) minus exports (Activities, Rest of the World [ROW]) and OHC (Activities, Households).

5. **(Domestic Taxes, Commodities):** 43,475—Sales taxes. Total sales tax as provided in the supplementary data to the *Revised National Accounts of Tanzania 1987–96* and double-checked with data from Table 2.1 of the Bank of Tanzania's (BOT) *Economic Bulletin,* 1997, 1st quarter, Dar es Salaam.

6. **(Tariffs, Commodities):** 23,451—Import duties. Total import duties as provided by the supplementary data to the *Revised National Accounts of Tanzania 1987–96*.

7. **(ROW, Commodities):** 553,363—Imports of goods and services. Total imports of goods and services at free on board (F.O.B.) prices as in Table 6(b) of URT (1997), adjusted by a 75 percent share of the *unrecorded trade and*

140

statistical discrepancy (TSh 19.023 million)—the remaining 25 percent is considered within the computation of total exports.

8. **(Households, Factors):** 841,879—Labor value-added. Total labor value-added will be generated for the microeconomic SAM[176] using the URT (1993). For the macrosam it is set at 60 percent of total value-added adjusted for 50 percent of net factor payments abroad (ROW, Factors).[177]

9. **(Enterprises, Factors):** 550,699—Value-added capital. Total value-added capital, including operating surplus and consumption of fixed capital, as a residual of total factor payment (Factors, Activities) minus labor value-added (Households, Factors) and adjusted for 50 percent of net factor payments abroad.

10. **(ROW, Factors):** 63,499—Net factor income paid abroad. Total net factor income paid abroad as calculated from Table 1 of the URT (1995a). The difference between GDP at f.c. and GNP at f.c. as a ratio to GDP at f.c. (all 1992) is applied to the new GDP at f.c. figure as in cell "Factors, Activities."

11. **(Activities, Households):** 273,340—OHC. Total OHC of agricultural produce as the equivalent of total nonmonetary agricultural GDP as in Table 1 of URT (1997).

12. **(Commodities, Households):** 913,213—Final household consumption. Total final household consumption as in Table 6(a) of URT (1997), minus OHC as in cell "Activities, Households" and adjusted according to the supplementary data to the *Revised National Accounts of Tanzania 1987–96.*

13. **(Government Recurrent, Households):** 16,656—Individual income taxes. Total individual income taxes paid by households, as in Table 2.1 of BOT, *Economic Bulletin,* 1997, 1st quarter, Dar es Salaam. Income taxes, other taxes, and nontax revenue are combined into one figure and shared between households and enterprises, according to their relative shares in 1990 as reported in Table 5.2 of World Bank (1996b).

14. **(Capital Account, Households):** 104,087—Household savings. Total household savings as a residual for balancing purposes.

15. **(Households, Enterprises):** 368,663—Operating surplus. Operating surplus distributed to households is calculated as the residual of total receipts of the enterprise account—value-added capital plus government transfers to enterprises—minus enterprise savings (Capital Account, Enterprises) and corporate taxes (Government Recurrent, Enterprises).

16. **(Government Recurrent, Enterprises):** 65,054—Corporate taxes. Total corporate taxes paid by enterprises as in Table 2.1 of BOT, *Economic Bulletin,* 1997, 1st quarter, Dar es Salaam. As described in paragraph 13, income taxes, other taxes, and nontax revenue are combined into one figure and

---

[176] A detailed description of the computations carried out for the generation of all value-added figures in the microsam is presented in the following section.

[177] See the discussion of the value-added split to labor, land, and capital under paragraph 2 (Factors, Activities) of the microsam documentation in Appendix C.

shared between households and enterprises, according to their respective shares from FY 1990 information in Table 5.2 of World Bank (1996b).

17. **(Capital Account, Enterprises):** 144,572—Enterprise Savings. Total enterprise savings as chosen for balancing purposes. Because the transfer of operating surplus from enterprises to households—paragraph 15 above—is calculated as a residual of total enterprise receipts minus corporate taxes and enterprise savings, enterprise savings can vary. The less enterprises save, the more operating surplus is transferred to households. As household expenditure on OHC, final commodity consumption, and income tax is given, household savings remain as the balancing cell of the household account. As a result, the less enterprises save the more households have to save and vice versa. This mechanism is used to adjust household and enterprise savings to obtain reasonable economywide rates. However, the sum of enterprise savings and household savings matches the reported magnitude of domestic private savings. As a percentage of adjusted GDP (market prices) for FY 1992 and FY 1993, these are 10.9 and 14.0 percent, respectively (IMF 1996a).

18. **(Government Recurrent, Domestic Taxes):** 70,507—Domestic tax collections. Total domestic tax collections of net indirect taxes (Domestic Taxes, Activities) and sales tax (Domestic Taxes, Commodities) paid to the government account.

19. **(Government Recurrent, Tariffs):** 23,451—Import duties collections. Total import duties collections (Tariffs, Commodities) paid to the government account.

20. **(Commodities, Government Recurrent):** 279,080—Government consumption. Total final government consumption as in the supplementary data to the *Revised National Accounts of Tanzania 1987–96.*

21. **(Enterprises, Government Recurrent):** 27,620—Government transfers to enterprises. Domestic government interest payments as reported for FY 1992 and FY 1993 in Table 11 of *Tanzania—Statistical Appendix* of the IMF Staff Country Report No. 96/2, adjusted in accordance with the applied final government consumption figure of the macrosam.

22. **(Government Investment, Government Recurrent):** 34,957—Government investment account deficit. Nonforeign-financed government spending within the development budget to balance the government investment account of the macrosam.

23. **(ROW, Government Recurrent):** 24,250—Government transfers to the ROW. Foreign interest payments by the government as reported for FY 1992 and FY 1993 in Table 11 of *Tanzania—Statistical Appendix* of the IMF Staff Country Report No. 96/2, adjusted in accordance with the applied final government consumption figure of the macrosam.

24. **(Capital Account, Government Recurrent):** –17,568—Government deficit. Total government deficit of recurrent government budget as a residual of total government revenue (Government Recurrent, Total) minus government consumption (Commodities, Government Recurrent), government transfers

to enterprises, the balancing position of the government investment account, and government transfers to the ROW.

25. **(Commodities, Government Investment)**: 52,521—Gross fixed capital formation (GFCF) by the government. Total GFCF by the government corresponding to government investment under the developing budget as in Table 5 of the statistical annex of Economic Research Bureau (1996).[178] The figure is adjusted to match the higher total GFCF applied in the macrosam.

26. **(Activities, ROW)**: 165,682—Exports of goods and services. Total exports of goods and services at cost, insurance, freight (C.I.F.) prices as in Table 6(b) of URT (1997), adjusted by the remaining 25 percent share of the *unrecorded trade and statistical discrepancy* (TSh 19,023 million).

27. **(Households, ROW)**: 96,755—Remittances. Net direct transfers to households from abroad as computed from Table 4.4 of BOT, *Economic Bulletin,* 1997, 1st quarter, Dar es Salaam, with respect to the relative household share of transfer inflows. This figure probably contains a large share of grants to nongovernmental organizations, which are assumed to be part of the institution category of households.

28. **(Government Recurrent, ROW)**: 172,671—Transfers to government from abroad. Net direct transfers to government from abroad as computed from Table 4.4 of BOT, *Economic Bulletin,* 1997, 1st quarter, Dar es Salaam, with respect to the relative government share of transfer inflows. This figure primarily represents foreign aid with a considerable grant component, including recurrent government budget support.

29. **(Government Investment, ROW)**: 17,564—Other transfers to government. Net official sector capital flows in U.S. dollars as in Table 23 of the reference tables in Economist Intelligence Unit (1996), applying the exchange rate reported in this publication.

30. **(Capital Account, ROW)**: 188,440—Net capital inflow. Net capital inflow from the ROW—not elsewhere specified in the ROW column—as a residual to balance the macroeconomic reference database and the implicitly generated current account.

31. **(Commodities, Capital Account)**: 419,532—Net private investment. Total private investment as in the supplementary data to the *Revised National Accounts of Tanzania 1987–96,* including *changes in inventory* as in the same data set, and adjusted for government investment as described in paragraph 24 (Commodities, Government Investment).

---

[178] Because in this database parastatals are not explicitly distinguished from private sector activities, the GFCF of parastatals, as stated in *Tanzanian Economic Trends,* is combined with the private sector GFCF, not with the GFCF financed by the government.

Documentation of Data Entries in the Microsam

Following the documentation in the macrosam chapter, each corresponding cell entry, vector, or submatrix of the microsam is discussed. Data sources are presented that provide clean data, raw data, or structural information for data adjustments. Decisions for data manipulations are justified in this section as well.

1.   **(Commodities, Activities):** To derive the intermediate demand matrix of the microsam, normalized input-output coefficients—coefficients of the intermediate demand subcolumns add up to one—apply to sectoral intermediate demand figures, given by the supplementary data to the *Revised National Accounts for Tanzania 1987–96*. The applied coefficients are adjusted values of the 1976 input-output table of Tanzania, the most recent available source of information. Consequently, the general production technology and economic structure assumed to characterize the Tanzanian economy is that of 1976. It provides a starting point ("prior") for the protosam and determines the estimation of the final technology of the microsam.

Because the 1976 input-output table covers domestically produced intermediates only and contains tax and subsidy information that does not match with the economic characteristics of the early 1990s, the coefficients have to be adjusted. Because the structure of subsidies changed completely between the mid-1970s and the early 1990s[179] the respective coefficients are netted out and subsidies are removed from the system.

An import matrix is developed to adjust the (domestic) intermediate demand coefficients for imported intermediate demands. Control totals for total imports per commodity are provided in the *Revised National Accounts for Tanzania 1987–96* (see also paragraph 7 [ROW, Commodities]). Shares of investment demand (capital goods), household and government demand (consumer

---

[179] In 1976 the share of subsidies in "Taxes on Production and Imports" was 5.6 percent and in 1990 only 1.4 percent (URT 1996b).

goods), and intermediate demand for imports are derived from Table 3.5 of the most recent World Bank country report on Tanzania (World Bank 1996b). On the basis of the domestically produced intermediate demand for each commodity with (strictly positive) imported intermediate demand, row coefficients are calculated and applied to imported intermediate demand totals. Imported intermediate demand is further adjusted using information from Balsvik and Brendemoen (1994), who compile intermediate demand use of imports for some crops on the basis of the annual crop reviews by the Marketing Development Bureau. The derived imported intermediate demand matrix is eventually combined with the matrix of domestically produced intermediate demands to obtain the "total" coefficients.

Because the *Revised National Accounts for Tanzania 1987–96* provide information on total intermediate demand of sector products,[180] row coefficients are calculated from the intermediate demands and applied to these control row totals. This technique ensures the consistency of sectoral production and absorption data and guarantees the correct magnitude of the total intermediate demand matrix.

The derived structure of the intermediate input matrix is translated into final (sub)column coefficients that can be applied to sectoral figures for total intermediate demand by sector. As the supplemental information on the latest national accounts publication distinguishes total expenditure on inputs and value-added, the two subtechnologies—intermediate use and generation of value-added—can be applied separately rather than applying the entire sector technology to the respective gross output.

For sectors with indirect taxes (Domestic Taxes, Activities), the intermediate demand entries of the respective column entries are reduced relatively, so that the sum of intermediate demand and indirect taxes meet the information in the *Revised National Accounts of Tanzania 1987–96*.

2. **(Factors, Activities):** Information on GDP at f.c. per sector is provided by supplementary data to the *Revised National Accounts of Tanzania 1987–96*. Data from the Labour Force Survey 1990/91 is used to calculate the value-added paid to the different labor factors. First, the survey provides detailed information on sectoral employment for nine different labor categories—for urban and rural areas, respectively—that have been aggregated to the five categories used in the microsam. Second, the survey differentiates primary and secondary occupations, including their respective average weekly working time in hours. Third, the survey provides average monthly wages for the different labor categories for rural and urban areas.[181] This employment and

---

[180] This is the intermediate use of a sectoral output by all sectors of the economy—for example, total intermediate use of cotton by all productive activities including cotton itself—and not the total intermediate use of inputs by the cotton sector.

[181] Many economic activities in low-income countries like Tanzania are carried out as secondary occupations by employees who either have a primary paid job or carry out an unpaid (mostly self-employed) main activity, such as farming.

wage information is used to compute a sector-specific spread of total labor value-added among the different labor categories. Subsequently, the sum of value-added to land and capital for each sector is calculated as the residual of sectoral GDP at f.c. and total labor value-added. Since information on the spread between land and capital value-added is unavailable, 40 percent is arbitrarily allocated to land and 60 percent to capital, following general practice in the literature.[182]

3. **(Domestic Taxes, Activities):** Indirect taxes related to the production process are calculated through their respective input-output coefficients.[183] The coefficients are applied to the sectoral gross output figures given by supplementary data to the *Revised National Accounts of Tanzania 1987–96* and subsequently adjusted to match total other indirect taxes as specified in the macrosam.

4.a. **(Activities, Commodities):** The entries of the main diagonal of this matrix represent the domestic supply of domestically produced goods. The off-diagonal entries are zero for all commodity accounts, because the present SAM does not include multicommodity-producing activities or multiple activities producing the same commodity. In other words, each activity produces exactly one good, which is exclusively supplied to its commodity market.[184] However, three marketing margin accounts are introduced to capture the transportation and marketing costs related to each commodity. As Tanzania's national accounts statistics categorize transportation and marketing costs for all commodities with the retail sector, the share of final demand for the retail sector is about 14 percent of total final demand. Consequently, each commodity is associated with a certain amount of transportation and marketing costs of the retail sector for its "delivery" to the destination of its final demand. Therefore, each commodity account buys its relevant transport and marketing costs out of the three marketing margin accounts, depending on its shares of domestic, imported, or exported production. Simultaneously, all final consumption and investment demands are adjusted for these additional costs and, in turn, the final demand for retail (the commodity CTRAD) is eliminated. To balance the three marketing margin accounts, their totals are bought out of the activity account *Trade* (ATRAD). The remaining flow from the commodity trade to the activity

---

[182] Information on the primary factor splits for agriculture derived from the Global Trade Analysis Project of the Center for Global Trade Analysis, Purdue University, indicates a 15:60:25 split of agricultural value-added between land, labor, and capital for SSA countries (Republic of South Africa and Republic of Zimbabwe). Consequently, a 40:60 split of nonlabor value-added between land and capital appears reasonably close to the reported 15:25, this is 37.5:62.5, split of the Global Trade Analysis Project data.

[183] As mentioned earlier, the applied coefficients are adjusted for their respective subsidy coefficients; these were substantial shares of gross output in 1976, but accounted for only 1 percent of GDP at f.c. in 1990.

[184] The only exception is the activity account for *Tourism,* which does not have a commodity account because all of its produce is exported and none enters the domestic market.

trade account (ATRAD, CTRAD) represents the part of gross output in trade that enters the domestic market for intermediate demand. The supply of domestic produce entries is obtained by subtracting OHC and exports— as described in paragraphs 10 and 26 below—from total sectoral gross output (obtained from previous calculations).

4.b.   **(Commodities, Commodities):** All commodity accounts showing marketing margins for domestic produce and/or imports buy their marketing margin values out of the respective marketing margin commodity accounts (CCOMD and CCOMI).[185] That way final household and investment demand for trade is eliminated and each commodity is associated with its own marketing margin.

5.   **(Domestic Taxes, Commodities):** Sales taxes are directly adopted from supplementary data to the *Revised National Accounts of Tanzania 1987–96.*

6.   **(Tariffs, Commodities):** Tariffs are directly adopted from supplementary data to the *Revised National Accounts of Tanzania 1987–96.*

7.   **(ROW, Commodities):** Import values for all 55 commodities are obtained from sectoral information in the supplementary data to the *Revised National Accounts of Tanzania 1987–96* and adjusted for the import control total given by Table 6(a) of the *Revised National Accounts of Tanzania 1987–96.* The import control total is increased by 75 percent of the *Unrecorded Trade and Statistical Discrepancy* figure reported in this table.[186] Further adjustments are made for the sectors *Machinery Equipment* and *Other Manufacturing.* The two sectors show higher exports than gross output figures, which implies negative domestic supply of domestic produce. This phenomenon indicates re-exports of imported goods because the economy exports more than its produced gross output. The two export figures are netted out, and their respective import figures are lowered by the equivalent values.

8.   **(Households, Factors):** Labor value-added is distributed to households according to the calculations described in paragraph 2 (Factors, Activities). The information on rural and urban employment allows the distribution of labor value-added to rural and urban households. Farm households (*HHRFA*

---

[185] The marketing margin flow for exports is considered under paragraph 1 (Commodities, Activities), because activities buy the marketing margin flow associated with their export component out of the marketing margin account "CCOME." This practice follows the assumption that exports are reported in F.O.B. prices including their respective marketing margin. As exports (at F.O.B. prices, including marketing margins) are bought out of activities (Activities, ROW), but the activity columns usually report on gross output at farm/factory gate prices (excluding marketing margins), the marketing margins for exports have to be incorporated somewhere in the production process (the column technology). However, this practice violates the clean definition of the column sum being sectoral gross output, because the net gross output figure of each column is adjusted by its respective export marketing margin flow. Consequently, gross output for Trade (ATRAD) is adjusted for the sum of all export marketing margin flows, and the ATRAD column entries are recalculated.

[186] The remaining 25 percent is deducted from total exports.

and *HHUFA*) are assumed to be endowed with the factor *Farming Labor* (*RURA*), and nonfarm households (*HHRNF* and *HHUNF*) are endowed with the remaining four labor factors. Consequently, household shares for each labor factor are calculated and applied to the respective total value-added by factor. Table C.1 presents the obtained distribution of labor value-added among household groups for the microsam after applying the cross-entropy balancing approach. Note that *Professional Labor* (*UPRO*) value-added decreases by 50 percent of *Net Factor Income Paid Abroad* as specified in paragraph 10 (ROW, Factors).[187] Furthermore, distribution of *Agricultural Labor* (*RURA*) value-added to nonfarm households (*HHUNF* and *HHRNF*) results from *Total Agricultural Own-Household Consumption* of the respective household.[188] Total land value-added is distributed to rural and urban farm households according to their relative labor income.

9. **(Enterprises, Factors):** Total capital value-added—net of 50 percent of *Net Factor Income Paid Abroad*—is transferred to enterprises for further distribution. The enterprise account represents all productive enterprises in the economy and acts as a collection point for total capital value-added. Besides value-added capital, the enterprise account receives transfers from the government. On the expenditure side, the enterprise account pays corporate taxes to the government and enterprise savings to the capital account, and distributes the remaining "operating surplus" to households (as described in paragraphs 14 to 16).

10. **(ROW, Factors):** Total net factor income is paid abroad, as described in paragraph 10 of the macrosam documentation. Because there is no information on which part of this factor payment is related to labor or capital, one-half of it is netted out from factor payments, *Professional*

Table C.1—Distribution of labor value-added (million TSh and percent)

Household group	UPRO	UWCO	UBCO	UNSK	RURA	Total	Percent
HHUFA	0	0	0	0	102,358	102,358	12.1
HHUNF	62,914	58,158	111,930	52,966	5,721	291,689	34.6
HHRFA	0	0	0	0	402,218	402,218	47.7
HHRNF	20,809	4,595	10,255	4,254	7,519	47,432	5.6

Source: Author.

---

[187] The remaining 50 percent of *Net Factor Income Paid Abroad* is deducted from the operating surplus paid from enterprises to households.

[188] The nonfarm households are assumed to have no *Agricultural Labor* endowment and, therefore, should not be considered in its value-added distribution. Nevertheless, most of the nonfarm households—although not commercially involved in agriculture—carry out some noncommercial farming for OHC, which is reported by the Household Budget Survey 1991/92. This production volume is also assumed to be considered in the informal sector GDP reported by the *Revised National Accounts of Tanzania 1987–96* and, as such, is considered part of value-added to *Agricultural Labor*.

Labor—considering the relative shares of different households—and one-half of it is netted out from factor payments, *Capital*.

11.   (**Activities, Households**): The disaggregation of *Own-Household Consumption* is calculated according to the respective household shares in *Own-Produced Food* as provided by the Household Budget Survey 1991/92. The survey not only reports on total household shares of nonmonetary food expenditures but also on the commodity distribution of these expenditures for each household. The sum of OHC and final household consumption must match the sector control total for total consumption for each household given by the supplementary national accounts data. Consequently, sector-specific coefficients are applied to these control totals, which are calculated on the basis of first estimates for the distribution of own and final household consumption.

OHC is a direct demand by private households for output of activities. The goods are produced by activities, but not fed through the commodity accounts to enter the domestic markets for intermediate or final consumption because OHC is assumed to be valued at producer prices, with no trade margins. In other words, OHC reduces sectoral gross output supplied to the domestic commodity market (as described under paragraph 4 [Activities, Commodities]).

The consideration of OHC within the SAM framework captures agricultural subsistence demand, an extremely important feature of the Tanzanian economy. Incorporating OHC into the SAM is important for policy analysis of its effects on household income, effective consumption, and welfare. Usually, this kind of transaction is netted out within the *Production Consumption Process* of a *Household Production Unit* and appears neither on the income nor the expenditure side. Consequently, reported income of small-scale farmers is often underestimated.

12.   (**Commodities, Households**): Total private household consumption reported in the *Revised National Accounts of Tanzania 1987–1996,* and adjusted for OHC, is distributed among the four household groups according to (1) the sectoral distribution of total household consumption in 1992 given by the supplementary national accounts data. and (2) the relative commodity distribution among households given by the Household Budget Survey 1991/92. As described in the previous paragraph, the distribution of final household consumption is calculated in connection with household spending on OHC. The coefficients derived from the first estimates of own and final household consumption are applied to the respective sector control totals. Because the relative sector spread of total household consumption is distorted by this procedure, the relative shares of total consumption expenditure among households in the microsam differ from their shares in the Household Budget Survey 1991/92, as is shown in Table C.2.

13.   (**Government Recurrent, Households**): Total individual income taxes, as computed in paragraph 13 of the macrosam documentation, are distributed among the four household groups according to their relative labor income.

149

Table C.2—Final household consumption (million TSh and percent)

	HHUFA	HHUNF	HHRFA	HHRNF	Total
Household budget survey 1991/92	136,563	197,244	348,782	27,527	710,116
Percent	19.2	27.8	49.1	3.9	100
Microsam	155,260	254,857	455,108	47,989	913,214
Percent	17.0	27.9	49.8	5.3	100

Source: Author.

Each labor type is taxed with a specific rate. In 1992 the Tanzanian income tax scheme ranged from 0 to 30 percent of monthly taxable income, and permitted several deductions. The ratio of total individual income taxes to total labor value-added shows an average income tax rate of only 2.1 percent for the economy as a whole. The enormous difference between this de facto average income tax rate and the nominal income tax rates is partly due to the high share in the economy of small-scale agriculture and informal sector activities, which are not taxed at all. Furthermore, extremely low administrative and technical standards affect the efficiency of tax collection. As a result, the substantial differences between the de facto and nominal income tax rates are not surprising.

A tax rate scheme is developed on the basis of the *Monthly Income Distribution of Government Employees According to the Individual Tax Rate Brackets* provided by the Tanzanian Income Tax Department. Although the sample contains government employees only (and thus does not represent the entire formal labor force) and the data relate to 1996 incomes, it delivers persuasive evidence for an extremely narrow range of effective income tax rates over all income brackets. For an aggregation of all nine income brackets to three brackets that represent the SAM labor categories, namely (1) professionals, (2) white and blue collar workers, and (3) unskilled and rural labor, the effective average income tax rates are 3.7, 3.4, and 1.1 percent, respectively. To guarantee a gradual progression across the three income groups in the microsam, tax rates of 5, 3, and 1 percent are applied to the respective income flows in the microsam. Finally, these rates are adjusted to match total individual income tax revenue of TSh 16,656 million for FY 1992. After the adjustment of the applied tax rates and the balancing procedure, the final income tax rates for the four household groups are 0.6, 1.0, 1.5, and 2.5 percent, respectively. Table C.3 shows individual household rates, values, and shares of total income taxes.

14.   **(Capital Account, Households):** Saving shares for different household groups are derived from nonconsumption expenditure information in Appendix 6 of the Household Budget Survey 1991/92. Table C.4 presents the saving shares and respective values for the four household groups after the balancing procedure.

150

Table C.3—Individual income tax (rates, values, and shares per household group in million TSh and percentage)

	HHUFA	HHUNF	HHRFA	HHRNF	Total/ Average
Rate (percent)	0.7	1.0	2.3	2.9	1.6
Value in TSh	1,258	2,845	11,011	1,542	16,656
Share (percent)	7.6	17.1	66.1	9.3	100.0

Source: Author.

15.   **(Households, Enterprises):** The distribution of operating surplus to households is calculated according to group-specific, income-expenditure deficits that result after all household expenditures and all household incomes, except capital income and remittances, are taken into account. The operating surplus distributed to households is calculated as a residual of total enterprise receipts net of enterprise savings and corporate taxes.

16.   **(Government Recurrent, Enterprises):** As the microsam contains only one representative enterprise—as in the macrosam—no changes occur in total corporate taxes being paid by enterprises to the recurrent government account of the order of TSh 65,054 million as described earlier.

17.   **(Capital Account, Enterprises):** Again, as the microsam contains only one enterprise account, no distribution of the macrosam figure for enterprise savings is necessary. After the balancing procedure, however, total enterprise savings equal TSh 195,335 million.

18.   **(Government Recurrent, Domestic Taxes):** Because no difference exists in the function of the intermediate tax collection accounts in the macrosam and the microsam, the flow from the intermediate tax account *Domestic Taxes* to the government account (representing the sum of all domestically collected taxes as described under paragraphs 3 and 5) is the same as described in the macrosam section.

19.   **(Government Recurrent, Tariffs):** The same argument applies to the *Tariffs* account. The flow of total collected tariffs, as described in paragraph 6, from the intermediate tax account *Tariffs* to the government account works in the same way as described in the macrosam section.

Table C.4—Household savings (rates, values, and shares per household group in million TSh and percent)

	HHUFA	HHUNF	HHRFA	HHRNF	Total/ Average
Rate (percent)	19.0	11.7	2.0	7.0	8.4
Value in TSh	36,476	33,923	9,443	3,603	83,445
Share (percent)	43.7	40.7	11.3	4.3	100.0

Source: Author.

20.   **(Commodities, Government Recurrent):** Final government consumption follows the supplementary national accounts information and consists of government demand for *Public Administration* only. This specification assumes none or little private demand for *Public Administration*[189] and that government consumes the major share and provides it to the public.[190]

21.   **(Enterprises, Government Recurrent):** Government transfers to enterprises as specified in the macrosam section remain a single-cell entry and are fixed at their initial value of TSh 27,620 million after the balancing procedure.

22.   **(Government Investment, Government Recurrent):** Government spending on the development budget remains one entry as specified in the macrosam counting for TSh 34,957 million after the cross-entropy.

23.   **(ROW, Government Recurrent):** Government spending on foreign interest payments remains a single entry in the microsam as well and remains at TSh 24,250 million after the balancing procedure.

24.   **(Capital Account, Government Recurrent):** Government saving in the microsam is calculated as the residual between total government revenue (that is the row total of the government account) and final government consumption, government transfers to enterprises, and payments to the government investment account as described in paragraphs 20 to 22. Because the macroeconomic control totals of all government revenue categories and the macroeconomic control totals for all other government expenditure categories are constrained during the balancing procedure, the government deficit remains at its initial value of TSh –17,586 million. However, if the government recurrent account payment to the government investment account were eliminated, the government recurrent account would show a surplus of TSh 17,389 million and the government investment account would show a deficit of TSh –34,957 million.

25.   **(Commodities, Government Investment):** GFCF by the government as specified in the macrosam, which remains as a single entry in the microsam, representing demand for construction at the same level as initialized.

26.   **(Commodities, ROW):** Export values for all 56 activities are obtained from sectoral information of the supplementary data to the *Revised National Accounts of Tanzania 1987–96* and adjusted for the export control total given by Table 6(a) of the *Revised National Accounts of Tanzania 1987–96*. The export control total is reduced by 25 percent of the *Unrecorded Trade and Statistical Discrepancy* figure reported in Table 6(a) as

---

[189] The SAM for Tanzania incorporates education and health services in *Public Administration*. The related private demand equals 2.5 percent of total government demand for *Public Administration*.

[190] There are two general practices to deal with public administration and government services. Either the government demands a bundle of commodities and provides these items to the public, or the public administration activity contains this consumption bundle as part of its intermediate demand. In the latter case, the government has no final demand for any other item than public services produced under the public administration activity.

mentioned in paragraph 7. Furthermore, the sectoral adjustments for *Machinery Equipment* and *Other Manufacturing* as described in paragraph 7 are taken into account.

27. **(Households, ROW):** Remittances from abroad to the four household groups are distributed according to their income-expenditure deficits as described for the distribution of operating surplus in paragraph 15 and remain at their initial level.

28. **(Government Recurrent, ROW):** Net direct transfers to the government from abroad as described in the macrosam section remain at their initial level.

29. **(Government Investment, ROW):** Capital inflows from abroad supporting the government development budget as described in the macrosam section remain at their initial level.

30. **(Capital Account, ROW):** Net capital inflows from the ROW as described in the macrosam section change to TSh 158,320 million after the balancing procedure.

31. **(Commodities, Capital Account):** Final private investment demand per sector as reported in the supplementary data to the *Revised National Accounts of Tanzania 1987–96* net of government investment in *Construction* (considered under the government investment account). As opposed to the procedure in the macrosam section, the values represent GFCF only and are net of changes in inventories, which are considered under a separate account as specified in paragraph 33 (Commodities, Change in Inventory).

32. **(Change in Inventory, Capital Account):** The flow represents the balancing of the *Change in Inventory* account through the *Capital Account*. The *Change in Inventory* account is not an explicit feature of the macrosam in which GFCF and changes in inventory are combined. However, for later modeling purposes, these two flows are separated in the microsam.

33. **(Commodities, Change in Inventory):** Change in inventory demand per sector is as reported in the supplementary data to the *Revised National Accounts of Tanzania 1987–96,* totaling TSh 4,146 million.

1992 Social Accounting Matrix for Tanzania

Table D.1—1992 social accounting matrix for Tanzania

Account	Code	ACOTT	ASISA	ATEA	ACOFF	ATOBA	ACASH	AMAIZ	AWHEA	APADD	ASORG	AOCER	ABEAN	ACASS	AROOT	AOILS	ASUGA
		ACTIVITIES															
Cotton	ACOTT																
Sisal	ASISA																
Tea	ATEA																
Coffee	ACOFF																
Tobacco	ATOBA																
Cashew nuts	ACASH																
Maize	AMAIZ																
Wheat	AWHEA																
Paddy	APADD																
Sorghum	ASORG																
Other cereal	AOCER																
Beans	ABEAN																
Cassava	ACASS																
Other roots and tubers	AROOT																
Oil seeds	AOILS																
Sugar	ASUGA																
Other horticulture	AOHOR																
Other crops	AOCRO																
Livestock	ALIVE																
Fishery	AFISH																
Forestry and hunting	AFOHU																
Mining	AMINE																
Meat and dairy products	AMEAT																
Other processed food	AFOOD																
Grain milling	AGRAI																
Beverages and tobacco	ABEVT																
Textiles	ATEXT																
Wearing apparel	AWEAR																
Leather products	ALEAT																
Wood and furniture	AWOOD																
Paper and publishing	APAPE																
Chemicals	ACHEM																
Fertilizer and pesticides	AFERT																
Fuel	AFUEL																
Rubber products	ARUBB																
Plastic products	APLAS																
Glass products	AGLAS																
Cement, clay, etc.	ACEME																
Iron and steel	AIRON																
Manufactured metal products	AFMPR																
Machinery equipment	AMAEQ																
Electrical equipment	AELEQ																
Transport equipment	ATREQ																
Other manufactures	AOMAN																
Electricity	AELEC																
Water	AWATE																
Construction	ACNST																
Wholesale and retail	ATRAD																
Tourism	ATOUR																
Hotels and restaurants	AHORE																
Transport and communication	ATR_C																
Financial institutions	AFI_I																
Real estate	AREAL																
Business services	ABUSI																
Public administration	APUBA																
Other private services	AOSER																
Cotton	CCOTT																
Sisal	CSISA		0.08														
Tea	CTEA																
Coffee	CCOFF				0.71												
Tobacco	CTOBA					0.11											
Cashew nuts	CCASH																
Maize	CMAIZ							17.83									
Wheat	CWHEA								2.02								
Paddy	CPADD									10.73							
Sorghum	CSORG										3.12						
Other cereal	COCER											1.03					
Beans	CBEAN												6.98				
Cassava	CCASS													0.80			
Other roots and tubers	CROOT														0.96		
Oil seeds	COILS															2.92	
Sugar	CSUGA																9.45
Other horticulture	COHOR																
Other crops	COCRO																
Livestock	CLIVE					0.73											1.04
Fishery	CFISH					0.81											1.19
Forestry and hunting	CFOHU					0.59											0.90
Mining	CMINE																
Meat and dairy products	CMEAT																
Other processed food	CFOOD																
Grain milling	CGRAI																
Beverages and tobacco	CBEVT																
Textiles	CTEXT	1.29			0.06	0.39	0.67	6.44	0.30	0.14	0.04	0.01	0.09	0.01	0.01	0.03	
Wearing apparel	CWEAR																
Leather products	CLEAT																
Wood and furniture	CWOOD																
Paper and publishing	CPAPE					0.22											
Chemicals	CCHEM	6.31		1.95	1.09	0.70	0.60	6.34		0.91	0.05	0.02	0.11	0.01	0.02	0.04	24.52
Fertilizer and pesticides	CFERT	1.36		0.42	0.24	0.15	0.13	1.38		0.20	0.01	0.00	0.02	0.00	0.00	0.01	1.76
Fuel	CFUEL			0.11	0.01				0.81		0.10						1.25
Rubber products	CRUBB																
Plastic products	CPLAS																
Glass products	CGLAS																
Cement, clay, etc.	CCEME																
Iron and steel	CIRON																
Manufactured metal products	CFMPR		0.31								0.07						2.34
Machinery equipment	CMAEQ		0.05								0.01						0.31
Electrical equipment	CELEQ																
Transport equipment	CTREQ		0.23	0.02	0.00												0.04
Other manufactures	COMAN																
Electricity	CELEC		1.64														
Water	CWATE		0.50														
Construction	CCNST																
Marketing margin export	CCOME			1.70	1.26	0.34	1.13	0.03					0.19			0.67	
Marketing margin domestic	CCOMD																
Marketing margin import	CCOMI																
Wholesale and retail	CTRAD	0.16	0.30	0.34	0.05	0.07	0.00	0.57		0.40	0.00	0.00	0.01	0.00	0.00	0.00	3.79
Hotels and restaurants	CHORE																
Transport and communication	CTR_C	0.64		0.07	0.11	0.22	0.05	3.88		3.78	0.03	0.01	0.07	0.01	0.01	0.03	14.98
Financial institutions	CFI_I	0.86	1.23	1.29	0.21	0.12	0.00	0.08		0.09	0.00	0.00	0.01	0.00	0.00	0.00	2.43
Real estate	CREAL																
Business services	CBUSI																
Public administration	CPUBA																
Other private services	COSER																
Urban professional labor	UPRO																
Urban white collar labor	UWCO																
Urban blue collar labor	UBCO																
Urban unskilled labor	UNSK																
Rural labor	RURA	8.41	0.66	2.27	5.16	5.58	6.07	101.38	2.58	22.86	8.16	1.89	34.24	18.30	21.79	19.18	16.98
Land	LAND	1.11	0.09	0.28	0.63	0.73	0.79	5.09	0.28	1.28	0.66	0.15	2.84	1.49	1.78	1.57	1.30
Capital	CAPITAL	0.75	0.06	0.19	0.42	0.49	0.53	3.87	0.19	0.89	0.45	0.10	1.97	1.01	1.21	1.07	0.82
Enterprises	ENTR																
Urban farm households	HHUFA																
Urban nonfarm households	HHUNF																
Rural farm households	HHRFA																
Rural nonfarm households	HHRNF																
Government recurrent	GOVR																
Government investment	GOVI																
Indirect taxes	ITAX					1.65											
Tariffs	TTAX																
Capital account	KACCOUN																
Change in stocks	DST																
Rest of the world	WORLD																
TOTAL		20.90	5.24	8.53	9.94	12.91	9.99	146.90	9.55	41.44	12.53	3.23	46.52	21.64	25.79	25.52	83.10

(continued)

155

Table D.1—Continued

	AOHOR	AOCRO	ALIVE	AFISH	AFOHU	AMINE	AMEAT	AFOOD	AGRAI	ABEVT	ATEXT	AWEAR	ALEAT	AWOOD	APAPE	ACHEM	AFERT	AFUEL	ARUBB	APLAS
														ACTIVITIES						
ACOTT																				
ASISA																				
ATEA																				
ACOFF																				
ATOBA																				
ACASH																				
AMAIZ																				
AWHEA																				
APADD																				
ASORG																				
AOCER																				
ABEAN																				
ACASS																				
AROOT																				
AOILS																				
ASUGA																				
AOHOR																				
AOCRO																				
ALIVE																				
AFISH																				
AFOHU																				
AMINE																				
AMEAT																				
AFOOD																				
AGRAI																				
ABEVT																				
ATEXT																				
AWEAR																				
ALEAT																				
AWOOD																				
APAPE																				
ACHEM																				
AFERT																				
AFUEL																				
ARUBB																				
APLAS																				
AGLAS																				
ACEME																				
AIRON																				
AFMPR																				
AMAEQ																				
AELEQ																				
ATREQ																				
AOMAN																				
AELEC																				
AWATE																				
ACNST																				
ATRAD																				
ATOUR																				
AHORE																				
ATR_C																				
AFI_I																				
AREAL																				
ABUSI																				
APUBA																				
AOSER																				
CCOTT													3.54							
CSISA													2.34							
CTEA							0.74													
CCOFF							1.52													
CTOBA										11.24										
CCASH							1.24													
CMAIZ									34.51	9.18										
CWHEA							0.93		7.11											
CPADD									23.04											
CSORG																				
COCER										1.26										
CBEAN																				
CCASS																				
CROOT																				
COILS							1.14													
CSUGA							24.31			11.01					0.13					
COHOR	7.41						5.77			11.40										
COCRO		2.13					0.81		6.37											
CLIVE			6.72				1.94		1.36				1.92							
CFISH				5.45			2.19													
CFOHU					2.29	0.10	1.17		2.41					4.72	0.79	0.12				
CMINE			0.04	0.03	0.01										0.33	0.01				
CMEAT			0.81	0.64	0.26								0.43							
CFOOD			0.44	0.35	0.15															
CGRAI			1.89	1.48	0.60															
CBEVT			0.88	0.68	0.27									0.00	0.02				0.00	
CTEXT	0.09	0.03	0.37	0.29	0.12	0.41	1.15				0.74									
CWEAR												3.29								
CLEAT													0.13							
CWOOD							0.99		2.00					1.26	0.78	0.03				
CPAPE						0.23	0.89	0.63	4.96	1.28				1.27	0.49	0.02	0.00		0.59	0.12
CCHEM	0.11	0.03				0.19		0.05		0.09		4.35	0.18	1.75	1.05	3.20	0.01			
CFERT	0.02	0.01																		
CFUEL			0.01	0.00	0.00	0.29	0.20	0.15	1.31	0.28	0.03	0.12	0.01	0.05	0.03	0.05	0.00	0.11	0.23	0.05
CRUBB														0.06					3.18	
CPLAS							0.71	1.45	0.06	0.25	0.01	0.10	0.06	0.86	0.03					2.17
CGLAS							0.25	0.52							0.03	0.29	0.01			
CCEME																				
CIRON																				
CFMPR			0.10	0.08	0.03		1.59	1.14	1.32	2.32	0.52	0.35	0.10	1.00	0.09	0.74	0.03	0.00	0.14	0.03
CMAEQ			0.01	0.01	0.01		0.21	0.16	0.31	0.31	0.09	0.02	0.14	0.11	0.00	0.00			0.36	0.08
CELEQ							0.58	0.39	3.17	0.83	0.19	0.92	0.04	0.35	0.22	0.27	0.01	0.01	0.36	
CTREQ			0.05	0.04	0.02		0.15	0.10	0.08	0.15	0.08	0.02	0.09	0.01	0.04	0.02	0.03	0.00	0.00	0.21
COMAN							0.04					0.35	0.08	0.09	0.00	0.04	0.03	0.00	0.04	0.01
CELEC						0.97	1.56	1.07	7.55	2.06	0.48	2.21	0.10	0.89	0.54	0.66	0.02	0.02	0.67	0.14
CWATE						0.28	0.45	0.30		0.56	0.17	0.64	0.03	0.26	0.16	0.20	0.01	0.01		0.20
CCNST			0.10	0.01										0.05						
CCOME	0.53	0.37	0.07			0.18	0.09	0.30		0.09	1.54	6.79	0.46	1.18	0.25	0.39	0.01		0.04	0.02
CCOMD																				
CCOMI																				
CTRAD	0.01	0.00	0.51	0.40	0.17	0.60	2.97	1.99	13.01	3.69	0.84	3.72	0.17	1.53	0.95	1.74	0.06	0.02	1.31	0.28
CHORE							1.34	0.96	1.95					0.39	0.73					
CTR_C	0.07	0.02	0.15	0.12	0.05	0.97	2.34	1.57	10.44	2.94	0.24	1.07	0.05	0.44	0.27	0.80	0.03	0.00	1.04	0.22
CFI_I	0.01	0.00	0.47	0.37	0.16		5.37	3.40	18.41	5.77	2.16	8.80	0.46	3.75	2.49	2.30	0.09	1.30	2.62	0.58
CREAL							1.23				2.75	12.80	0.55	3.11	2.93	0.11		1.55	3.26	0.69
CBUSI							0.07	0.41	0.29	0.57	0.14	0.68	0.03	0.27	0.16	0.15	0.01	0.08	0.17	0.04
CPUBA							0.99													
COSER							1.44	0.11	0.50	0.18	1.25	0.02	0.18	0.53	0.02					
UPRO						0.56	0.63	0.38	0.32	0.74	0.17	0.26	0.03	0.62	0.11	0.06	0.00	0.02	0.02	0.01
UWCO						0.20	0.47	0.29	0.25	0.58	0.13	0.20	0.02	0.48	0.09	0.05	0.00	0.04	0.02	0.01
UBCO						29.39	5.11	3.27	2.94	6.61	1.37	2.15	0.21	5.01	0.94	0.47	0.02	0.12	0.19	0.11
UNSK						1.32	0.67	0.40	0.33	0.86	0.18	0.28	0.03	0.67	0.12	0.06	0.00	0.02	0.02	0.01
RURA	68.08	17.32	44.72	33.18	54.40		7.60	4.66	3.60	8.75										
LAND	5.79	1.41	4.46	3.28	5.45															
CAPITAL	4.17	0.96	3.15	2.28	3.88	11.09	12.88	8.16	7.07	16.21	2.87	4.43	0.45	10.41	1.98	2.36	0.09	0.63	0.95	0.57
ENTR																				
HHUFA																				
HHUNF																				
HHRFA																				
HHRNF																				
GOVR																				
GOVI																				
ITAX				0.19	3.98	10.40	0.34	0.45	0.53	0.43	0.18	0.41	0.04	0.35	0.12	0.19	0.00	0.04	0.14	0.03
TTAX																				
KACCOUN																				
DST																				
WORLD	86.30	22.28	64.85	48.87	72.04	59.98	50.92	72.32	146.57	108.14	20.98	55.23	5.47	40.66	15.47	21.07	0.60	4.02	15.41	5.21

(continued)

Table D.1—Continued

	AGLAS	ACEME	AIRON	AFMPR	AMAEQ	AELEQ	ATREQ	AOMAN	AELEC	AWATE	ACNST	ATRAD	ATOUR	AHORE	ATR_C	AFI_I	AREAL	ABUSI	APUBA	AOSER
ACOTT																				
ASISA																				
ATEA																				
ACOFF																				
ATOBA																				
ACASH																				
AMAIZ																				
AWHEA																				
APADD																				
ASORG																				
AOCER																				
ABEAN																				
ACASS																				
AROOT																				
AOILS																				
ASUGA																				
AOHOR																				
AOCRO																				
ALIVE																				
AFISH																				
AFOHU																				
AMINE																				
AMEAT																				
AFOOD																				
AGRAI																				
ABEVT																				
ATEXT																				
AWEAR																				
ALEAT																				
AWOOD																				
APAPE																				
ACHEM																				
AFERT																				
ARUBB																				
APLAS																				
AGLAS																				
ACEME																				
AIRON																				
AFMPR																				
COCRO								0.00						0.25					3.10	
CLIVE														2.37					17.94	
AMAEQ																				
AELEQ																				
ATREQ																				
AOMAN																				
AELEC																				
AWATE																				
ACNST																				
ATRAD																				
ATOUR																				
AHORE																				
ATR_C																				
AFI_I																				
AREAL																				
ABUSI																				
APUBA																				
AOSER																				
CCOTT																				
CSISA								0.00												
CTEA																				
CCOFF																				
CTOBA																				
CCASH																				
CMAIZ																			2.56	
CWHEA																				
CPADD																				
CSORG																				
COCER														0.18						
CBEAN																			10.67	
CCASS																			6.46	
CROOT																			6.04	
COILS																			4.59	
CSUGA																				
COHOR														1.74					18.22	
CFISH														2.69					22.36	
CFOHU											5.63								19.42	
CMINE	1.16	8.06		0.02				0.00			61.93									
CMEAT														0.28					0.45	
CFOOD														0.16					0.25	
CGRAI														0.79						
CBEVT	0.00								0.01				1.88	0.30		0.03	0.01	0.00		0.04
CTEXT				0.66			1.44							0.42		0.39				0.83
CWEAR				0.25			0.55							0.13		0.13				0.37
CLEAT																				
CWOOD	0.12		0.80	0.58	0.13	0.26	1.27	0.03			0.44	3.45	0.15	0.32		0.34	0.07		7.48	0.73
CPAPE	0.08	0.50	0.50	0.37	0.08	0.16	0.80	0.02		0.11	0.12	0.30		0.19	2.66	0.84	0.20	0.04	5.03	0.46
CCHEM				0.17				0.25	0.14	0.15	0.69	2.29	0.12	0.26	0.29		0.02		11.87	2.79
CFERT																			1.55	
CPLAS			0.05	0.04								0.30	0.02		0.02				2.52	
CGLAS	0.41				0.00	0.01					1.30			0.02					0.96	
CCEME		2.84									22.14									
CIRON			20.63	10.64	0.11	0.23	1.30	0.24			13.86									
CFMPR	0.13			0.22	0.10	0.19	0.72				4.17									
CMAEQ	0.02	0.13		0.76	0.69				0.09		0.60	0.12	0.01	0.02	0.02	0.08	0.10	0.01	0.16	0.08
CELEQ	0.05	0.31			1.74	0.27			0.09		1.42	0.30	0.02	0.08	0.01	0.03	0.05	0.01	0.40	0.08
CTREQ	0.03	0.18	0.11		0.07	0.14				0.06	0.96	0.54	0.04	0.09	2.94	0.16	0.05	0.01	1.74	0.20
COMAN	0.00	0.03		0.76	0.69	0.57	0.07		0.02	0.07		0.17	0.03	0.00	0.01	0.01	0.00		0.04	0.01
CELEC	0.09	0.56	0.54	0.40	0.09	0.18	0.30	0.02	1.27		0.44	4.86	0.30	0.68	5.74	1.54	0.40	0.09	7.48	2.89
CWATE	0.03	0.18	0.18	0.13	0.03	0.06	0.09	0.02		7.80	0.12	1.06	0.09	0.20	1.38	0.44	0.12	0.03	1.61	0.83
CCNST	0.01	0.07	0.01						1.57	1.30	1.44	1.22	0.09	0.20	15.73	6.98	1.76	0.39	5.22	1.97
CCOME	0.05	0.41		0.52																
CCOMD																				
CCOMM																				
CTRAD	0.17	1.10	1.17	0.87	0.21	0.41	1.63	0.05	1.26	1.11	2.33	4.94	0.41			0.77	0.22	0.05	7.05	0.65
CHORE	0.07		0.50	0.37	0.08	0.16		0.28	0.02	1.56	0.46	1.82	59.53	6.74	1.39	12.08	0.29	0.09	6.20	0.35
CTR_C	0.14	0.88	0.40	0.30	0.07	0.14	0.47	0.06	0.37	1.36	0.72	4.87	0.68	10.18	20.13	3.93	0.99	0.24	10.63	1.02
CFI_I	0.36	2.15	1.27	0.96	0.24	0.47	1.91	0.06	0.37		1.00	15.42	0.88	2.01	6.63				2.39	3.27
CREAL			1.68																	
CBUSI	0.02	0.15	0.10	0.07	0.01	0.03	0.12	0.00	0.02		0.08	0.97	0.05	0.10	0.40		3.85	0.96	0.16	0.18
CPUBA																				
COSER		0.10	0.60	0.37	0.05	0.11	0.31	0.01	0.29	10.88	0.74	0.02	0.05	0.75	0.71	0.08			3.97	8.97
UPRO	0.02	0.10	0.05	0.11	0.02	0.03	0.04	0.00	1.30	0.22	1.94	27.65	2.05	6.45	10.67	6.04	8.90	1.17	34.25	12.71
UWCO	0.02	0.08	0.04	0.08	0.02	0.03	0.03	0.00	1.71	0.29	0.78	17.89	1.24	3.94	10.99	3.71	5.47	0.71	8.76	4.15
UBCO	0.17	0.85	0.45	0.87	0.15	0.28	0.30	0.04	5.18	0.88	17.81	3.33	0.23	0.74	20.40	0.89	1.30	0.17	7.18	3.05
UNSK	0.02	0.11	0.06	0.11	0.02	0.04	0.04	0.00	0.48	0.08	3.17	25.10	1.78	5.63	7.82	0.67	0.98	0.13	4.36	1.65
RURA																				
LAND																				
CAPITAL	0.84	4.29	2.24	4.40	0.78	1.42	1.52	0.19	23.15	3.99	54.66	121.05	4.83	14.28	50.50	33.86	49.88	6.66	49.68	1.14
ENTR																				
HHUFA																				
HHUNF																				
HHRFA																				
HHRNF																				
GOVR																				
GOVI																				
ITAX	0.03	0.21	0.21	0.19	0.09	0.05	0.09	0.01	0.11		0.34	0.94	0.15		3.82	0.79	0.16	0.02	0.02	0.31
TTAX																				
KACCOUN																				
DST																				
WORLD	4.06	23.49	31.61	24.24	4.05	8.10	15.82	1.11	50.11	18.26	200.96	297.35	26.45	61.46	205.40	73.63	75.69	10.77	295.75	51.13

(continued)

Table D.1—Continued

	COMMODITIES																			
	CCOTT	CSISA	CTEA	CCOFF	CTOBA	CCASH	CMAIZ	CWHEA	CPADD	CSORG	COCER	CBEAN	CCASS	CROOT	COILS	CSUGA	COHOR	COCRO	CLIVE	CFISH
ACOTT	3.54																			
ASISA		2.43																		
ATEA			4.70																	
ACOFF				4.05																
ATOBA					11.71															
ACASH						6.08														
AMAIZ							78.28													
AWHEA								9.47												
APADD									37.29											
ASORG										6.01										
AOCER											2.08									
ABEAN												25.17								
ACASS													6.58							
AROOT														9.63						
AOILS															24.02					
ASUGA																58.75				
AOHOR																	69.27			
AOCRO																		16.86		
ALIVE																			36.81	
AFISH																				43.75
AFOHU																				
AMINE																				
AMEAT																				
AFOOD																				
AGRAI																				
ABEVT																				
ATEXT																				
AWEAR																				
ALEAT																				
AWOOD																				
APAPE																				
ACHEM																				
AFERT																				
AFUEL																				
ARUBB																				
APLAS																				
AGLAS																				
ACEME																				
AIRON																				
AFMPR																				
AMAEQ																				
AELEQ																				
ATREQ																				
AOMAN																				
AELEC																				
AWATE																				
ACNST																				
ATRAD																				
ATOUR																				
AHORE																				
ATR_C																				
AFI_I																				
AREAL																				
ABUSI																				
APUBA																				
AOSER																				
CCOTT																				
CSISA																				
CTEA																				
CCOFF																				
CTOBA																				
CCASH																				
CMAIZ																				
CWHEA																				
CPADD																				
CSORG																				
COCER																				
CBEAN																				
CCASS																				
CROOT																				
COILS																				
CSUGA																				
COHOR																				
COCRO																				
CLIVE																				
CFISH																				
CFOHU																				
CMINE																				
CMEAT																				
CFOOD																				
CGRAI																				
CBEVT																				
CTEXT																				
CWEAR																				
CLEAT																				
CWOOD																				
CPAPE																				
CCHEM																				
CFERT																				
CFUEL																				
CRUBB																				
CPLAS																				
CGLAS																				
CCEME																				
CIRON																				
CFMPR																				
CMAEQ																				
CELEQ																				
CTREQ																				
COMAN																				
CELEC																				
CWATE																				
CCNST																				
CCOME																				
CCOMD			0.37	2.62	3.35	1.86	17.27			4.81	1.01	3.39	2.73	1.62	3.69	17.10	14.61	1.47	9.54	15.48
CCOMI															0.06		0.06		0.27	
CTRAD																				
CHORE																				
CTR_C																				
CFI_I																				
CREAL																				
CBUSI																				
CPUBA																				
COSER																				
UPRO																				
UWCO																				
UBCO																				
UNSK																				
RURA																				
LAND																				
CAPITAL																				
ENTR																				
HHUFA																				
HHUNF																				
HHRFA																				
HHRNF																				
GOVR																				
GOVI																				
ITAX			0.18	0.59			0.11				0.57				0.01		0.00		0.07	
TTAX											0.39				0.02	0.01	0.02		0.08	
KACCOUN																				
DST								0.63			3.94			1.38	0.22		0.19		0.95	
WORLD	3.54	2.43	5.25	7.25	15.07	7.93	95.55	10.20	37.29	10.82	7.99	28.56	9.31	12.64	28.00	75.86	84.15	18.33	47.73	59.22

(continued)

Table D.1—Continued

	COMMODITIES																			
	CFOHU	CMINE	CMEAT	CFOOD	CGRAI	CBEVT	CTEXT	CWEAR	CLEAT	CWOOD	CPAPE	CCHEM	CFERT	CFUEL	CRUBB	CPLAS	CGLAS	CCEME	CIRON	CFMPR
ACOTT																				
ASISA																				
ATEA																				
ACOFF																				
ATOBA																				
ACASH																				
AMAIZ																				
AWHEA																				
APADD																				
ASORG																				
AOCER																				
ABEAN																				
ACASS																				
AROOT																				
AOILS																				
ASUGA																				
AOHOR																				
AOCRO																				
ALIVE																				
AFISH																				
AFOHU	46.89																			
AMINE		58.32																		
AMEAT			50.09																	
AFOOD				29.50																
AGRAI					146.50															
ABEVT						107.59														
ATEXT							7.77													
AWEAR								39.95												
ALEAT									4.28											
AWOOD										33.57										
APAPE											13.97									
ACHEM												21.07								
AFERT													0.60							
AFUEL														4.02						
ARUBB															15.30					
APLAS																5.09				
AGLAS																	3.74			
ACEME																		21.02		
AIRON																			30.38	
AFMPR																				21.12
AMAEQ																				
AELEQ																				
ATREQ																				
AOMAN																				
AELEC																				
AWATE																				
ACNST																				
ATRAD																				
ATOUR																				
AHORE																				
ATR_C																				
AFI_I																				
AREAL																				
ABUSI																				
APUBA																				
AOSER																				
CCOTT																				
CSISA																				
CTEA																				
CCOFF																				
CTOBA																				
CCASH																				
CMAIZ																				
CWHEA																				
CPADD																				
CSORG																				
COCER																				
CBEAN																				
CCASS																				
CROOT																				
COILS																				
CSUGA																				
COHOR																				
COCRO																				
CLIVE																				
CFISH																				
CFOHU																				
CMINE																				
CMEAT																				
CFOOD																				
CGRAI																				
CBEVT																				
CTEXT																				
CWEAR																				
CLEAT																				
CWOOD																				
CPAPE																				
CCHEM																				
CFERT																				
CFUEL																				
CRUBB																				
CPLAS																				
CGLAS																				
CCEME																				
CIRON																				
CFMPR																				
CMAEQ																				
CELEQ																				
CTREQ																				
COMAN																				
CELEC																				
CWATE																				
CCNST																				
CCOME																				
CCOMD	6.95		9.83	2.13	11.25	1.99	0.72	0.16	4.30	1.72	2.58				0.92	0.46	0.47	2.69		2.21
CCOMI	0.12		0.22	5.53	0.45	2.12	0.44	0.60	0.11	1.23	5.18			0.41	1.32	3.99	0.24	0.45		2.62
CTRAD																				
CHORE																				
CTR_C																				
CFI_I																				
CREAL																				
CBUSI																				
CPUBA																				
COSER																				
UPRO																				
UWCO																				
UBCO																				
UNSK																				
RURA																				
LAND																				
CAPITAL																				
ENTR																				
HHUFA																				
HHUNF																				
HHRFA																				
HHRNF																				
GOVR																				
GOVI		0.21	3.53	4.23	0.05	10.96	2.47	1.48	0.53	0.01	0.39	0.86	0.00	0.43	1.01	0.14	0.12	4.61	0.10	1.18
ITAX	0.04	0.53	0.13	2.71	0.16	0.24	2.15	0.63	0.45	0.02	0.29	0.65	0.00	0.34	0.46	0.20	0.07	0.21	0.87	0.59
TTAX																				
KACCOUN																				
DST	0.41	12.66	1.55	40.45	13.99	3.16	14.27	2.82	4.18	0.87	9.22	39.20	6.41	25.74	9.71	30.56	1.76	3.28	29.35	19.59
WORLD	54.40	71.71	65.35	84.56	160.71	133.65	30.76	46.03	10.21	38.89	26.82	69.53	7.01	30.94	28.72	40.44	6.40	32.26	60.69	47.31

(continued)

Table D.1—Continued

	COMMODITIES																	
	CMAEQ	CELEQ	CTREQ	COMAN	CELEC	CWATE	CCNST	CCOME	CCOMD	CCOMI	CTRAD	CHORE	CTR_C	CFI_I	CREAL	CBUSI	CPUBA	COSER
ACOTT																		
ASISA																		
ATEA																		
ACOFF																		
ATOBA																		
ACASH																		
AMAIZ																		
AWHEA																		
APADD																		
ASORG																		
AOCER																		
ABEAN																		
ACASS																		
AROOT																		
AOILS																		
ASUGA																		
AOHOR																		
AOCRO																		
ALIVE																		
AFISH																		
AFOHU																		
AMINE																		
AMEAT																		
AFOOD																		
AGRAI																		
ABEVT																		
ATEXT																		
AWEAR																		
ALEAT																		
AWOOD																		
APAPE																		
ACHEM																		
AFERT																		
AFUEL																		
ARUBB																		
APLAS																		
AGLAS																		
ACEME																		
AIRON																		
AFMPR																		
AMAEQ	4.05																	
AELEQ		8.10																
ATREQ			15.82															
AOMAN				1.11														
AELEC					50.11													
AWATE						18.26												
ACNST							200.96											
ATRAD								18.21	152.82	58.86	67.46							
ATOUR																		
AHORE																		
ATR_C												50.45						
AFI_I													196.26					
AREAL														73.56				
ABUSI															75.69			
APUBA																10.77		
AOSER																	295.59	25.22
CCOTT																		
CSISA																		
CTEA																		
CCOFF																		
CTOBA																		
CCASH																		
CMAIZ																		
CWHEA																		
CPADD																		
CSORG																		
COCER																		
CBEAN																		
CCASS																		
CROOT																		
COILS																		
CSUGA																		
COHOR																		
COCRO																		
CLIVE																		
CFISH																		
CFOHU																		
CMINE																		
CMEAT																		
CFOOD																		
CGRAI																		
CBEVT																		
CTEXT																		
CWEAR																		
CLEAT																		
CWOOD																		
CPAPE																		
CCHEM																		
CFERT																		
CFUEL																		
CRUBB																		
CPLAS																		
CGLAS																		
CCEME																		
CIRON																		
CFMPR																		
CMAEQ																		
CELEQ																		
CTREQ																		
COMAN																		
CELEC																		
CWATE																		
CCNST																		
CCOME																		
CCOMD	0.51	0.97	1.92	0.13														
CCOMI	7.37	5.73	18.08	2.27														
CTRAD																		
CHORE																		
CTR_C																		
CFI_I																		
CREAL																		
CBUSI																		
CPUBA																		
COSER																		
UPRO																		
UWCO																		
UBCO																		
UNSK																		
RURA																		
LAND																		
CAPITAL																		
ENTR																		
HHUFA																		
HHUNF																		
HHRFA																		
HHRNF																		
GOVR																		
GOVI																		
ITAX	2.38	1.41	4.28	0.81	0.18	0.56												0.00
TTAX	1.42	1.12	9.16	0.48														
KACCOUN																		
DST																		
WORLD	55.39	43.00	78.08	16.99								7.38	5.05	25.26	45.73			
	71.13	60.32	127.34	21.79	50.29	18.81	200.96	18.21	152.82	58.86	67.46	57.83	201.31	98.82	121.42	10.77	295.59	25.23

(continued)

Table D.1—Continued

	FACTORS								HOUSEHOLDS				OTHER INSTITUTIONS							
	UPRO	UWCO	UBCO	UNSK	RURA	LAND	CAPITAL	ENTR	HHUFA	HHUNF	HHRFA	HHRNF	GOVR	GOVI	ITAX	TTAX	KACC	DST	WORLD	TOTAL
ACOTT																			17.36	20.90
ASISA																			2.81	5.24
ATEA																			3.83	8.53
ACOFF																			5.89	9.94
ATOBA																			1.20	12.91
ACASH																			3.91	9.99
AMAIZ									3.27	1.71	62.06	1.50							0.08	146.90
AWHEA																			0.08	9.55
APADD									0.15	0.08	3.85	0.07								41.44
ASORG									0.41	0.22	5.67	0.20							0.02	12.53
AOCER									0.20	0.12	0.72	0.09							0.02	3.23
ABEAN									0.54	0.36	19.01	0.95							0.49	46.52
ACASS									0.33	0.20	13.43	0.57							0.53	21.64
AROOT									0.39	0.23	14.82	0.67							0.05	25.79
AOILS																			1.50	25.52
ASUGA											23.85	0.49								83.10
AOHOR									1.21	0.72	12.57	0.93							1.60	86.30
AOCRO									0.18	0.17	4.13	0.10							0.83	22.28
ALIVE									1.23	0.75	25.35	0.49							0.23	64.85
AFISH									0.24	0.10	3.23	0.08							1.48	48.87
AFOHU									1.57	0.84	21.64	0.65							0.45	72.04
AMINE																			1.67	59.98
AMEAT																			0.83	50.92
AFOOD									0.35	0.23	39.72	0.71							1.82	72.32
AGRAI																			0.07	146.57
ABEVT																			0.55	108.14
ATEXT																			13.22	20.98
AWEAR																			15.28	55.23
ALEAT																			1.19	5.47
AWOOD																			7.09	40.66
APAPE																			1.50	15.47
ACHEM																				21.07
AFERT																				0.60
AFUEL																				4.02
ARUBB																			0.11	15.41
APLAS																			0.12	5.21
AGLAS																			0.33	4.06
ACEME																			2.47	23.49
AIRON																			1.23	31.61
AFMPR																			3.13	24.24
AMAEQ																				4.05
AELEQ																				8.10
ATREQ																				15.82
AOMAN																				1.11
AELEC																				50.11
AWATE																				18.26
ACNST																				200.96
ATRAD																				297.35
ATOUR																			26.45	26.45
AHORE																			11.01	61.46
ATR_C																			9.14	205.40
AFI_I																			0.07	73.63
AREAL																				75.69
ABUSI																				10.77
APUBA																			0.16	295.75
AOSER																			25.91	51.13
CCOTT																				3.54
CSISA																				2.43
CTEA									1.02	1.67	1.69	0.13								5.25
CCOFF									1.04	1.76	2.10	0.13								7.25
CTOBA									0.91	1.45	1.22	0.12								15.07
CCASH									1.09	1.94	3.53	0.13								7.93
CMAIZ									12.93	6.35	10.88	1.30						0.01		95.55
CWHEA									0.01	0.02	0.08	0.00						0.03		10.20
CPADD									0.94	1.62	0.81	0.16								37.29
CSORG									1.20	3.23	3.10	0.17								10.82
COCER									0.60	1.56	3.26	0.09								7.99
CBEAN									2.39	3.98	4.27	0.27								28.56
CCASS									0.54	0.76	0.64	0.10								9.31
CROOT									1.47	2.10	1.81	0.26								12.64
COILS									3.90	7.00	7.75	0.57						0.00		28.00
CSUGA									6.79	10.49	11.33	1.86						0.61		75.86
COHOR									10.63	15.83	11.31	1.84								84.15
COCRO									1.38	2.15	1.79	0.20						0.15		18.33
CLIVE									2.24	3.37	4.02	0.61						3.46		47.73
CFISH									5.39	7.04	10.80	1.31								59.22
CFOHU									2.96	4.57	8.05	0.68								54.40
CMINE																		0.12		71.71
CMEAT									10.52	22.69	26.64	2.84						-0.22		65.35
CFOOD									9.12	17.93	49.37	2.92						3.86		84.56
CGRAI									25.59	55.90	70.42	6.78						-2.74		160.71
CBEVT									15.02	12.84	91.21	8.67						1.77		133.65
CTEXT									1.57	2.32	5.81	0.56					2.81	1.25		30.76
CWEAR									5.37	8.26	25.57	1.82						0.30		46.03
CLEAT									1.31	2.03	6.37	0.44						-0.08		10.21
CWOOD									0.42	0.78	1.33	0.13					14.55	0.43		38.89
CPAPE									0.68	1.06	2.13	0.23						-0.43		26.82
CCHEM									3.01	5.97	7.67	0.98						-20.83		69.53
CFERT																		-0.26		7.01
CFUEL									1.97	4.36	5.56	0.54								30.94
CRUBB									0.05	0.10	0.31	0.02					2.23	-1.07		28.72
CPLAS									2.17	4.25	9.73	0.62					15.18	-0.15		40.44
CGLAS									0.21	0.41	1.15	0.05					0.89	-0.10		6.40
CCEME									0.63	1.57	4.23	0.12						0.73		32.26
CIRON																		13.67		60.69
CFMPR									0.84	1.84	2.37	0.22					26.87	-2.25		47.31
CMAEQ									0.01	0.01	0.03	0.00					62.22	2.60		71.13
CELEQ									0.42	0.84	0.87	0.11					46.45	-0.72		60.32
CTREQ									1.06	2.03	2.08	0.28					112.89	0.15		127.34
COMAN									0.87	1.86	2.02	0.25					12.92	-0.07		21.79
CELEC									0.07	0.10	0.25	0.01						1.43		50.29
CWATE									0.20	0.13	0.33	0.04						-0.03		18.81
CCNST									0.01	0.01	0.04	0.00		52.52			109.70	0.12		200.96
CCOME																				18.21
CCOMD																				152.82
CCOMI																				58.86
CTRAD																				67.46
CHORE									1.16	10.51	10.01	1.83						0.16		57.83
CTR_C									3.05	4.92	11.76	5.58					8.67	2.34		201.31
CFI_I									0.08	0.17	0.30	0.02						0.01		98.82
CREAL									10.85	12.33	24.37	2.72						0.01		121.42
CBUSI									0.10	0.19	0.20	0.03						-0.10		10.77
CPUBA									0.88	1.30	2.29	0.18	279.08							295.59
COSER									0.57	1.26	2.25	0.06								25.23
UPRO																				117.63
UWCO																				62.75
UBCO																				122.19
UNSK																				57.22
RURA																				517.82
LAND																				40.45
CAPITAL																				537.99
ENTR							508.40						27.62							536.02
HHUFA					102.36	8.61		68.98											23.12	203.06
HHUNF	62.91	58.16	111.93	52.97	5.72			4.36											1.30	297.35
HHRFA					402.22	31.85		192.43											99.10	725.59
HHRNF	20.81	4.60	10.26	4.25	7.52			9.86											3.36	60.65
GOVR								65.05	1.26	2.85	11.01	1.54			70.51	23.45			172.67	348.34
GOVI													34.96						17.56	52.52
ITAX																				70.51
TTAX																				23.45
KACCOUN								195.33	36.48	33.92	9.44	3.60	-17.57						158.32	419.53
DST																	4.15			4.15
WORLD	33.91						29.59						24.25							641.11
	117.63	62.75	122.19	57.22	517.82	40.45	537.99	536.02	203.06	297.35	725.59	60.65	348.34	52.52	70.51	23.45	419.53	4.15	641.11	

Source: Author.

Structure of the Economy

Table E.1—Structure of the economy

	Composition (percent)				Ratios (percent)		Elasticities	
	X share	VA share	E share	M share	E/X	M/Q	SIGT	SIGC
ACOTT	0.7	0.7	11.8	n.a.	83.1	n.a.	5.0	3.0
ASISA	0.2	0.1	1.9	n.a.	53.7	n.a.	5.0	3.0
ATEA	0.2	0.2	1.4	n.a.	31.2	n.a.	5.0	3.0
ACOFF	0.3	0.4	3.1	n.a.	53.4	n.a.	5.0	3.0
ATOBA	0.4	0.6	0.6	n.a.	6.8	n.a.	5.0	3.0
ACASH	0.3	0.5	1.9	n.a.	31.4	n.a.	5.0	3.0
AMAIZ	5.1	7.2	0.0	n.a.	0.0	n.a.	1.2	3.0
AWHEA	0.3	0.2	0.1	0.1	0.8	6.2	1.2	2.0
APADD	1.4	1.6	n.a.	n.a.	n.a.	n.a.	n.a.	3.0
ASORG	0.4	0.6	0.0	n.a.	0.1	n.a.	1.2	3.0
AOCER	0.1	0.2	0.0	0.7	0.6	58.3	1.2	3.0
ABEAN	1.6	2.6	0.2	n.a.	0.6	n.a.	1.2	3.0
ACASS	0.8	1.4	0.4	n.a.	2.5	n.a.	1.2	3.0
AROOT	0.9	1.6	0.0	0.2	0.2	11.0	1.2	3.0
AOILS	0.9	1.4	0.6	0.0	3.3	0.8	1.2	3.0
ASUGA	2.9	1.3	n.a.	n.a.	n.a.	n.a.	n.a.	3.0
AOHOR	3.0	5.1	0.7	0.0	1.3	0.3	1.2	3.0
AOCRO	0.8	1.3	0.3	n.a.	2.1	n.a.	1.2	3.0
ALIVE	2.3	3.4	0.1	0.2	0.3	2.2	1.2	3.0
AFISH	1.7	2.5	1.0	n.a.	3.0	n.a.	1.2	3.0
AFOHU	2.5	4.4	0.2	0.1	0.4	0.8	1.2	3.0
AMINE	2.1	3.5	1.1	2.3	2.8	18.4	1.2	1.5
AMEAT	1.8	2.0	0.5	0.3	1.5	2.7	1.2	1.5
AFOOD	2.5	1.4	1.0	7.5	2.1	53.7	1.2	1.5
AGRAI	5.1	1.0	0.0	2.5	0.0	8.8	1.2	1.5
ABEVT	3.8	3.0	0.3	0.6	0.4	2.8	1.2	1.5
ATEXT	2.5	1.2	14.2	4.2	28.7	29.7	1.2	1.5
AWOOD	1.9	1.4	4.9	1.8	13.1	15.9	1.2	1.5
ACHEM	0.9	0.4	n.a.	12.5	n.a.	68.1	n.a.	1.5
ARUBB	1.7	1.0	1.7	8.0	5.2	45.4	1.2	1.5
AIRON	1.9	0.7	2.6	8.7	6.9	47.2	1.2	1.5
AMAEQ	1.0	0.9	n.a.	35.7	n.a.	75.7	n.a.	1.5
AELEC	2.4	2.5	n.a.	n.a.	n.a.	n.a.	n.a.	1.5
ACNST	7.0	5.2	n.a.	n.a.	n.a.	n.a.	n.a.	1.5
ATRAD	10.4	12.8	n.a.	n.a.	n.a.	n.a.	n.a.	1.5

(continued)

Table E.1—Continued

	Composition (percent)				Ratios (percent)		Elasticities	
	X share	VA share	E share	M share	E/X	M/Q	SIGT	SIGC
ATOUR	0.9	0.7	17.9	n.a.	100.0	n.a.	0.5	n.a.
AHORE	2.1	2.3	7.5	1.3	17.9	12.8	0.5	1.5
ATR_C	7.2	6.6	6.2	0.9	4.4	2.5	0.5	1.5
AFI_I	2.9	3.5	0.0	4.4	0.1	23.1	0.5	1.5
AREAL	2.6	4.4	n.a.	7.9	n.a.	37.7	n.a.	1.5
APUBA	10.3	6.8	0.1	n.a.	0.1	n.a.	0.5	1.5
AOSER	1.8	1.5	17.6	n.a.	50.7	n.a.	0.5	1.5
Total Ag	27.0	37.3	24.3	1.4	4.7	1.3	n.a.	n.a.
Total NAg	73.0	62.7	75.7	98.6	5.3	21.8	n.a.	n.a.

Source: Author.

Notes: n.a. = Not applicable.

The 42-sector structure of this table is more aggregated in the nonagriculture sector than the microsam. X = Output, VA = Value-added, E = Exports, M = Imports, Q = Absorption, SIGT = Elasticity of transformation, SIGC = Elasticity of substitution, Ag = Agriculture, and NAg = Nonagriculture.

Supplementary Tables on the Policy Bias against Agriculture

Table F.1—Policy bias experiments from initial base: Free exchange rate

	tm	*te*	*tx*	*tc*	**All**
AG_M^{TOT}	103.8	103.8	103.8	103.7	97.1
P_M^{AG}	101.2	101.2	101.4	101.5	95.2
P_M^{AGN}	97.5	97.5	97.7	97.9	98.0
AG_E^{TOT}	100.1	100.1	99.9	99.8	99.8
P_E^{AG}	101.5	101.5	101.2	101.0	101.2
P_E^{AGN}	101.4	101.4	101.2	101.2	101.3
AG_Q^{TOT}	100.8	100.8	100.6	98.9	98.6
P_Q^{AG}	100.1	100.1	100.1	98.9	98.7
P_Q^{AGN}	99.3	99.3	99.5	100.0	100.1
AG_X^{TOT}	100.2	100.2	99.7	97.4	97.2
P_X^{AG}	100.2	100.2	99.7	98.1	98.0
P_X^{AGN}	99.9	99.9	100.1	100.7	100.8
AG_{VA}^{TOT}	100.1	100.1	97.3	93.6	93.4
P_{VA}^{AG}	100.3	100.3	100.6	98.7	98.5
P_{VA}^{AGN}	100.2	100.2	103.4	105.4	105.5
Real exchange rate	1.013	1.013	1.013	1.014	1.015

Source: Author.

Table F.2—Policy bias experiments from initial base: Fixed exchange rate

	tm	te	tx	tc	All
AG_M^{TOT}	103.8	103.8	103.7	103.7	97.1
P_M^{AG}	100.0	100.0	100.1	100.2	93.8
P_M^{AGN}	96.3	96.3	96.5	96.6	96.6
AG_E^{TOT}	100.0	100.0	99.9	99.8	99.8
P_E^{AG}	100.0	100.0	99.7	99.4	99.4
P_E^{AGN}	100.0	100.0	99.8	99.7	99.7
AG_Q^{TOT}	101.8	101.8	101.6	99.9	99.7
P_Q^{AG}	100.6	100.6	100.6	99.5	99.3
P_Q^{AGN}	98.9	98.9	99.0	99.6	99.6
AG_X^{TOT}	101.1	101.1	100.6	98.3	98.2
P_X^{AG}	100.8	100.8	100.4	98.8	98.7
P_X^{AGN}	99.7	99.7	99.8	100.5	100.5
AG_{VA}^{TOT}	101.3	101.3	98.5	94.8	94.6
P_{VA}^{AG}	101.2	101.2	101.5	99.7	99.6
P_{VA}^{AGN}	99.9	99.9	103.1	105.1	105.2
Real exchange rate	1.000	1.000	1.000	1.000	1.000

Source: Author.

Table F.3—Policy bias experiments from synthetic base: Free exchange rate

	tm	te	tx	tc	All
AG_M^{TOT}	115.4	115.4	115.3	115.3	115.3
P_M^{AG}	103.9	103.1	103.3	103.4	103.4
P_M^{AGN}	90.0	89.3	89.6	89.7	89.7
AG_E^{TOT}	100.2	102.2	102.0	101.9	101.9
P_E^{AG}	104.7	105.8	105.6	105.4	105.4
P_E^{AGN}	104.4	103.6	103.5	103.4	103.4
AG_Q^{TOT}	104.2	105.1	104.8	103.1	103.1
P_Q^{AG}	101.1	101.5	101.5	100.4	100.4
P_Q^{AGN}	97.0	96.6	96.8	97.3	97.3
AG_X^{TOT}	101.8	102.7	102.2	99.9	99.9
P_X^{AG}	101.3	102.0	101.6	99.9	99.9
P_X^{AGN}	99.5	99.3	99.4	100.0	100.0
AG_{VA}^{TOT}	101.6	102.8	100.0	96.3	96.3
P_{VA}^{AG}	102.9	103.9	104.2	102.3	102.3
P_{VA}^{AGN}	101.3	101.0	104.2	106.2	106.2
Real exchange rate	1.041	1.033	1.033	1.034	1.034

Source: Author.

Table F.4—Policy bias experiments from synthetic base: Fixed exchange rate

	tm	te	tx	tc	All
AG_M^{TOT}	115.3	115.3	115.2	115.2	115.2
P_M^{AG}	100.0	100.0	100.1	100.2	100.2
P_M^{AGN}	86.7	86.7	86.9	87.0	87.0
AG_E^{TOT}	100.0	102.0	101.8	101.7	101.7
P_E^{AG}	100.1	102.1	101.7	101.5	101.5
P_E^{AGN}	100.0	100.1	99.9	99.7	99.7
AG_Q^{TOT}	107.4	107.6	107.4	105.6	105.6
P_Q^{AG}	102.8	102.9	102.9	101.7	101.7
P_Q^{AGN}	95.7	95.6	95.8	96.3	96.3
AG_X^{TOT}	104.7	105.1	104.5	102.2	102.2
P_X^{AG}	103.5	103.7	103.3	101.6	101.6
P_X^{AGN}	98.8	98.7	98.8	99.4	99.4
AG_{VA}^{TOT}	105.5	106.0	103.1	99.2	99.2
P_{VA}^{AG}	106.1	106.4	106.7	104.8	104.8
P_{VA}^{AGN}	100.5	100.4	103.6	105.6	105.6
Real exchange rate	1.000	1.000	1.000	1.000	1.000

Source: Author.

Table F.5—Real sectoral value-added: Experiment series one

Sector	Base	tm	te	tx	tc	All
agexp	34.2	34.2	34.2	34.0	36.2	36.3
agfood	373.1	373.3	373.3	372.3	370.6	370.7
aglffh	154.8	154.7	154.7	155.8	155.3	155.1
nagfood	92.8	93.1	93.1	92.9	94.3	94.4
nagmanu	45.5	45.0	45.0	44.8	44.9	44.9
nagmmuc	171.6	171.0	171.0	173.6	173.3	173.3
nagserv	584.0	584.7	584.7	582.5	581.3	581.3
Total	1,456.0	1,456.0	1,456.0	1,456.0	1,456.0	1,456.0

Source: Author.
Note: agexp = traditional agricultural exports
agfood = nonexport agriculture except aglffh
aglffh = livestock, forestry, fishing, and hunting
nagfood = processed food
nagmanu = manufactures
nagmmuc = mining, metal, machinery, utilities, and construction
nagserv = private and public services

Table F.6—Real sectoral value-added: Experiment series two

Sector	Base	*tm*	*te*	*tx*	*tc*	**All**
agexp	34.2	34.2	34.2	34.0	36.2	36.3
agfood	373.1	373.3	373.3	372.3	370.6	370.7
aglffh	154.8	154.7	154.7	155.8	155.3	155.1
nagfood	92.8	93.1	93.1	92.9	94.3	94.4
nagmanu	45.5	45.0	45.0	44.8	44.9	44.9
nagmmuc	171.6	171.0	171.0	173.6	173.3	173.3
nagserv	584.0	584.7	584.7	582.5	581.3	581.3
Total	1,456.0	1,456.0	1,456.0	1,456.0	1,456.0	1,456.0

Source: Author.
Note: See Table F.5 for definitions.

Table F.7—Real sectoral value-added: Experiment series three

Sector	Base	*tm*	*te*	*tx*	*tc*	**All**
agexp	26.8	34.6	36.1	36.1	38.2	38.2
agfood	358.8	352.6	351.4	350.4	348.6	348.6
aglffh	148.8	146.7	146.3	147.3	146.8	146.8
nagfood	91.6	90.6	90.6	90.3	91.7	91.7
nagmanu	46.9	45.6	45.5	45.3	45.4	45.4
nagmmuc	173.7	172.2	172.2	174.8	174.6	174.6
nagserv	578.6	582.4	582.4	580.2	579.0	579.0
Total	1,425.2	1,424.6	1,424.5	1,424.5	1,424.3	1,424.3

Source: Author.
Note: See Table F.5 for definitions.

Table F.8—Real sectoral value-added: Experiment series four

Sector	Base	*tm*	*te*	*tx*	*tc*	**All**
agexp	26.8	29.1	31.5	31.3	33.3	33.3
agfood	358.8	357.5	355.6	354.7	353.0	353.0
aglffh	148.8	147.7	147.1	148.2	147.7	147.7
nagfood	91.6	93.1	92.7	92.5	93.9	93.9
nagmanu	46.9	45.0	45.1	44.9	44.9	44.9
nagmmuc	173.7	171.1	171.4	174.0	173.7	173.7
nagserv	578.6	581.4	581.6	579.4	578.2	578.2
Total	1,425.2	1,425.0	1,424.9	1,424.9	1,424.8	1,424.8

Source: Author.
Note: See Table F.5 for definitions.

Table F.9—Nominal GDP indices: Experiment series one

Index	Base	*tm*	*te*	*tx*	*tc*	**All**
Consumption	100.0	99.5	99.5	99.8	97.4	97.3
Investment	100.0	97.7	97.7	97.3	95.4	95.5
Inventory	100.0	91.0	91.0	92.4	83.4	83.0
Government	100.0	100.1	100.1	101.1	101.1	101.1
Exports	100.0	101.3	101.3	101.3	101.4	101.5
Imports	100.0	101.3	101.3	101.3	101.4	101.5
GDP	100.0	98.6	98.6	98.9	96.4	96.4

Source: Author.

Table F.10—Nominal GDP indices: Experiment series two

Index	Base	*tm*	*te*	*tx*	*tc*	**All**
Consumption	100.0	99.6	99.6	99.9	97.5	97.4
Investment	100.0	96.9	96.9	96.4	94.6	94.6
Inventory	100.0	92.7	92.7	94.2	85.3	85.1
Government	100.0	100.1	100.1	101.1	101.1	101.1
Exports	100.0	100.0	100.0	100.0	100.0	100.0
Imports	100.0	100.0	100.0	100.0	100.0	100.0
GDP	100.0	98.8	98.8	99.1	96.6	96.6

Source: Author.

Table F.11—Nominal GDP indices: Experiment series three

Index	Base	*tm*	*te*	*tx*	*tc*	**All**
Consumption	100.0	98.7	98.8	99.1	96.7	96.7
Investment	100.0	92.2	91.6	91.3	89.5	89.5
Inventory	100.0	116.1	117.5	119.5	107.4	107.4
Government	100.0	100.4	100.4	101.3	101.4	101.4
Exports	100.0	104.1	103.3	103.3	103.4	103.4
Imports	100.0	104.1	103.3	103.3	103.4	103.4
GDP	100.0	95.8	95.9	96.2	93.8	93.8

Source: Author.

Table F.12—Nominal GDP indices: Experiment series four

Index	Base	tm	te	tx	tc	All
Consumption	100.0	99.0	99.0	99.3	96.9	96.9
Investment	100.0	89.8	89.7	89.3	87.6	87.6
Inventory	100.0	123.6	123.5	125.5	113.7	113.7
Government	100.0	100.4	100.4	101.4	101.4	101.4
Exports	100.0	100.0	100.0	100.0	100.0	100.0
Imports	100.0	100.0	100.0	100.0	100.0	100.0
GDP	100.0	96.4	96.3	96.6	94.2	94.2

Source: Author.

Table F.13—Percentage change of deflated household consumption: Experiment series one

Household group	Base value	tm	te	tx	tc	All
HHUFA	162.1	–0.5	–0.5	–1.9	–3.9	–4.0
HHUNF	255.6	0.7	0.7	4.4	8.2	8.3
HHRFA	689.5	–0.1	–0.1	–1.1	–2.0	–2.1
HHRNF	54.2	0.2	0.2	1.8	3.8	3.8
Total	1,161.4	0.0	0.0	0.2	0.2	0.2

Source: Author.
Notes: Base value in billion TSh
           HHUFA = urban farm
           HHUNF = urban nonfarm
           HHRFA = rural farm
           HHRNF = rural nonfarm

Table F.14—Percentage change of deflated household consumption: Experiment series two

Household group	Base value	tm	te	tx	tc	All
HHUFA	162.1	1.2	1.2	–0.2	–2.1	–2.0
HHUNF	255.6	0.4	0.4	4.2	7.9	8.1
HHRFA	689.5	1.2	1.2	0.3	–0.6	–0.5
HHRNF	54.2	0.6	0.6	2.3	4.3	4.4
Total	1,161.4	1.0	1.0	1.2	1.3	1.4

Source: Author.
Note: See Table F.13 for definitions.

Table F.15—Percentage change of deflated household consumption: Experiment series three

	Base value	*tm*	*te*	*tx*	*tc*	All
HHUFA	159.6	−1.6	−1.5	−3.0	−5.0	−5.0
HHUNF	252.3	2.8	2.5	6.3	10.1	10.1
HHRFA	676.3	−0.3	−0.2	−1.2	−2.2	−2.2
HHRNF	53.6	0.8	0.6	2.2	4.2	4.2
Total	1,141.9	0.2	0.2	0.4	0.4	0.4

Source: Author.
Note: See Table F.13 for definitions.

Table F.16—Percentage change of deflated household consumption: Experiment series four

	Base value	*tm*	*te*	*tx*	*tc*	All
HHUFA	159.6	3.6	2.8	1.4	−0.5	−0.5
HHUNF	252.3	2.0	1.9	5.7	9.5	9.5
HHRFA	676.3	3.9	3.3	2.3	1.5	1.5
HHRNF	53.6	2.3	1.8	3.5	5.5	5.5
Total	1141.9	3.4	2.8	3.0	3.1	3.1

Source: Author.
Note: See Table F.13 for definitions.

Sensitivity of the Modeling Results with Respect to CES and CET Elasticities

The CES import aggregation and CET export transformation functions describe the substitution possibilities for the traded commodities of the model. The choice of elasticities determines the intensity of the substitution mechanisms between (1) domestic supply and imports and (2) domestic production and exports. In Tanzania, economywide information on the required sectoral substitution elasticities is unavailable, and sufficient time-series data for their econometric estimation do not exist. Estimating these parameters relies on general assumptions about behavior typical of the developing country regarding production and trade. To assess how sensitive the simulation results are to differences in the underlying elasticities, a single devaluation experiment is carried out applying two series of different elasticity variations. The first experiment series considers a 25 percent reduction of the trade balance, implying a devaluation of the exchange rate, and variation of the CES import aggregation elasticity, σ_{Comm}^{C}, from 75 to 175 percent in 25 percent increments. The second experiment series considers the same reduction of the trade balance and the same percentage variation on the CET export transformation elasticity, σ_{activ}^{T}, while fixing the CES elasticities, σ_{Comm}^{C}, at their initial values.

Table G.1 shows the exchange rate results in the two experiment series. A 25 percent reduction of the trade balance under initial elasticity conditions (100 percent) causes a 9.6 percent devaluation of the exchange rate. Decreasing either one of the elasticities, σ_{Comm}^{C} or σ_{activ}^{T}, means diminished trade opportunities and, consequently, requires a greater depreciation to obtain the given reduction of the trade balance (10.4 and 10.6 percent, respectively). By contrast, the gradual increase of the substitution and transformation elasticities requires significantly lower depreciation rates to achieve the imposed trade balance constraint. Table G.1 shows significant but moderate effects of the elasticity variation on the percentage deviation from the devaluation experiment (Table G.2). The 25 percent variation of the elasticities in both directions on the same devaluation experiment

Table G.1—Elasticity variation and exchange rate depreciation

	Variation of elasticities as a percentage of their initial value				
	75	100	125	150	175
EXR (σ_{comm}^{C})	10.4	9.6	9.0	8.4	8.0
EXR (σ_{activ}^{T})	10.6	9.6	8.9	8.3	7.8

Source: Author.

Table G.2—Percentage deviation of the depreciation rates with respect to the experiment with initial elasticity values

	Variation of elasticities as a percentage of their initial value				
	75	100	125	150	175
$\Delta\,EXR$ (σ_{comm}^{C})	8.0	0.0	−6.7	−12.4	−17.3
$\Delta\,EXR$ (σ_{activ}^{T})	10.2	0.0	−7.8	−14.1	−19.3

Source: Author.

would cause the exchange rate to vary by not more than 10 percent compared with the devaluation experiment under the initial elasticity values.

Because of the exchange rate behavior of the different scenarios (assuming the trade balance is fixed, but trade volumes differ), the values of aggregate foreign trade change accordingly, but the general trade pattern remains the same. Compared with the CGE base run, the GDP shares of total exports and imports for both experiment series show a 3.3 percent increase in exports and a 2.8 percent decrease in imports to achieve the trade balance reduction under existing elasticity conditions (compare the "100%" column in Table G.3 with the "Base" column).

The second row of Table G.3 shows that the higher the CES substitution elasticity, the lower the share of imports in the composition GDP at market prices. For the entire series of variation on the elasticity values, however, the changes in GDP share of total imports range from 2.6 percent to 3.4 percent. Because the trade balance for the experiment is fixed, the GDP shares of total exports differ accordingly. Similar observations are made for the second experiment series in which a gradual increase of the CET transformation elasticities causes increasing GDP shares of total exports, ranging from 3.1 to 3.7 additional percentage points.

For production, similar differences occur throughout the two experiment series. Table G.4 presents the percentage deviations in real value-added for the variety of CES substitution elasticities, σ^{C}, regarding their base values for the seven-sector disaggregation. The "100%" column shows the deviations in real value-added caused by the 25 percent devaluation under initial base values for the substitution elasticities. Lowering all σ^{C} by 25 percent causes absolute percentage deviations in the changes of sectoral real value-added between 1.1 percent and 6.8 percent from what the changes are in case

Table G.3—Real GDP shares of foreign trade

| | Base | Variation of elasticities as a percentage of their initial value | | | | |
		75	100	125	150	175
Exp (σ^C_{comm})	10.7	14.3	14.0	13.8	13.6	13.5
Imp (σ^C_{comm})	35.7	33.1	32.9	32.7	32.5	32.3
Exp (σ^T_{activ})	10.7	13.8	14.0	14.2	14.3	14.4
Imp (σ^T_{activ})	35.7	32.7	32.9	33.0	33.1	33.3

Source: Author.

Table G.4—Percentage change of real value-added to the base run in terms of the variation of the CES elasticities of substitution

| | Variation of σ^C as a percentage of their initial value | | | | |
	75	100	125	150	175
agexp	41.1	38.9	37.1	35.5	34.1
agfood	–3.0	–2.8	–2.7	–2.5	–2.4
aglffh	–2.4	–2.4	–2.3	–2.2	–2.2
nagfood	–2.9	–2.7	–2.6	–2.5	–2.3
nagmanu	3.0	3.1	3.2	3.2	3.2
nagmmuc	–2.5	–2.5	–2.4	–2.4	–2.4
nagserv	0.9	0.9	0.8	0.8	0.8

Source: Author.
Note: See Table F.5 for definitions.

of the initial values of σ^C. Accordingly, when increasing all σ^C by 25 percent, changes in sectoral real value-added deviate by 1.2 to 5.6 percent. Table G.5 presents similar results for the experiment variation on the CET elasticities of transformation, σ^T, and shows that the deviations are even less distinct than they are for the σ^C variation.

The means by which the deviations develop for the two experiment series throughout the entire 75 to 175 percent variation of the CES and CET elasticities can also be observed from two figures derived from Tables G.4 and G.5. Figures G.1 and G.2 show that the deviations of the sectoral changes in real value-added diminish with each additional 25 percentage point increase of either one of the elasticity groups. Examining the last stages (175 percent) of the two experiment series reveals that even with a 75 percent increase of all sectoral elasticities the modeling results do not change by more than 18 percent.

The sensitivity analysis shows that the qualitative results of this study's analysis remain the same under a wide range of different CES and CET parameters. Although the quantitative results might differ up to 20 percent from their observed values, the policy results are relatively robust, and their interpretation and conclusions apply to the entire spectrum of parameter variation.

Table G.5—Percentage change of real value-added to the base run in terms of the variation of the CES elasticities of transformation

| | Variation of σ^c as a percentage of their initial value | | | | |
	75	100	125	150	175
agexp	38.3	38.9	39.2	39.3	39.2
agfood	–2.8	–2.8	–2.8	–2.9	–2.9
aglffh	–2.3	–2.4	–2.4	–2.3	–2.3
nagfood	–2.5	–2.7	–2.9	–3.1	–3.2
nagmanu	3.0	3.1	3.2	3.4	3.5
nagmmuc	–2.6	–2.5	–2.4	–2.4	–2.3
nagserv	0.9	0.9	0.9	0.9	0.9

Source: Author.
Note: See Table F.5 for definitions.

Figure G.1—Percentage change of real value-added deviations with respect to σ^c variation

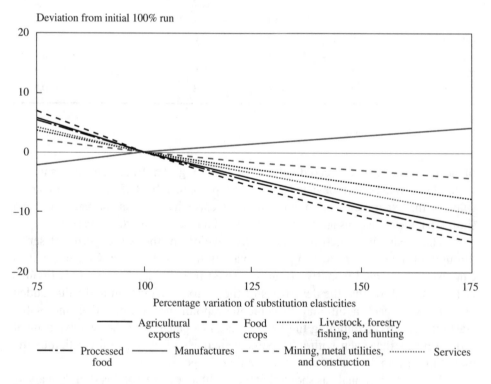

Source: Author.

Figure G.2—Percentage change of real value-added deviations with respect to σ^T variation

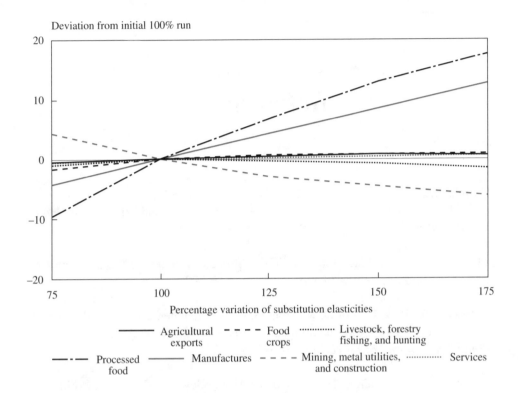

Deviation from initial 100% run

Percentage variation of substitution elasticities

Agricultural exports —— Food crops – – – Livestock, forestry fishing, and hunting ·········

Processed food —·— Manufactures —— Mining, metal utilities, and construction – – – Services ·········

Source: Author.

References

Abbink, G. A., M. C. Braber, and S. I. Cohen. 1995. A SAM-CGE demonstration model for Indonesia: Static and dynamic specifications and experiments. *International Economic Journal* 9 (3): 15–33.

Adams, F. G., and I. Park. 1995. A CGE approach to modeling the development ladder. *Journal of Asian Economics* 6 (2): 177–199.

Adams, P. D., P. B. Dixon, D. McDonald, G. A. Meagher, and B. R. Parmenter. 1994. Forecasts for the Australian economy using the MONASH model. *International Journal of Forecasting* 10 (4): 557–571.

Adelman, I., and P. Berck. 1988. Food security policy in a stochastic world. Department of Agricultural and Resource Economics Working Paper 478. University of California at Berkeley, Berkeley, Calif., U.S.A.

Adelman, I. and S. Robinson. 1978. *Income distribution policy in developing countries: A case study of Korea.* Stanford, Calif., U.S.A.: Stanford University Press.

———. 1987. Macroeconomic adjustment and income distribution: Alternative models applied to two economies. Department of Agricultural and Resource Economics Working Paper 385. University of California at Berkeley, Berkeley, Calif., U.S.A.

Adelman, I., J. M. Bournieux, and J. L. Waelbroeck. 1986. Agricultural development led industrialization in a global perspective. Department of Agricultural and Resource Economics Working Paper 478. University of California at Berkeley, Berkeley, Calif., U.S.A.

Akinboade, O. A. 1994. Technical efficiency change in Kenyan agriculture and the poor: A computable general equilibrium analysis. *Canadian Journal of Development Studies* 15 (1): 55–74.

Anderson, K., B. Dimaranan, T.W. Hertel, and W. Martin. 1997. *Economic growth and policy reform in the APEC region: Trade and welfare implications by 2005.* Centre for Economic Policy Research Discussion Paper 1605. London: Centre for Economic Policy Research.

Ardeni, P. G. 1989. Does the law of one price really hold for commodity prices? *American Journal of Agricultural Economics* 71 (3): 661–669.

Armington, P. S. 1969. A theory of demand for products distinguished by place of production. *IMF Staff Papers* 16: 159–176.

Arndt, C., S. Robinson, and F. Tarp. 1999. *Parameter estimation for a computable general equilibrium model: A maximum entropy approach.* Trade and Macroeconomics Division Discussion Paper No. 40. Washington, D.C.: International Food Policy Research Institute.

Arrow, K. J. 1952. An extension of the basic theorems of classical welfare economics. In *Proceedings of the second Berkeley symposium on mathematical statistics*, ed. J. Neyman. Berkeley, Calif., U.S.A.: University of California Press.

Arrow, K. J., and F. H. Hahn. 1971. *General competitive analysis.* San Francisco, Calif.: Holden-Day.

Ashimogo, G. 1995. *Peasant grain storage and marketing in Tanzania: A case study of maize in Sumbawanga District.* Schriften zur internationalen Agrarentwicklung, Bd. 15. Berlin: Humbold University.

Aune, J. B., and R. Lal. 1995. The tropical soil productivity calculator—A model for assessing effects of soil management on productivity. In *Soil management: Experimental basis for sustainability and environmental quality*, ed. R. Lal and B. A. Steward. Boca Raton, Fla., U.S.A.: CRC Press.

Aune, J. B., S. Glomsrod, V. Iversen, and H. Wiig. 1997. *Structural adjustment and soil degradation in Tanzania: A CGE-model approach with endogenous soil productivity.* Research Department Discussion Papers No. 189. Oslo: Statistics Norway.

Azis, I. J. 1997. Impacts of economic reform on rural-urban welfare: A general equilibrium framework. *Review of Urban and Regional Development Studies* 9 (1): 1–19.

Baffes, J. 1991. Some further evidence on the law of one price: The law of one price still holds. *American Journal of Agricultural Economics* 73 (4): 1264–1273.

Balsvik, R. and A. Brendemoen. 1994. *A computable general equilibrium model for Tanzania: Documentation of the model, the 1990 – Social Accounting Matrix and Calibration.* Statistisk sentralbyra Reports 94/20. Oslo: Statistics Norway.

Bandara, J. S. 1991. Computable general equilibrium models for policy analysis in developing LDCs. *Journal of Economic Surveys* 5 (1): 3–69.

Bautista, R. M., and S. Robinson. 1996. *Income and equity effects of crop productivity growth under alternative foreign trade regimes: A CGE analysis for the Philippines.* Trade and Macroeconomics Division Discussion Paper No. 4. Washington, D.C.: International Food Policy Research Institute.

————. 1997. Income and equity effects of crop productivity growth under alternative foreign trade regimes: A CGE analysis for the Philippines. *Asian Journal of Agricultural Economics* 2 (2): 177–194.

Bautista, R. M., and A. Valdes. 1993. *The bias against agriculture: Trade and macroeconomic policies in developing countries.* San Francisco, Calif.: Institute for Contemporary Studies Press.

Bautista, R. M., S. Robinson, F. Tarp, and P. Wobst. 2001. Policy bias and agriculture: Partial and general equilibrium measures. *Review of Development Economics* 5 (1): 89–104.

Bell, C. L. G., and T. N. Srinivasan. 1984. On the uses and abuses of economy-wide models in development policy analysis. In *Economic structure and performance,* ed. M. Syrquin, L. Taylor, and L. E. Westphal. New York: Academic Press.

Benjamin, N. 1996. Adjustment and income distribution in an agricultural economy: A general equilibrium analysis of Cameroon. *World Development* 24 (6): 1003–1013.

Bevan, D. L., P. Collier, and J. W. Gunning. 1986. *Consequences of a commodity boom in a controlled economy.* Oxford Applied Economics Discussion Paper 6. Oxford: Institute of Economics and Statistics.

BOT (Bank of Tanzania). Various quarterly issues. *Economic Bulletin.* Dar es Salaam.

Bourguignon, F. 1994. Comment (on A financial computable general equilibrium model for the analysis of stabilization programs by A. Fargeix and E. Sadoulet). In *Applied general equilibrium and economic development: Present achievements and future trends,* eds., J. Mercenier and T. N. Srinivasan. Ann Arbor, Mich., U.S.A.: University of Michigan Press.

Bourguignon, F, W. H. Branson, and J. de Melo. 1992. Adjustment and income distribution: A micro-macro model for counterfactual analysis. *Journal of Development Economics* 38 (1): 17–39.

Brooke, A., D. Kendrick, and A. Meeraus. 1988. *GAMS: A user's guide*. San Francisco, Calif., U.S.A.: Scientific Press.

Brown, D. K. 1992. The impact of a North American free trade area: Applied general equilibrium models. In *North American free trade: Assessing the impact*, ed. N. Lustig, B. P. Bosworth, and R. Z. Lawrence. Washington, D.C.: Brookings Institution.

Brown, D. K., A.V. Deardorff, A. K. Fox, and R. M. Stern. 1996. The liberalization of service trade: Potential impact in the aftermath of the Uruguay Round. In *The Uruguay Round and the developing countries*, ed. W. Martin and A. Winters. Cambridge: Cambridge University Press.

Bryceson, D. F. 1993. *Liberalizing Tanzania's food trade: Public and private faces of urban marketing policy, 1939–1988*. Geneva: United Nations Research Institute for Social Development.

Ceglowski, J. 1994. The law of one price revisited: New evidence on the behavior of international prices. *Economic Inquiry* 32: 407–418.

Chenery, H. B. 1975. The structuralist approach to development policy. *American Economic Review* 65 (2): 310–316.

Chenery, H. B., S. Robinson, and M. Syrquin. 1986. *Industrialization and growth: A comparative study*. New York: Oxford University Press.

Coetzee, Z. R., J. J. Swanepoel, and W. A. Naude. 1997. A minimalist CGE model for analyzing trade liberalization in South Africa. *Journal for Studies in Economics and Econometrics* 21 (1): 37–56.

Coetzee, Z. R., K. Gwaranda, W. A. Naude, and J. J. Swanepoel. 1997. Currency depreciation, trade liberalization and economic development. *South African Journal of Economics* 65 (2): 165–190.

Condon, T., H. Dahl, and S. Devarajan. 1987. *Implementing a computable general equilibrium model on GAMS: The Cameroon model*. DRD Discussion Paper 290. Washington, D.C.: World Bank.

Coopers and Lybrand. 1994. *Tanzanian government 1994/1995 budget summary*. Dar es Salaam: Coopers and Lybrand.

————. 1995. *Tanzanian government 1995/1996 budget summary.* Dar es Salaam: Coopers and Lybrand.

————. 1996. *Tanzanian government 1996/1997 budget summary.* Dar es Salaam: Coopers and Lybrand.

Davies, R., and J. Rattso. 1996. Growth, distribution, and environment: Macroeconomic issues in Zimbabwe. *World Development* 24 (2): 395–405.

Davies, R., J. Rattso, and R. Torvik. 1994. The macroeconomics of Zimbabwe in the 1980s: A CGE analysis. *Journal of African Economics* 3 (2): 153–198.

————. 1998. Short-run consequences of trade liberalization: A computable general equilibrium model of Zimbabwe. *Journal of Policy Modeling* 20 (3): 305–333.

Deardorff, A. V., and R. M. Stern. 1990. *Computational analysis of global trading arrangements.* Ann Arbor, Mich., U.S.A.: University of Michigan Press.

Debreu, G. 1951. The coefficient of resource utilization. *Econometrica* 19 (3): 273–292.

————. 1959. *Theory of value: An axiomatic analysis of economic equilibrium.* New York: Wiley.

Decaluwe, B., and A. Martens. 1988. CGE modeling and developing economies: A concise empirical survey of 73 applications to 26 countries. *Journal of Policy Modeling* 10 (4): 529–568.

Decaluwe, B., and F. Nsengiyumva. 1994. Policy impact under credit rationing: A real and financial CGE of Rwanda. *Journal of African Economics* 3 (2): 262–308.

de Janvry, A., A. Fargeix, and E. Sadoulet. 1988. The welfare effects of stabilization policies and structural adjustment programs analyzed in CGE frameworks: Results and agenda. Department of Agricultural and Resource Economics Working Paper 460. University of California at Berkeley, Berkeley, Calif., U.S.A.

Delgado, C. L., and N. W. Minot. 2000. *Agriculture in Tanzania since 1986: Follower or leader of growth?* World Bank country study. Washington, D.C.: World Bank.

de Maio, L., F. Stewart, and R. van der Hoeven. 1999. Computable general equilibrium models, adjustment and the poor in Africa. *World Development* 27 (3): 453–470.

de Melo, J. 1988. Computable general equilibrium models for trade policy analysis in developing countries: A survey. *Journal of Policy Modeling* 10 (4): 469–503.

de Melo, J., and S. Robinson. 1985. Product differentiation and trade dependence of the domestic price system in computable general equilibrium trade models. In *International trade and exchange rates in the late eighties*, ed. T. Peeters, P. Praet, and P. Reding. Amsterdam: North-Holland.

―――. 1989. Product differentiation and the treatment of foreign trade in computable general equilibrium models of small economies. *Journal of International Economics* 27: 47–67.

de Melo, J., and D. Tarr. 1992. *A general equilibrium analysis of U.S. foreign trade policy*. Cambridge, Mass., U.S.A. and London: Massachusetts Institute of Technology Press.

Dervis, K., J. de Melo, and S. Robinson. 1982. *General Equilibrium Models for Development Policy*. Cambridge: Cambridge University Press.

Devarajan, S., J. D. Lewis, and S. Robinson. 1986. A Bibliography of computable general equilibrium (CGE) models applied to developing countries. Department of Agricultural and Resource Economics Working Paper 400. University of California at Berkeley, Berkeley, Calif., U.S.A.

―――. 1990. Policy lessons from trade-focused, two-sector models. *Journal of Policy Modeling* 12: 625–657.

―――. 1991. From stylized to applied models: Building multisector CGE models for policy analysis. Department of Agricultural and Resource Economics Working Paper 616. University of California at Berkeley, Berkeley, Calif., U.S.A.

―――. 1993. External shocks, purchasing power parity, and the equilibrium real exchange rate. *World Bank Economic Review* 7 (1): 45–63.

―――. 1994. Getting the model right: The general equilibrium approach to adjustment policy. World Bank and International Food Policy Research Institute, Washington, D.C. Draft manuscript.

Devarajan, S., D. S. Go, J. D. Lewis, S. Robinson, and P. Sinko. 1997. Simple general equilibrium modeling. In *Applied methods for trade policy analysis: A handbook*, ed. J. F. Francois and K. A. Reinert. Cambridge: Cambridge University Press.

Diao, X., E. Yeldan, and T.L. Roe. 1998. A simple dynamic applied general equilibrium model of a small open economy: Transitional dynamics and trade policy. *Journal of Economic Development* 23 (1): 77–101.

Dixon, P.B., B. R. Parmenter, A. A. Powell, and P. J. Wolcoxen. 1992. *Notes and problems in applied general equilibrium economics.* Amsterdam: North-Holland.

Dixon, P. B., B. R. Parmenter, J. Sutton, and D. P. Vincent. 1982. *ORANI: A multisectoral model for the Australian economy.* Amsterdam: North-Holland.

Dorfman, R., P. A. Samuelson, and R. M. Solow. 1958. *Linear programming and economic analysis.* New York: McGraw-Hill.

Economic Research Bureau. 1996. *Tanzanian economic trends: A bi-annual review of the economy*, vol. 8, nos. 1 and 2. Dar es Salaam: University of Dar es Salaam.

Economist Intelligence Unit. 1996. *County profile: Tanzania/Comoros 1995–96.* London.

FAO (Food and Agriculture Organization of the United Nations). 1998a. *Special report: FAO/WFP crop and food supply assessment mission to Tanzania. 3 August 1998.* <http://www.fao.org/giews>.

———. 1998b. *Special Report: FAO/WFP crop and food supply assessment mission to the United Republic of Tanzania. 19 February 1998.* <http://www.fao.org/giews>.

———. 1998c. The *FAOSTAT* database. <http://apps.fao.org>.

———. 1999. *Special Report: FAO/WFP crop and food supply assessment mission to Tanzania. 15 February 1999.* <http://www.fao.org/giews>.

Fargeix, A., and E. Sadoulet. 1994. A financial computable general equilibrium model for the analysis of stabilization programs. In *Applied general equilibrium and economic development: Present achievements and future trends*, ed. J. Mercenier and T. N. Srinivasan. Ann Arbor, Mich., U.S.A.: University of Michigan Press.

Felderer, B., and S. Homburg. 1984. *Makroökonomik und neue makroökonomik.* Berlin: Springer-Verlag.

Frisch, R. 1959. A complete scheme for computing all direct and cross demand elasticities in a model with many sectors. *Econometrica* 27: 177–196

Gibson, B., and D. E. van Seventer. 1996. Trade, growth and distribution in the South African economy. *Development Southern Africa* 13 (5): 771–792

Ginsburgh, V. A., and L. Van der Heyden. 1985. *Equilibrium with government price support policies and mathematical programming.* CORE Discussion Paper 8511. Louvain la Neuve, Belgium: Catholic University of Louvain.

Ginsburgh, V. A. and J. L. Waelbroeck. 1981. *Activity analysis and general equilibrium modelling*. Amsterdam: North-Holland.

Go, D. S. 1994. External shocks, adjustment policies and investment in a developing economy: Illustrations from a forward-looking CGE model of the Philippines. *Journal of Development Economics* 44 (2): 229–261.

Golan, A. 1998. Entropy, likelihood, and uncertainty: A comparison. In *Maximum entropy and bayesian methods*, ed. G. Erickson. The Netherlands: Kluwer Academic Publishers, forthcoming.

Golan, A., and G. G. Judge. 1996. A maximum entropy approach to empirical likelihood estimation and inference. Working Paper. University of California at Berkeley, Berkeley, Calif., U.S.A.

Golan, A., G. G. Judge, and D. Miller. 1996. *Maximum entropy econometrics: Robust estimation with limited data*. New York: John Wiley & Sons.

Golan, A., G. G. Judge, and S. Robinson. 1994. Recovering information from incomplete or partial multisectoral economic data. *Review of Economics and Statistics* 76: 541–549.

Goldin, I., O. Knudsen, and D. van der Mensbrugghe. 1993. *Trade liberalization: Global economic implications*. Paris and Washington, D.C.: Organization for Economic Cooperation and Development and World Bank.

Grepperud, S., H. Wiig, and F. R. Aune. 1999. *Maize trade liberalization vs. fertilizer subsidies in Tanzania: A CGE model analysis with endogenous soil fertility*. Research Department Discussion Papers No. 249. Oslo: Statistics Norway.

Gunning, J. W., and M. Keyser. 1993. Applied general equilibrium models for policy analysis. In *Handbook of development economics*, ed. H. Chenery and T. N. Srinivasan. Amsterdam: North-Holland.

Harrison, W. J., and K. R. Pearson. 1994. *Computing solutions for large general equilibrium models using GEMPACK*. Centre of Policy Studies and the Impact Project Working Paper IP-64. Clayton, Australia: Monash University.

Heidhues, F. 1998. Developing countries and globalization: Convergence or divergence? *Quarterly Journal of International Agriculture* 37 (3): 175–179.

Hertel, T. W. 1997a. Applied general equilibrium analysis of agricultural policies. Department of Agricultural Economics, Purdue University, Purdue, Ind., U.S.A.

————. 1997b. *Global trade analysis: Modeling and applications*. New York: Cambridge University Press.

————. 1999. *GTAP preparatory course on applied equilibrium analysis*. Department of Agricultural Economics, Purdue University. <http://www.agecon.purdue.edu/gtap/gtaponline>.

Hicks, J. R. 1939. *Value and capital: An inquiry into some fundamental principles of economic theory*. Oxford: Clarendon Press.

Hinojosa, O., and S. Robinson. 1992. Labor issues in a North American trade area. Department of Agricultural and Resource Economics Working Paper 632. University of California at Berkeley, Berkeley, Calif., U.S.A.

Huff, K. M. 1995. *Medium-run consequences for Australia of an APEC free-trade area: CGE analysis using the GTAP and Monash models*. Centre of Policy Studies and the Impact Project Working Paper G-111. Clayton, Australia: Monash University.

IDA/IMF (International Development Association/International Monetary Fund). 2000. *Tanzania: Decision point document under the enhanced heavily indebted poor country (HIPC) initiative*. Washington, D.C.

IMF (International Monetary Fund). 1996a. *Tanzania: Staff report for the 1996 Article IV consultation*. African Department, Washington, D.C.

————. 1996b. *Tanzania: Statistical appendix*. IMF Staff Country Report No. 96/2. Washington, D.C.

————. 1996c. *Tanzania: Selected issues and statistical appendix, SM/96/267*. Washington, D.C.

————. 1998. *Tanzania: Statistical appendix*. IMF Staff Country Report No. 98/5. Washington, D.C.

————. 1999. *IMF concludes Article IV consultations with Tanzania*. Public Information Notice (PIN) No. 99/28. <http://www.imf.org>.

————. Various years. *Press Releases*. Several issue numbers. <http://www.imf.org>.

Isard, P. 1977. How far can we push the "law of one price"? *American Economic Review* 67 (5): 942-948.

Isard, W. 1960. *Methods of regional analysis: An introduction to regional science.* New York: Technology Press of Massachusetts Institute of Technology and Wiley.

Isard, W., I. J. Azis, M. P. Drennan, R. E. Miller, S. Saltzman, and E. Thorbecke. 1998. *Methods of interregional and regional analysis.* Aldershot: Ashgate.

Johansen, L. 1960. *A multisectoral study of economic growth.* Amsterdam: North-Holland.

Keller, W. J. 1980. *Tax incidence: A general equilibrium approach.* Amsterdam: North-Holland.

Keuschnigg, C., and W. Kohler. 1995. Dynamic effects of tariff liberalization: An intertemporal CGE approach. *Review of International Economics* 3 (1): 20–35.

King, B. B. 1985. What is a SAM? In *Social accounting matrices: A basis for planning*, ed. G. Pyatt and J. I. Round. Washington, D.C.: World Bank.

Krueger, A. O. 1992. *The political economy of agricultural pricing policy: A synthesis of the political economy in developing countries*, vol. 5. World Bank: Washington, D.C.

Krueger, A. O., M. Schiff, and A. Valdes. 1988. Agricultural incentives in developing countries: Measuring the effect of sectoral and economywide policies. *World Bank Economic Review* 2 (3): 255–271.

Kullback, S., and R. A. Leibler. 1951. On information and sufficiency. *Annual Mathematical Studies* 4: 99–111.

Leontief, W. W. 1941. *The structure of the American economy, 1919–1929.* New York: Oxford University Press.

Lewis, J. D. 1994. Macroeconomic stabilization and adjustment policies in a general equilibrium model with financial markets: Turkey. In *Applied general equilibrium and economic development: Present achievements and future trends*, ed. J. Mercenier and T. N. Srinivasan. Ann Arbor, Mich., U.S.A.: University of Michigan Press.

Lewis, J. D., S. Robinson, and Z. Wang. 1995. Beyond the Uruguay round: The implications of an Asian free trade area. *China Economic Review* 6 (1): 35–90.

Lipton, M. 1977. *Why poor people stay poor: Urban bias in world development.* Cambridge, Mass., U.S.A.: Harvard University Press.

Löfgren, H., and S. Robinson. 1999. *Spatial networks in multi-region computable general equilibrium models*. Trade and Macroeconomics Division Discussion Paper No. 35. Washington, D.C.: International Food Policy Research Institute.

Lora, E. 1994. Comments (on Macroeconomic stabilization and adjustment policies in a general equilibrium model with financial markets: Turkey by J. D. Lewis). In *Applied general equilibrium and economic development: Present achievements and future trends*, eds., J. Mercenier and T. N. Srinivasan. Ann Arbor, Mich., U.S.A.: University of Michigan Press.

Lyon, C. C., and G. D. Thompson. 1993. Temporal and spatial aggregation: Alternative marketing margin models. *American Journal of Agricultural Economics* 75: 523–536.

Malakellis, M. 1993. *Illustrative results from ORANI-INT: An intertemporal CGE model of the Australian economy*. Centre of Policy Studies and the Impact Project Working Paper OP-77. Clayton, Australia: Monash University.

Mas-Colell, A. 1985. *The theory of general economic equilibrium: A differentiable approach*. Cambridge: Cambridge University Press.

Mercenier, J., and T. N. Srinivasan, eds. 1994. *Applied general equilibrium and economic development: Present achievements and future trends*. Ann Arbor, Mich., U.S.A.: University of Michigan Press.

Mitra, P. K. 1994. *Adjustment in oil-importing developing countries: A comparative economic analysis*. Cambridge: Cambridge University Press.

Mundlak, Y., and D. F. Larson. 1992. On the transmission of world agricultural prices. *The World Bank Economic Review* 6 (3): 399–422.

Naude, W.A. and P. Brixen. 1993. Currency depreciation, trade liberalization, and economic development. *South African Journal of Economics*, 61(3): 153-165.

Ndulu, B. J. 1994. Tanzania's economic development: Lessons from the experience and challenges for the future. In *Development challenges and strategies for Tanzania: An agenda for the 21st century*, ed. L. A. Msambichaka, H. P. B. Moshi, and F. P. Mtatifikolo. Dar es Salaam: University of Dar es Salaam Press.

Negishi, T. 1960. Welfare economics and existence of an equilibrium for a competitive economy. *Metroeconomica* 12: 92–97.

OECD (Organization for Economic Cooperation and Development). 1990. *Modelling the effects of agricultural policies*. OECD Economic Studies Special Issue No. 13. Paris.

Oygard, R. 1995. Structural adjustment policies and the management of natural resources. *Norwegian Journal of Agricultural Sciences*, Supplement No. 21: 7–12.

Pareto, V. 1909. *Manuel d'economie politique*. Paris: V. Giard & E. Briere.

Pereira, A. M., and J. B. Shoven. 1988. Survey of dynamic computational general equilibrium models for tax policy evaluation. *Journal of Policy Modeling* 10 (3): 401–436.

Pfeiffer, S. 1989. *Der IWF und Tansania: Die Konditionalität der Bereitschaftskreditvereinbarung des Internationalen Währungsfonds mit Tansania vom, September 1980*. Hamburger Beiträge zur Afrika-Kunde No. 71. Hamburg: Institut für Afrika-Kunde.

Phlips, L. 1974. *Applied consumption analysis*. Amsterdam and New York: North-Holland and American Elsevier Publishing Co., Inc.

Pyatt, G. and J. I. Round. 1985. *Social accounting matrices: A basis for planning*. Washington, D.C.: World Bank.

Rattso, J., and R. Torvik. 1998. Zimbabwean trade liberalization: Ex post evaluation. *Cambridge Journal of Economics* 22 (3): 325–346.

Reinert, K. A., and D. W. Roland-Holst. 1997. Social accounting matrices. In *Applied methods for trade policy analysis*, ed. J. F. Francois and K. A. Reinert. Cambridge: Cambridge University Press.

Robinson, S. 1989. Multisectoral models. In *Handbook of development economics*, ed. H. Chenery and T. N. Srinivasan. Amsterdam: North-Holland.

———. 1990. Analyzing agricultural trade liberalization with single-country computable general equilibrium models. Department of Agricultural and Resource Economics Working Paper 524. University of California at Berkeley, Berkeley, Calif., U.S.A.

———. 1991. Macroeconomics, financial variables, and computable general equilibrium models. *World Development* 19 (11): 1509–1525.

Robinson, S., A. Cattaneo, and M. El-Said. 1998. Estimating a social accounting matrix using cross entropy methods. Trade and Macroeconomics Division Discussion Paper No. 33. International Food Policy Research Institute, Washington, D.C.

———. 2000. Updating and estimating a social accounting matrix using cross entropy methods. Trade and Macroeconomic Division Discussion Paper No. 58. International Food Policy Research Institute, Washington, D.C.

Rutayisire, L., and R. Vos. 1991. A SAM for Tanzania. Working Paper Sub-Series on Money, Finance, and Development No. 39. Institute of Social Studies, The Hague.

Rutherford, T. F. 1987. *A modeling system for applied general equilibrium analysis*. Cowles Foundation for Research in Economics Discussion Paper No. 836. New Haven, Conn., U.S.A.: Yale University Press.

Sahn D. E., P. Dorosh, and S. Younger. 1996. Exchange rate, fiscal and agricultural policies in Africa: Does adjustment hurt the poor? *World Development* 24 (4): 719–747.

————. A reply to De Maio, Stewart, and van der Hoeven. *World Development* 27 (3): 471–475.

Salter, W. 1959. Internal and external balance: The role of price and expenditure effects. *Economic Record* 35: 226–238.

Sarris, A. H. 1994a. *A social accounting matrix for Tanzania*. Cornell Food and Nutrition Policy Program Working Paper 62. Ithaca, New York, U.S.A.: Cornell University Press.

————. 1994b. *Macroeconomic policies and household welfare: A dynamic computable general equilibrium analysis for Tanzania*. Cornell Food and Nutrition Policy Program Working Paper 68. Ithaca, New York, U.S.A.: Cornell University Press.

————. 1996. Macroeconomic policies and household welfare in Tanzania. In *Economic reform and the poor in Africa*, ed. D. E. Sahn. Oxford: Clarendon Press.

Scarf, H. E. 1967a. The approximation of fixed points of a continuous mapping. *SIAM Journal of Applied Mathematics* 15 (5): 328–343.

————. 1967b. On the computation of equilibrium prices. In *Ten essays in honor of Irving Fisher*, ed. W. Fellner. New York: Wiley & Sons.

————. 1973. *The computation of economic equilibria*. New Haven, Conn., U.S.A.: Yale University Press.

Schiff, M., and A. Valdes. 1992. *The political economy of agricultural pricing policy: A synthesis of the economics in developing countries*, vol. 4. World Bank Comparative Study. Baltimore, Md.: Johns Hopkins University Press.

Semboja, H. H. 1994. The effect of energy taxes on the Kenyan economy: A CGE analysis. *Energy Economics* 16 (3): 205–215.

Shannon, C. E. 1948. A mathematical theory of communication. *Bell Systems Technical Journal* 27: 379–423.

Shoup, C. S. 1990. Choosing among types of VATs. In *Value added taxation in developing countries*, ed. M. Gillis, C. S. Shoup, and G. P. Sicat. World Bank Symposium. Washington, D.C.: World Bank.

Shoven, J. B., and J. Whalley. 1972. A general equilibrium calculation of the effects of differential taxation of income from capital in the U.S. *Journal of Public Economics* 1: 281–321.

―――. 1973. General equilibrium with taxes: A computational procedure and an existence proof. *Review of Economic Studies* 40: 475–489.

―――. 1974. On the computation of competitive equilibrium on international markets with tariffs. *Journal of International Economics* 4: 341–354.

―――. 1984. Applied general-equilibrium models of taxation and international trade. *Journal of Economic Literature* 22 (3): 1007–1051.

―――. 1992. *Applying general equilibrium.* Cambridge: Cambridge University Press.

Srinivasan, T. N. 1982. General equilibrium theory, project evaluation and economic development. In *The theory and experience of economic development: Essays in honor of Sir W. Arthur Lewis*, ed. M. Gersovitz and W. A. Lewis. London: George Allen and Unwin.

Swan, T. 1960. Economic control in a dependent economy. *Economic Record* 36: 51–66.

Taube, G. 1992. *Wirtschaftliche Stabilisierung und Strukturanpassung in Tanzania: Die Auswirkungen des Economic Recovery Programme 1986–1989 im Ländlichen Bereich. Fallstudie West-Usambara-Berge, Distrikt Lushoto.* Hamburger Beiträge zur Afrika-Kunde No. 41. Hamburg: Institut für Afrika-Kunde.

Taylor, L. 1975. Theoretical foundations and technical implications. In *Economy-wide models of development planning*, ed. C. R. Blitzer, P. B. Clark, and L. Taylor. London: Oxford University Press.

―――. 1990. Structuralist CGE models. In *Socially relevant policy analysis: Structuralist computable general equilibrium models for the developing world*, ed. L. Taylor. Cambridge, Mass., U.S.A., and London: Massachusetts Institute of Technology Press.

―――. 1991. *Income distribution, inflation, and growth: Lectures on structuralist macroeconomic theory.* Cambridge, Mass., U.S.A., and London: Massachusetts Institute of Technology Press.

―――. 1994. Comment (on A financial computable general equilibrium model for the analysis of stabilization programs by A. Fargeix and E. Sadoulet). In *Applied general equilibrium and economic development: Present achievements and future trends,* eds., J. Mercenier and T. N. Srinivasan. Ann Arbor, Mich., U.S.A.: University of Michigan Press.

Taylor, L., and I. Adelman. 1996. *Village economies: The design, estimation, and use of villagewide economic models.* Cambridge: Cambridge University Press.

Taylor, L., and S. L. Black. 1974. Practical general equilibrium estimation of resource pulls under trade liberalization. *Journal of International Economics* 4: 35–58.

Taylor, L., and F. J. Lysy. 1979. Vanishing income redistributions: Keynesian clues about model surprises in the short run. *Journal of Development Economics* 6 (1): 11–30.

Theil, H. 1967. *Economics and information theory.* Amsterdam: North-Holland.

Unemo, L. 1995. *Environmental impact on governmental policies and external shocks in Botswana: A CGE modeling approach.* Environmental Papers. Washington, D.C.: World Bank.

UNDP (United Nations Development Programme). 1996. Development cooperation report – Tanzania: 1995 report. Dar es Salaam and New York.

URT (United Republic of Tanzania). Planning Commission. 1986. *The economic recovery programme.* Dar es Salaam.

―――. Bureau of Statistics and Labour Department. 1993. *Labour force survey 1990/91.* Dar es Salaam.

―――. Bureau of Statistics. 1995a. *National accounts of Tanzania 1976–94.* Dar es Salaam.

―――. Ministry of Lands, Housing and Urban Development. 1995b. *National land policy.* Dar es Salaam.

―――. Bureau of Statistics. 1995c. *Selected statistical series: 1951–93.* Dar es Salaam.

———. Bureau of Statistics. 1995d. *Revised national accounts of Tanzania 1976–1990*. Dar es Salaam.

———. Bureau of Statistics. 1996a. *Household budget survey 1991/92*, vol. 4. Dar es Salaam.

———. Bureau of Statistics. 1996b. *Statistical abstract 1994*. Dar es Salaam.

———. Tanzania Revenue Authority. 1996c. *Structural and operational features of Tanzania value added tax (VAT) and (VAT) demonstration notes*. Dar es Salaam.

———. Bureau of Statistics. 1997. *Revised national accounts of Tanzania 1987–1996*. Dar es Salaam.

URT, IMF, and World Bank (United Republic of Tanzania, International Monetary Fund). 1996. *Tanzania: Policy framework paper for 1996/97–1998/99*. Dar es Salaam and Washington, D.C.

———. 1999. *Tanzania: Enhanced structural adjustment facility policy framework paper for 1998/99–2000/01*. <http://www.imf.org>.

U.S. Central Intelligence Agency. 1998. *World factbook 1998*. <http://www.cia.gov/cia>.

U.S. International Trade Commission. 1998. *The economic implications of liberalizing APEC tariff and nontariff barriers to trade*. Investigation No. 3332-372, Publication 3101. Washington, D.C.

Wald, A. 1936. Über einige Gleichungssysteme der mathematischen Ökonomie. *Zeitschrift für Nationalökonomie* 7: 637–670.

Walras, L. 1874. *Elements d'economie politique pure, ou, Theorie de la richesse sociale*. Lausanne: L. Corbaz.

Wang, Z., and F. Zhai. 1998. Tariff reduction, tax replacement, and implications for income distribution on China. *Journal of Comparative Economics* 26 (2): 358–387.

Weintraub, E. R. 1983. On the existence of a competitive equilibrium: 1930–54. *Journal of Economic Literature* 21: 1–39.

———. 1985. General equilibrium analysis. Cambridge: Cambridge University Press.

Wenzel, H. D., and R. Wiedemann. 1989. *Tanzania's economic performance in the eighties*. Studies in Applied Economics and Rural Development No. 20. Heidelberg, Germany: Research Centre for International Agrarian Development.

Winters, P., R. Murgai, E. Sadoulet, A. de Janvry, and G. Frisvold. 1998. Economic and welfare impacts of climate change on developing countries. *Environmental and Resource Economics* 12 (1): 1–24.

World Bank. 1981. *Accelerated development in Sub-Saharan Africa: An agenda for action.* Washington, D.C.: World Bank.

———. 1994a. *Tanzania: Agriculture.* World Bank country study. Washington, D.C.

———. 1994b. *Tanzania: Agriculture sector memorandum*, vol. 2, main report. Washington, D.C.

———. 1996a. *African development indicators 1996.* Washington, D.C.

———. 1996b. *Tanzania – The challenge of reforms: Growth, incomes and welfare*, vol. 2. Washington, D.C.

———. 1998. World development indicators 1998. Washington, D.C. CD-ROM.

———. 1999a. *Countries: Tanzania.* <http://www.worldbank.org>.

———. 1999b. World development indicators 1999. Washington, D.C. CD-ROM.

———. 2000a. *World Bank and IMF support debt relief for Tanzania under enhanced HIPC initiative.* News Release No: 2000/281/S. <http://www.worldbank.org>

———. 2000b. World development indicators 2000. Washington, D.C. CD-ROM.

Yeldan, A. E. 1997. Financial liberalization and fiscal repression in Turkey: Policy analysis in a CGE model with financial markets. *Journal of Policy Modeling* 19 (1): 79–117.

About the Author

Peter Wobst is a postdoctoral fellow in the Trade and Macroeconomics Division of IFPRI. He received his Ph.D. in economics from the University of Hohenheim, Germany. His research focuses on the design and implementation of computable general equilibrium and macroeconomic models for policy analysis in Southern African countries, particularly Tanzania and Malawi.